Living Traditions
of the
Bible

Living Traditions
of the
Bible

Scripture in Jewish, Christian, and Muslim Practice

James E. Bowley, editor

Chalice Press
St. Louis, Missouri

Cover: Grady Gunter
Cover art: Detail from "Saint John the Evangelist on Patmos" by Titian.
Samuel B. Kress Collection, © 1998 Board of Trustees National Gallery of
Art, Washington, D.C.
Interior design: Rhonda Dohack

This book is printed on acid-free, recycled paper.

Visit Chalice Press on the World Wide Web at
www.chalicepress.com

10 9 8 7 6 5 4 3 2 1   99 00 01 02 03

Library of Congress Cataloging–in–Publication Data

Living traditions of the Bible : scripture in Jewish, Christian, and
Muslim practice / edited by James E. Bowley.
      p.   cm.
Includes bibliographical references.
ISBN 0-8272-2127-4
  1. Bible--History. 2. Bible--Use.   3. Theology, Doctrinal.   4. Judaism-
-Doctrines.   5. Islam--Doctrines.   I. Bowley, James E.
  BS445.L58   1999   99–29735
220' .09--dc21   C1P

Printed in the United States of America

To the Students of King College,
Devotees of the
Fine Art of
Disciplined Curiosity

Contents

Contributors

James E. Bowley
Associate Professor of Bible and Religion, King College

Demetrios J. Constantelos
Charles Cooper Townsend, Sr., Distinguished Professor of History and Religious Studies, Richard Stockton College

Joseph A. Fitzmyer, S.J.
Professor Emeritus, Department of Biblical Studies, Catholic University of America

Kathryn Johnson
Associate Professor of Religious Studies, University of North Carolina, Charlotte

Adam Kamesar
Professor of Judaeo-Hellenistic Literature, Hebrew Union College–Jewish Institute of Religion, Cincinnati

James S. McClanahan
Associate Professor of Bible and Religion, King College

Bruce M. Metzger
Professor Emeritus of New Testament Language and Literature, Princeton Theological Seminary

Michael A. Meyer
Adolph S. Ochs Professor of Jewish History, Hebrew Union College–Jewish Institute of Religion, Cincinnati

John C. Reeves
Blumenthal Professor of Judaic Studies, University of North Carolina, Charlotte

David C. Steinmetz
Amos Ragan Kearns Professor of the History of Christianity, Duke University Divinity School

Acknowledgments

I would like to thank members of the Presbyterian Church (USA) and Duncan Ferguson, of the denomination's higher education program staff, for the funding that underwrote the lecture series, "Living Traditions of the Bible: The History of Biblical Interpretation," in the spring of 1997 at King College. Those funds turned a dream into the reality out of which this book grew. I am thankful for each of the other contributors to this volume who have made this project enjoyable, and who have enriched and influenced the world of scholarship by their many years of dedication. Each one was chosen for his or her widely acknowledged expertise in the field.

Numerous persons of King College should be mentioned, including Russell Repass, Zach Garner, Josh Cole, Cindy Miles, Lila Ray with the entire library staff, the Faculty Development Committee, and the supportive faculty and staff in our learning community. I am happy to acknowledge my debt to Brandon Forbes for initial preparation of the diagrams, to the ever-curious Frank Blanton for encouragement and proofreading, to my always congenial colleague Jim McClanahan and the Bible and Religion department for frequent help and interest, to Chalice Press editor Jon L. Berquist for direction and patience, and especially to my understanding wife Bonnie for transcribing, proofreading, and giving her steadfast support to me in this project.

J. E. B.
Bristol, Tennessee
October 1998

Introduction

Living Traditions of the Bible

James E. Bowley

A Story

This is a storybook. A book of three stories, to be more exact. The story begins in the pages of an ancient book we call the Bible, and it is mediated in three different monotheistic religions: Judaism, Christianity, and Islam. Over half the world's population of the late twentieth century share traditions that place themselves in continuity with this story.

The history of the Bible and its interpretation is really the history of communities who not only worship the God of the Bible, but all see themselves as part of the story that begins in Genesis. These three communities and the colorful myriad of denominations, groups, and individuals of which they are composed, all relate themselves in some way to the story contained in the Bible. Biblical characters are spoken of as patriarchs and matriarchs, as if they were blood relatives. Christian children sing a popular song called "Father Abraham." Its chorus declares, "I am one of them [the children of Abraham] and so are you!" Now few of these children (and certainly not their parents) are prepared to present their genealogical credentials demonstrating their blood ties to the most famous character from the pages of Genesis. So what do they mean?

They mean that they too worship the same God whom Abraham and Sarah worshiped, and that the story on the pages of Genesis is their story, not just in the sense that they own the book, but that they are actually, somehow, characters in that same story, following in the footsteps of Abraham. Or, to put it another way, the story *is still* being written, and Abraham, as a founding character of the story, stands as an

1

ancestor of faith. That they themselves, millennia later, are in the same story is crucial for their valuing of the document we call the Bible. By calling Abraham father they are akin to the spirit of the Qur'ān, which declares that "the nearest of kin to Abraham are those who follow him" in his submission (*islam*) to God (3:67–68) and to the notion of Paul, who proclaimed that even Gentiles may become the descendants of Abraham (Rom. 4:16). As characters in the continuing saga of the story begun in the Bible, these communities might be labeled "People of the Book." This is, in fact, the sobriquet given to Jews and Christians in the Qur'ān, and it is fitting in many respects.[1]

This book, *Living Traditions of the Bible*, is about those communities who relate themselves in particular and peculiar ways to the story found in the Bible. The communities are Jewish, Christian, and Muslim. All three communities worship the God of Abraham. All three communities claim to be, in some sense, children of Abraham. All three communities believe that they are, to this day, people of this same God.

We must hasten to add that groups within each of these communities may well understand the nature of the continuity between the biblical story and their own history in a variety of ways. They may even understand the biblical story itself in ways very different from their fellow adherents (e.g., historical or fictional). But these sorts of differences, which will be displayed in later chapters of this book, qualify rather than abrogate the connection with the biblical story and with the ancient communities who wrote it. In that sense, the traditions of the Bible are still living. They live on in our world as the readings, stories, characters, rituals, ideals, ideas, and artistry of the Bible continues to affect and shape these communities directly and indirectly.

Same Beginning, Different Endings

My son has a book that begins a story and then allows the reader to choose one of several endings. Imagine with me what could happen to the story of "Goldilocks and the Three Bears." In chapter one the golden-haired adorable rascal enters the bears' house and proceeds to try the chairs, porridge, and beds, finally falling asleep in Baby Bear's bed. But after that, imagine having various options. In ending A, she awakes in a fright and runs away from the bears' house. But if you are in the mood for something more gruesome (read any Stephen King lately?), you might choose ending B, where she is mauled to death and fed to the wolves. In version C, more to my liking, she awakens and teaches the bears Hebrew and they become her grateful students.

Jews, Christians, and Muslims begin their stories essentially the same. They share colorful characters from the pages of scripture such as Adam, Noah, Abraham, kings, and prophets. But by the end of the story, all three are reading radically different chapters of this storybook.

One has a chapter about a nation who was chosen by God in the person of Abraham and commanded by God in the person of Moses. For them, the Jews, Torah is God's ultimate instruction—the rich and living text and centerpiece through which all of life is read. The Torah (and Abraham and Moses) also figures in the Christian and Muslim stories, but not as the central chapter of the story.

One has a chapter about a son of Abraham and of God who came, died, and was raised by God. And though he never wrote so much as a paragraph, he is for them, the Christians, the rich and living event, the Word, through which all events and all texts before and after him are read.

One has a chapter about the greatest and last prophet from God, named Muhammad. For them, the Muslims, the perfection of revelation is the rich and living Qur'ān, which overshadows all previous revelations to all previous prophets, including Moses and Jesus.

None of these stories is said to be finished. Jews, Christians, and Muslims are waiting for final chapters about messiahs or second comings or kingdoms or triumphant victories or universal redemption. These Bible-begun stories are all in mid-sentence; they are still being written. They are "*Living* Traditions of the Bible." The story that begins, "In the beginning God…" has not yet come to "The End."[2]

The central chapter of each story (Torah, Christ, Qur'ān), around which all the other parts are structured, provides what is sometimes called "the rule of faith" or "central myth" of each tradition. The word *myth* is frequently misunderstood or opposed (in fact, we may have just lost some readers) because its popular usage is different than its literary-critical usage. Rather than "fraudulent" or "untrue," myth, as used in academic discourse, is employed in a largely positive and functional way. A dominant myth of any culture is a story that provides a basic vision of the structure of reality and informs people about themselves and about their relation to God(s), nature, and destiny. Myths often include a story of salvation, provide patterns for behavior, and are reenacted in ritual.[3] This usage *says nothing* about whether any given myth is historical or fictional.

The rule of faith, or dominant myth, explains why these three large religious communities, all of whom worship the God of Abraham and relate their own story to the Bible, may read (or choose not to read) the very same texts so differently. The Bible begins the story and continues to have its effect on each community. But it is a two-way street. These historical communities of faith have impacted the understanding of the Bible and the Bible itself—the way it looks, what it includes and excludes, what is primary and secondary, and whether it needs to be read at all. For example, in Judaism the Torah is the living center of the Bible in a manner completely foreign to most Christians. Christianity, for its part, added twenty-seven peculiarly Christian books to the Bible, an unauthorized action at best, to most Jews. The status of the Qur'ān in Islam is so superlative that the Bible is overshadowed and not usually approached directly.

Yes, the histories and understandings of these communities have, in distinct and vibrant ways, grown out of the biblical story. Yes, these ancient texts, collected and canonized as sacred, have been the source of authority, controversy, and inspiration. Yes, the Bible has so indelibly marked these communities that they can be collectively called the three biblical faiths. But the communities themselves have also so indelibly marked the biblical traditions with their unique experience and divergent understanding that they must also be called different religions. Their use of the Bible, with widely varing interpretations and significations, constantly demonstrates this.

This book is about how people of Judaism, Christianity, and Islam have read and continue to read the early chapters of their story, the Bible. It is also about how the Bible *came to be* the Bible and the remarkable differences it now exhibits in the ways that it *is*. The purpose is twofold: (1) to provide an understanding of the broad historical developments of each community's relationship to the Bible and (2) to allow each tradition to speak for itself regarding the Bible.

The early chapters of the book progress historically. First are the issues of how the great story of ancient Israel came to be written in the forms in which we have it today (chap. 1). In chapter 2 we consider the journey that the Hebrew Bible made from a Hebrew, Eastern, and Jewish culture to a Greek, Western, and Christian culture. Chapter 3 speaks to us of the Bible from the standpoint of Early Judaism and rabbinic teachers of the Bible. Next is the intriguing process by which Christians determined the extent of the New Testament (chap. 4). These first four chapters contain historical and literary surveys that set the stage for the more specific discussions of how the Bible lives in today's communities of faith. Chapters 5 through 10 meet the second goal by presenting clearly and concisely the role of Scripture in Islam (chap. 5), the Orthodox Church (chap. 6), Roman Catholicism (chap. 7), the Reformation and modern Protestantism (chaps. 8–9), and modern Judaism (chap. 10). Each chapter is intentionally freestanding and can be read beneficially without reference to the others.

In light of the goal of allowing each tradition to speak with integrity from its own categories and conceptions, I thought it appropriate to forego uniformity of expression and terminology among the various authors, which in other circumstances an editor might desire. Thus, for example, I have not altered personal preferences regarding the notation of the era (B.C. or B.C.E.; A.D. or C.E.). I trust that whatever minor difficulty may be caused by a lack of consistency will be pardoned for the sake of authentic expression.

It is my sincere hope that this book will serve to promote not only knowledge of the past, but also wisdom for the present among all the children of Abraham.

---

[1] It is also problematic. John Barton (*People of the Book?* [Philadelphia: Westminster, 1988]) has stressed that Christianity is not a book-centered religion.

[2] Unfortunately, there have always been attempts to write the other groups out of the story. Sometimes these attempts have been accompanied by serious ethical violations or even unspeakable cruelties.

[3] Ian Barbour, *Myths, Models, and Paradigms* (New York: Harper, 1974).

1

A Library of Tradition: The Beginnings of the Bible

James E. Bowley

The Story and the Books

From beginning to end, the Bible is a human book. It did not fall out of heaven, and then, by our good fortune or divine providence, someone happened upon it and called a news conference. Like all other books, it has a human history behind every letter—all the more so, in fact. That is, to a degree far beyond the average book on any modern shelf, its history is complicated with a web of intricacies, the stuff that makes human life and its creations complex and interesting.

The Bible is also, and here we state the obvious in a rather banal way, a book embraced by religious communities, millennia after its formation, as much more than a human book. It carries impressive titles and epithets, such as Holy Bible, Sacred Scripture, Divinely Inspired Scripture, even Word of God. Indeed, the word *bible*, has become a term meaning "authoritative written source," as when a sports fan might say, "He wrote the bible of baseball hitting technique." And though *bible* is a word of Greek origin simply meaning "books," it is considered proper form to capitalize *Bible* as a title and proper name. How did these ancient "books" come to be the Bible, The Book?

It is first of all important to realize that the written document we call the Bible only exists because of the communities and stories described in the Introduction. The Bible has survived and enjoys the status it does because communities of faith considered the preservation of these writings valuable for the community. Because Jews, and then Christians, were committed to remembering and preserving their story, the story was told and retold, written and rewritten, acted and reenacted. A story repeated in any medium becomes a tradition. A tradition develops, continues, and survives in practice because communities—not just individuals—consider it valuable for the present, not because it is an interesting museum piece.[1] As James Kugel has described it, the biblical tradition developed as the community combined the value of the past with the needs of the present.[2]

It is within the context of a large multifaceted tradition that the scriptures must be situated in order to realize that they are organically a part of a larger whole. The Israelite tradition was the story of relationship with their God, YHWH, a relationship that involved an "ongoing discourse," that is, communications of various sorts between YHWH and the Israelites.[3] For example, Israelites built sanctuaries, sacrificed, confessed, praised, and acted in appropriate ways. God acted, commanded, and directed. This discourse was carried out both publicly and privately, though, of course, the vast majority of the evidence for the tradition is of the public variety. The discourse, both sides of it, was preserved in several media. The medium of physical activity, such as the activities of the Israelite cult (institution of the social worship of God including temple and priests) and festivals, rehearsed in word and deed the actions of God and expressed the Israelite response. For example, in Exodus the keeping of the Sabbath was a communal activity meant to preserve the tradition of YHWH's creative power (Ex. 20:8–11). In Deuteronomy Sabbath observance is a communal activity meant to preserve the tradition of YHWH's rescue from slavery (Deut. 5:12–15).

Another medium for preserving the tradition was oral speech. The stories of the past were on the lips of parents, elders, community leaders, and priests. Laws and judicial decisions in the name of YHWH were promulgated in teaching and speech by priests (Deut. 17:8–13; 33:10) and kings (1 Sam. 30:23–25). Prophets often spoke formally in the name of God (e.g., Isa. 7:7; Jer. 46:1) and were called upon by kings for a divine word (2 Kgs. 22:1–28). Many ancient cultures, including Israel, are dubbed "oral cultures" because of the supreme value that was placed on the spoken word. We must also mention the mysterious *urim* and *thummim* or *ephod* devices, which were used under priestly auspices as a means of discerning YHWH's answer to direct oral inquiries (Ex. 28:30; 1 Sam. 23:9–12; 30:7–8).

Another medium in the service of tradition was the written text. Israelite culture was literate, and Israel was surrounded by literate peoples.[4] Documents were written, many of which no longer exist. The

"Book of the Wars of YHWH" (Num. 21:14) doubtless preserved material about YHWH's deeds in the past. The authors of Joshua and 2 Samuel excerpted poems from a certain "Book of Jashar" (Josh. 10:12–13; 2 Sam. 1:17–27). At best we have snippets of these most ancient written traditions. The book of Judges contains what is thought to be, based on linguistic criteria, one of the oldest texts preserved in the Bible, the Song of Deborah (Jud. 5:2–31), from the eleventh century B.C.E. Its language is archaic and at variance with the rest of the book, indicating its differing origin. Thus the book of Judges, which probably took its basic final form in the sixth century B.C.E., preserves material preceding it by several centuries. By the time of the writing of Chronicles (ca. fourth century B.C.E.), dozens of books are mentioned, such as the "Acts of Nathan the Prophet" (1 Chr. 29:29) and the "Commentary on the Book of Kings" (2 Chr. 24:27). Israel's priests and kings, in harmony with surrounding nations, wrote laws and publicized them in written form. Many of these laws, dating to various periods, are preserved in the legal portions of Exodus, Leviticus, Numbers, and Deuteronomy.

It is important to recognize that these media were not mutually exclusive, and there was undoubtedly interaction between them. In the history of Israel, the growth in importance of the written tradition can be traced, but the written word never replaced other media. Even in the second century C.E., a Christian leader of Phrygia named Papias (70–140) prefers the oral traditions about Jesus—"utterances of a living surviving voice"—to information from books.[5] So, too, rabbinic Judaism highly valued the oral law alongside the written.

As moderns we sometimes jump to the conclusion that every reference to "law" (*torah*) or the divine "word" in the Bible is a reference to written law, but by so doing we underestimate the value of orality in ancient Israel. In the historical books such as Samuel and Kings, kings of Israel are more often depicted as going to prophets for a *spoken* word of YHWH than they are going to a text. In an episode representing the late seventh century B.C.E., a written legal text is clearly involved, but even here an appeal is made to the oral authority of a prophet to mediate the written word (see 2 Kgs. 22:8–16). In any case, texts that are now a part of what we call the Bible were one medium used by ancient Israelites to maintain their tradition(s), their story, their ongoing discourse with YHWH. It is the written medium, and it is one of several media that still continue in all three biblical religions.

A Book of Books

The journey of stories and writings from the immensely different world of ancient Palestine to the desks, kitchen tables, and bookstores of today is part of the subject of this book. In fact, as the Introduction made clear, we could say that the Bible has actually made several different journeys to a variety of destinations. There are parts of the Bible's journey to our world that are shrouded in the proverbial cobwebs of history that will probably never be known. For example, who is the author of Ruth? While much might be reasonably inferred *about* the person, her or his actual identity is not hotly contested because the evidence to be disputed is so meager.

Other aspects of our Bible's history are quite easily documented because of the preservation of thousands of ancient biblical manuscripts. For example, who is responsible for the verse divisions and numbers in most modern Bibles? Answer: Robert Estienne (also known as Stephanus), a famous Bible printer of the sixteenth century, whose 1551 edition of a Greek-Latin New Testament was the first with such divisions. His 1553 French Bible was the first to use his versification for the whole Bible.[6] Surely it is easy to recognize how different a Bible might read without this late intrusion of numbers, especially for those modern versions that treat each of Estienne's verses as if it were a new paragraph. Furthermore, if it were not for Robert Estienne, American sport spectators would not be "treated" to the now infamous "JOHN 3:16" banners at major sporting events. I wonder, what would Estienne think of his numbering project if he were to return and see such a sign? Not to mention the author of John!

Finally, many details of the Bible's journey remain in the wide middle ground between the dark shadows of ignorance and the light of reasonable certainty. For example, what was Ezra's (ca. fifth century B.C.E.) role in the formation of the Pentateuch? Ezra's scribal activity has been described, discussed, debated, and denied for millennia, and the presses are still rolling.

The first thing that should be made clear is that the Bible was not always called "the Bible". The ancient Greek word *biblion* is properly translated "book" and is used in ancient literature, including the New Testament documents, to refer to a treatise (much like the way we usually use "book") or a subdivision of a treatise (much like our "volume"). In a famous declaration, to which students may readily relate, the Greek poet Callimachus (305–240) opined that "a big book (*biblion*) is a big evil." Biblion derives from the Greek name of the stalk of the papyrus plant, *byblos*, from which paper was made. Originally biblion was a diminutive of *biblos*, but by the time of the New Testament writings biblion and biblos could be used synonymously. The plural form of biblion is *biblia*. We find it, for example, in the last sentence of the gospel of John, where readers are told that "the whole world could not contain the books" (biblia) that could be written about Jesus' many deeds.

It is from the Greek plural biblia that the English (through Latin and then French) word "Bible" comes. But, of course, as used today its original plural sense is not maintained. In fact, already before the English use, the word biblia was used in Latin not as a plural but as a singular. Exactly when the shift from a plural meaning to a singular occurred is unknown, though it was prior to the ninth century.[7] This linguistic shift, which occurred long after all parts of what we call the Bible were written and long after the Bible could be bound as one document between two covers, is a symptom of the conceptual change to regarding the many biblia as one work. This conceptual shift may have some positive value, but it also has a deleterious effect on the popular understanding of the Bible and its history.

In many ways the Bible is more a library of sacred books than a single book, at least as we usually conceive a single book. It was written by dozens of authors over many centuries. The word *anthology* is a picturesque and accurate term for the Bible. Anthology is from two Greek words (*anthos* and *logo*) that together mean a gathering of flowers, a bouquet. It was used in antiquity to refer to a collection of poems, and it is a felicitous description of the Bible, which is, after all, a beautiful bouquet of diverse literary creations. Each flower has its own integrity and unique beauty but also a position in the larger bouquet. The communities of faith have arranged the bouquet differently, sometimes discarding, sometimes adding, sometimes putting into the background what another places in a prominent position.

An Ancient Library

The ancient biblion was not quite a book as we think of it. I suspect that most readers today, when seeing the word "book," picture pages of writing between two covers. But that is not the picture in the mind of an ancient, whether Israelite or Greek. It was not until the end of the first century C.E. that the codex form, the pages and cover format, was used.[8] Individual books were often written on individual scrolls. A particularly long book could be divided, again for convenience, into separate scrolls or "books"—the equivalent of our multivolume composition. For example, one might consider the books of Samuel, Kings, and Chronicles. On the other hand, short books might be written consecutively on the same scroll for convenience sake. Already in the second century B.C.E., this was the case for the group known as the twelve minor prophets (Hosea, Joel, Amos, Obadiah, Jonah, Micah, Nahum, Habakkuk, Zephaniah, Haggai, Zechariah, and Malachi).[9]

It should be clear now that Jesus, or any other ancient worthy of his day or earlier, cannot be pictured as walking around Galilee with his Bible under his arm or sitting in a synagogue with an opened Bible on his lap. Such an image is an anachronism. In his day, the Bible, as *a book* (pages between two covers), did not exist. Instead, the writings that make up our Bible existed as independent scrolls, each one independently copied by hand. Few individuals would have had their own copy of any, much less all, of these scrolls. Instead, synagogues (see Lk. 4:16–20), undoubtedly the temple, and perhaps other formal institutions such as libraries or houses of instruction, would have had collections of scrolls. In what follows we will consider several of the various terms that were used to refer to such collections, but there was no single title equivalent to our "Bible," which referred to a defined collection of these scrolls. In the days of Jesus, and certainly of Jeremiah (sixth century B.C.E.), the word biblia was centuries away from becoming the title for this collection.

It would not be inappropriate then to speak of the Bible as a sacred library—a collection of writings deemed holy by a particular community. This terminology, in addition to more accurately reflecting biblia as plural, also provides a better mental image for understanding the many different referents the word Bible may have. The Samaritans and the Ethiopian Christian Church both hold the Bible as sacred. An enterprising publisher might hope to serve both communities by publishing one book, one Bible. What a surprise to learn that the former's Bible contains five books and the latter's eighty-one! If we think of the Bible as a library, instead of a single book, this great divergence and all of those in between are easily grasped. When we enter the Roman Catholic library, we will find seventy-three volumes; the Greek Orthodox "shelves" hold seventy-six; the Protestant Bible, since the mid-seventeenth century, has usually included sixty-six books;[10] and the Jewish bookroom has twenty-four. As table 1 shows, each community of faith has its own sacred library, its own collection of biblia, and each library has books in common as well as major and minor differences. Finally, recognizing the Bible as a library will also aid us in interpreting each book as a composition with its own integrity and viewpoint.

Writing an Ancient Book

Unfortunately for the curious modern, the Bible's early history—the writing, copying, and so on, of its various books—is not the subject of any ancient writer contemporary with biblical authors. Neither the Bible nor its individual books come with an ancient Preface that provides details about the author, explains his or her purpose, and thanks spouse and children for their patience and colleagues for their contributions. No ancient traveler, such as the fifth-century B.C.E. Greek historian Herodotus, describes Jewish sacred texts in a traveler's log. Archaeologists have turned up no ancient personal diary of Luke noting on what day he purchased his copy of Mark's Gospel from the local Barnes and Noble, and upon reading it, decided to compose his own gospel. Instead, what we know about the earliest history of this library comes not from explicit ancient testimony about its writings but from clues in the Bible itself.

Table 1: The Books and Arrangement of Biblical Libraries (using common English names)

The Jewish Sacred Library

1. Genesis
2. Exodus
3. Leviticus
4. Numbers
5. Deuteronomy
6. Joshua
7. Judges
8. Samuel
9. Kings
10. Isaiah
11. Jeremiah
12. Ezekiel
13. The Twelve (Hosea, Joel, Amos, Obadiah, Jonah, Micah, Nahum, Habakkuk, Zephaniah, Haggai, Zechariah, Malachi)
14. Psalms
15. Proverbs
16. Job
17. Song of Songs
18. Ruth
19. Lamentations
20. Ecclesiastes
21. Esther
22. Daniel
23. Ezra-Nehemiah
24. Chronicles

The Roman Catholic Sacred Library

1. Genesis
2. Exodus
3. Leviticus
4. Numbers
5. Deuteronomy
6. Joshua
7. Judges
8. Ruth
9. 1 Samuel
10. 2 Samuel
11. 1 Kings
12. 2 Kings
13. 1 Chronicles
14. 2 Chronicles
15. Ezra
16. Nehemiah
17. Tobit
18. Judith
19. Esther (with Greek chapters)
20. 1 Maccabees
21. 2 Maccabees
22. Job
23. Psalms
24. Proverbs
25. Ecclesiastes
26. Song of Songs
27. Wisdom of Solomon
28. Sirach (=Ecclesiasticus =Ben Sira)
29. Isaiah
30. Jeremiah
31. Lamentations
32. Baruch (includes Letter of Jeremiah)
33. Ezekiel
34. Daniel (with Greek chapters)
35. Hosea
36. Joel
37. Amos
38. Obadiah
39. Jonah
40. Micah
41. Nahum
42. Habakkuk
43. Zephaniah
44. Haggai
45. Zechariah
46. Malachi
47. Matthew
48. Mark
49. Luke
50. John
51. Acts
52. Romans
53. 1 Corinthians
54. 2 Corinthians
55. Galatians
56. Ephesians
57. Philippians
58. Colossians
59. 1 Thessalonians
60. 2 Thessalonians
61. 1 Timothy
62. 2 Timothy
63. Titus
64. Philemon
65. Hebrews
66. James
67. 1 Peter
68. 2 Peter
69. 1 John
70. 2 John
71. 3 John
72. Jude
73. Revelation

The Orthodox Sacred Library

is identical to the Roman Catholic except
(1) The Letter of Jeremiah is a separate book, and
(2) the following are variously included by various Orthodox communions:

3 and 4 Maccabees are added after 2 Maccabees;

1 Esdras (a work combining parts of 2 Chronicles and Nehemiah, all of Ezra, and original material) is added after 2 Chronicles

The Prayer of Manasseh is included at the end of 2 Chronicles

Psalm 151 is included at the end of Psalms

The Protestant Sacred Library

1. Genesis
2. Exodus
3. Leviticus
4. Numbers
5. Deuteronomy
6. Joshua
7. Judges
8. Ruth
9. 1 Samuel
10. 2 Samuel
11. 1 Kings
12. 2 Kings
13. 1 Chronicles
14. 2 Chronicles
15. Ezra
16. Nehemiah
17. Esther
18. Job
19. Psalms
20. Proverbs
21. Ecclesiastes
22. Song of Songs
23. Isaiah
24. Jeremiah
25. Lamentations
26. Ezekiel
27. Daniel
28. Hosea
29. Joel
30. Amos
31. Obadiah
32. Jonah
33. Micah
34. Nahum
35. Habakkuk
36. Zephaniah
37. Haggai
38. Zechariah
39. Malachi
40. Matthew
41. Mark
42. Luke
43. John
44. Acts
45. Romans
46. 1 Corinthians
47. 2 Corinthians
48. Galatians
49. Ephesians
50. Philippians
51. Colossians
52. 1 Thessalonians
53. 2 Thessalonians
54. 1 Timothy
55. 2 Timothy
56. Titus
57. Philemon
58. Hebrews
59. James
60. 1 Peter
61. 2 Peter
62. 1 John
63. 2 John
64. 3 John
65. Jude
66. Revelation

The erroneous picture of Jeremiah or Hillel or Paul flipping through the pages of a Bible underscores the importance of recognizing the vast cultural differences that separate us from the ancient world of Israel and ancient Judaism. One difficult aspect of studying an ancient biblical text is letting go of modern conceptions of books and bookmaking. For starters, the majority of books in the Bible were written anonymously. This manner of presentation is not unknown today, but it is certainly unusual. Ancient Israelite culture did not value authorship in the manner we do. Copyrights, royalties, plagiarism, and "ownership" of expression were foreign concepts. While surely this seems obvious, the implications for our understanding of biblical literature are by no means insignificant; they are profound. As much as we would like to know who wrote the book of Genesis, for example, the book itself does not say. There is no informative entry in an ancient Israelite Library of Congress to aid us, nor is there an ancient copyright page with Moses' name. Unlike the typical Greek historian of antiquity, the Israelite author of Genesis did not begin with a bit of autobiography. Genesis and the other four "Books of Moses" are all presented anonymously, and though the association with Moses in later tradition is easily understood, the books themselves actually carry no claim of Mosaic authorship.[11] The anonymity of so many books certainly complicates our understanding of their authorship, but it also opens our minds to a manner of book writing different from our own.

Another reality of biblical literature that diverges from the way we publish books is the common practice of using the words of another without attribution. In some cases sources are given (e.g., Josh. 10:13 and Mt. 2:17); but more frequently they are not. For example, the texts of Micah 4:1–3 and Isaiah 2:2–4 are nearly identical. One of these texts has obviously been "borrowed" from the other, or, perhaps, the two authors both borrowed from a third and older source. Regardless of which explanation we may choose, we find no footnote to give credit where credit is due. The same is true of hundreds of other biblical passages, including much of the work of Chronicles, which borrows heavily from Samuel and Kings, and the New Testament gospels, which share many materials.[12] In a modern classroom, such blatant plagiarism is disapproved; yet scholars, rabbis, and ministers today do not even mildly criticize the biblical author(s) for such behavior. Why not? Because it would be, of course, ludicrous to expect ancient authors to follow modern conventions of copyright and book writing. This practice, too, has important implications for how we conceive the composition of our Bible.

The common practice of borrowing words from other writings introduces the ancient practice of composite authorship. This simply means that a given book of the Bible may be the product of more than one author, just as it is clear that much of Chronicles originated in Samuel and Kings.[13] Someone—scholars call such a person an editor or redactor—brought various sources together and composed the book we know as Chronicles. The amount of material that is culled from earlier sources may vary from nearly everything to next to nothing, but the composite nature of many biblical books is a standard feature explaining the history of many biblical texts. For example, the traditional prophetic books, such as Isaiah and Amos, frequently reflect distinct historical and political realities indicating different periods of composition for different sections of the same book. In ancient Israel prophets were often part of "schools," with masters and students and scribes. Students and scribes would remember and record the utterances of a prophet, and they might also supplement that written text with oracles from others (or themselves) years later. The book called Isaiah reflects periods from the eighth century B.C.E., when a prophet named Isaiah lived in a quasi-independent Jerusalem beset by the international complications of a world in the shadow of the Assyrian empire (see Isa. 1—12). But the book also contains material from the sixth century, reflecting a world dominated by the very different Persian empire (see Isa. 45). The practice of supplementing collections of oracles was a perfectly natural enterprise for prophets and their disciples, who were not concerned with providing a pristine museum piece for later generations to admire, but rather were intent on giving a living and written testimony to the dialogue of YHWH with Israel.

The obvious implication of composite authorship is that books were composed diachronically. That is, they were supplemented, altered, and edited over time—in some cases apparently long periods of time. A book was not a static entity to be altered only by the original author in whose name the copyright is found. The realities that enabled the continuing growth of authoritative tradition are observed throughout the biblical texts themselves. For example, the book of Deuteronomy depicts the priests as those who supplement the law based on their own court decisions (17:8–13), and David, in the aftermath of a battle is depicted as establishing a long-held rule of gathering the spoil (1 Sam. 30:21–25). The diachronic composition explains what scholars often call the layers of the text, which come from different periods. This also helps to explain the numerous anachronisms and editorial remarks in biblical texts. For example, Genesis 14:14 depicts Abram pursuing enemy kings "as far as Dan." The city or region now known as Dan was certainly not called Dan in Abram's day as is clear from Judges 18. It is clear that, however old the tradition of Abram's pursuit is (and there is too little evidence to even hazard a guess), the use of "Dan" is a historical anachronism coming from a later time. Similarly, an editor of 1 Samuel has added a note of explanation for his readers about a word used in an older source that his modern readers might find confusing (1 Sam. 9:9).

This notion of composite and diachronic composition is not merely a modern scholar's imaginative construct based on a few narrative hints. There is more than a little hard evidence for diachronic composition/ compilation by several hands contained in numerous ancient manuscripts. For example, the book of Psalms, as we have it in most modern English Bibles, has 150 separate psalms. The tradition of most English Bibles follows that of the Jewish Masoretic tradition. The Masoretes were Jewish scholars who carefully studied and meticulously copied biblical manuscripts in Tiberias on the Lake of Galilee from the sixth to ninth centuries C.E. The earliest Masoretic manuscripts that survive—some only partially—are from the late ninth to early eleventh centuries. Thus, these earliest of Hebrew texts are still some 2,000–1,200 years removed from the original writings of the Hebrew Bible. This fact should make clear the importance of the Dead Sea Scrolls for the history and study of the Bible, because those scrolls, found in caves near the northwest end of the famed Salt Sea, provide us with biblical manuscripts that predate the Masoretic texts by more than 1,000 years. A few Psalms scrolls that were found among the Dead Sea Scrolls, dating to the first century C.E., differ from the Masoretic edition in the following ways: (1) The order of individual psalms diverges, (2) some psalms contained in the Masoretic text are not found, (3) psalms not in the Masoretic book of Psalms but known from elsewhere (e.g., 2 Sam. 23:7; Sirach 51) are included, and (4) psalms unattested elsewhere are included. These differences are observed mainly in the last third of the collection of Psalms and are solid evidence that even in the first century C.E. the book of Psalms existed in differing edited forms and that Psalms was still a work in progress centuries after the earliest individual psalms were composed.

The book of Jeremiah also serves as an excellent illustration. Most modern English Bibles translate the Hebrew Masoretic (tenth-century) version of Jeremiah. But a much earlier translation from Hebrew into Greek (probably made in the second century B.C.E.) differs in significant ways from the Masoretic edition. The Greek translation of the Hebrew Bible is known as the Septuagint (meaning seventy and abbreviated LXX) and is so important in the history of the Bible that the next chapter in this book, written by Professor Adam Kamesar, deals extensively with it. When New Testament authors quote scripture, they usually use the LXX version. It is most intriguing to note that the LXX Jeremiah is about one-seventh shorter than the Masoretic (Hebrew) Jeremiah. The shortening involves what appears to be wholesale omission and condensation. The LXX Jeremiah also has dozens of sections of the book in a different order than our current Hebrew and English editions (e.g., the Hebrew Jer. 46:2–28 is found in the LXX Jer. 26:2–28). Recently it has become clear—again thanks to the Dead Sea Scrolls—that these two significantly divergent versions of Jeremiah existed side by side *in Hebrew* during the first century. In fact, it has now been convincingly shown that the Masoretic version (and thus most modern English editions) is the younger of the two versions and that the LXX tradition did not omit material from the text, but rather the Masoretic tradition of Jeremiah expanded and rearranged the book. Thus, in the first century, there were at least two different versions of Jeremiah, an older shorter version and a younger longer version. Jews and Christians who used the Greek Bible were using a translation of the older shorter version, whereas among Jews who used Hebrew the older version was eventually displaced by the younger longer version.[14] To this day the difference is still observed, for the Orthodox Church follows the LXX while Jews and the Western Church (Roman Catholic and Protestant) base their translations on the Masoretic text.

But we did not need the Dead Sea Scrolls to teach us that biblical writings were often supplemented over time. Any comparison between the ancient Greek translation (LXX) with the Masoretic text will show, in addition to the differences in Jeremiah, there are many others, including large additions to Daniel (stories and poetry) and Esther (a rewriting making the book much more pious), and a widely divergent text of Samuel. Short and long forms exist also for Job and Sirach, and each one's textual history is highly complicated. These differences are still observable today, as the Orthodox and Roman Catholic churches follow the practice of the majority of ancient churches by including the Esther and Daniel additions. The New Testament also contains such additions, as anyone with a modern translation of the gospels of Mark and John can see. Some of the oldest manuscripts of the book of Mark (fourth century C.E.) close the book at Mark 16:8 but later manuscripts, including that used for the King James Version, include longer endings. John 7:53—8:11 is the famous story of Jesus and the woman accused of adultery. This entire section was added to the gospel and is not included in the most ancient manuscripts. A note to this effect in now a part of most modern New Testaments, including the *New Revised Standard Version* and the *New International Version*.

One final difference in ancient and modern form is observed in the ancient literary device of writing in the name of another, or pseudepigraphy. In Jewish antiquity this was not an uncommon practice, variously motivated and not necessarily censured as deception, especially in the centuries surrounding the turn of the era. A text could be penned as if written by an ancient worthy, such as Enoch, Abraham, or even Moses. There are many examples preserved in both Jewish and Christian provenance.[15] It is within this tradition that books (or parts of books) such as Ecclesiastes, Proverbs, Song of Songs, and Wisdom of Solomon are considered "Solomonic." This possibility must be considered in all evaluations of authorship. In one sense, the practice of pseudepigraphy is an extension of the practice of supplementing the traditional writings of a master such as Isaiah and is a practice that once again underscores the *living* and dynamic nature of the tradition.

These are some of the crucial differences between modern writing conventions and those of ancient Israel. The actual process for every book of the sacred library called scripture must be investigated on an individual basis—words such as composite or pseudepigraphic cannot be indiscriminately applied. It has been my experience as a teacher that holding ancient authors to modern conventions of writing and book-making stands as one of the major impediments to exploring the history of the Bible. It is also an impediment that is patently fallacious and in need of discarding. When the ancient writers are freed from the bonds of our modern customs, they obtain liberty to live and write as ancient Jews and Christians. In fact, they were free to do just that, and moderns have only shackled modern minds and precluded a proper understanding of the Bible and the ancient world.

A Sacred Library

By now some readers might be saying, "Certainly the Bible is an ancient book or library, with all that that implies, but it is so much more than that." Indeed, the Bible is not just any ancient book. It is different. In a word, it is *sacred*: The Holy Bible. It is different than others. It is special. Many customs in our modern Western world, and even whole cultures, honor this superior status. We even have our presidents and judges and witnesses take their oaths upon it. Why swear "on a stack of Bibles"?

It is not because the Bible does not share the full humanity of all other books. It may be considered divine, but that is not because its manuscripts were physically produced in a heavenly scriptorium. Like other books, every letter of every word was penned by human hands. Explanations for the Bible's superior status, its sacredness, vary between traditions and even within the same religious tradition. A common theological explanation is that the Bible is divinely inspired. That is, it is the product of divine impetus. Again, just how the divine operated in/on/through the human authors/editors is divergently explained, depending on sectarian and personal theologies. For some, the divine activity would be considered very direct, for others, quite indirect, and for still others the sacredness of scripture would be considered only a product of wise human choices. In the Christian tradition, some early authors metaphorically pictured the scriptures (referring to Jewish pre-New Testament Scriptures) as "God-breathed" (*theopneustos*, 2 Tim. 3:16) or the fruit of the movement of the Holy Spirit upon individual speakers (2 Pet. 1:21). Statements of the divine source of the scriptures are found in Jewish and Islamic writings as well.[16] Of course, these are not really explanations; they do not technically answer the question, How are scriptures inspired? Instead they are affirmations that in some way the divine spirit worked through humans to create these writings, rendering them sacred, holy. It is at this point that the various traditions, Jewish, Christian, and Muslim, will come forward with their several theologies of revelation and inspiration.

The nature of the sacred writings, however one explains their origin, always carries some implication of authority.[17] How this authority is worked out in theory and practice varies widely between and within the biblical faiths. Many a Jew and Christian would consider "Remember the Sabbath day to keep it holy" (Ex. 20:8) to be an authoritative command of Sacred Scripture. Yet if one were to spend a Saturday shadowing a Christian, an Orthodox Jew, and a Reform Jew, one would soon realize that their common heritage of this sacred command does not make for common practice of the Sabbath. We need not lay out in complete detail the life of a pious Jew, a devout Roman Catholic, and a committed Shi'ite Muslim in order to illustrate that though rabbinic writings, church doctrine, and the Qur'ān all have a sense of biblical literature as revelation with authority, the communities have worked out that idea in remarkably different ways!

Building the Sacred Library of Ancient Israel

It is clear, then, that the belief or lack of belief in the divine inspiration (however defined) of scripture does not adequately explain the differences between Judaism, Christianity, and Islam. It also does not account for why the particular books in the Bible are there. That is, it is incredible to think that inspiration imparted a recognizable watermark or stamp to the texts themselves that made clear to all that they ought to be given status in the sacred library of Israel. How were the texts distinguished? Why these and not others? Why does the Bible take very different forms in Judaism and Christianity, the two faiths that still read the Bible directly? Why is the Bible of different Christian groups composed of different books? Even if one holds that in some way the divine spirit worked through prophets, sages, and apostles to create these special, sacred writings, the question must still be asked, Which writings? None would apply the term sacred to all ancient writings; no one has suggested recently that the Babylonian *Enuma Elish* be added to modern scriptures. Do the scriptures include all ancient Israelite writings? Of course not. The Gezer calendar and numerous other inscriptions are not candidates for the Bible's pages. Even older writings that are clearly authoritative sources for biblical authors are not considered sacred today. There is no search on for the lost Book of Jashar (Josh. 10:13; 2 Sam. 1:18) or any of the several dozens of writings mentioned throughout the Bible for the purpose of completing the Bible. Most Christians do not include the readily available *Book of Enoch* in their scriptures even though those very scriptures clearly refer to that pseudepigraph as an authoritative work (Jude 14–15). Apparently antiquity and authoritative citation are not the determining criteria.

No list bearing the heading "Divinely Inspired Books" has yet fallen out of heaven, nor do individual books of the Bible have the Holy Spirit's monogram on the first page. Given the anonymity of so many books, the piety or character of the author cannot serve as the essential criterion of whether the book should be granted holy status. It also will not do to argue that the books whose content is most pious or intrinsically religious are considered scripture, for that question is fraught with subjectivity and would certainly not explain the presence of Esther (the Hebrew version), Song of Songs, and Ecclesiastes. I would hazard a guess that most Protestants would find Sirach more "agreeable" in its piety than Ecclesiates, Esther, or Song of Songs, yet it is not in their Bible and the others are. Finally, one cannot simply look for claims to divine inspiration, for most biblical books contain no such claim, and, ironically, books contemporary with biblical writings that do claim inspired status are often not considered scriptural (e.g., *Jubilees*, 4 Ezra).[18]

If these were not the determining criteria, how does one account for the current collection and shape of the Bible? The short answer comes in the words of Tevye, that lovable father of Joseph Stein's *Fiddler on the Roof:* Tradition! It is only in the sometimes foggy world of ancient communal traditions that the writings that are called sacred today came to be regarded as such by our religious ancestors. The writings themselves did not come stamped in large red letters, "Authoritative." Instead, over time the apparent usefulness of individual scrolls for the larger religious community proved them worthy of preservation. Priests, religious leaders, and scribes must have had a major impact on what books were to be edited, copied, and granted the highest status.[19] This growth of the library is known formally as the growth of the *canon*, a word that has come to mean a list of and/or collection of authoritative books. But canon, in the sense of "formal list," is a problematic term to use for the early stages of the library's growth. The term itself comes from antiquity, but was not used in the sense of a list of books regarded as authoritative until the late fourth century C.E., and then only by Christians.[20] Such a list necessarily excludes some books and, unless it has a statement to the contrary, it implies the closing of the canon simply by ending. The fixed nature of such a list is anachronistic if applied to stages of the library when books were considered authoritative, but there was no sense of definite closure to the category of sacred texts. The ancient library of Israel became, through the streams of tradition, the ancient libraries of several Jewish groups and later several Christian groups. When these libraries are thought by their own respective communities to be closed, with little or no opportunity for deletion or addition, then we can say that the canon is formed.

Of course, to say that the library was formed by tradition is hardly a satisfying answer. For a more complete account we need to return to the initial stages in the growth of this sacred library. We will leave to Dr. Metzger in chapter 4 the discussion of the addition of the Christian "shelf," the New Testament books, to the library.

The concern for the remainder of this chapter is the Israelite development of the library. Admittedly, the earliest of stages of the library have not left a paper trail of evidence; the "librarians" of ancient Israel did not leave us the minutes of their acquisition meetings. Generally speaking, the closer to the present one comes in this history of the progress of the sacred library, the clearer the accounting and details become.

It must first be pointed out that the growth of the library we call the Bible is a stage neither chronologically nor logically separate from the writing and editing of individual documents within that library. Not all the books had been written before other books began to be collected. It is clear that, for example, the five books of the Torah were considered sacred texts with a certain authority before some books of the Hebrew Bible were written (Ezra, Daniel, and others) and long before all books of the New Testament were penned. Furthermore, a place in the sacred library does not necessarily indicate that the individual writing was actually fixed or static. Alongside the drive to preserve was the desire to make the text serve the needs of the intended audience, namely, Jews (and later Christians) in relationship with the God of Abraham. This creative tension resulted in a textual tradition that involved both respect for the inherited tradition and the freedom to supplement and alter, examples of which we considered above.

Finally, in speaking of the growth of a sacred library we ought not to think that there was only growth. There are clear references in our biblical writings to texts that were sacred or authoritative to one degree or another, yet were later discarded, some of them undoubtedly having been incorporated into our biblical texts. Thus, again we mention the Book of Jashar, twice quoted as an authoritative source for knowing divine actions on behalf of Israel (Josh. 10:13; 2 Sam. 1:18) and the "Book of the Wars of YHWH" (Num. 21:14). We have no sense of how widespread was the use of these works or what was their status vis-à-vis other writings, but we do know that at some point they were not retained by later generations of scribes for the use of Israel. If, for example, the Book of the Covenant mentioned in Exodus 24:7 ever existed as a separate document, as many scholars speculate, it certainly held authoritative status. Today it forms part of our book of Exodus. The result is that the library of ancient Israel's sacred and authoritative literature did not begin with the collection of the books found in our biblical library. Rather, our library attests, albeit in tantalizing obscurity, to the existence of sacred documents earlier in Israel's history.

In speaking of the growth of the library, we may give the false impression that ancient Israel had one official library, in downtown Jerusalem perhaps. The historical situation is much more complicated than that. Israel first became a politically settled entity around the year 1000 B.C.E. under the leadership of David. It is in such settled situations, with the growth of formal social institutions, that Israelite society was afforded the luxury of storing, copying, maintaining, and collecting scrolls. Indeed, the demands of governmental bureaucracy would have encouraged and underwritten such activity. It is not that Israel was an illiterate people prior to this time, that they had no writings, and only around 1000 B.C.E. began to "make up" their traditions. Certainly, Israelite traditions had been passed down orally and quite possibly even in written form prior to this. However, it is at the time of the stable monarchy that the necessary conditions are in place for the long term *preservation* of written materials by governmental and religious leaders. Within this monarchical setting there also arose other institutions, such as prophetic groups, with their schools of disciples and scribes (1 Sam. 19:20; 22:6; Isa. 8:16; Jer. 36:4). This time frame correlates well with the chronological work of the scholars of Hebrew language who have, on linguistic grounds, dated the oldest parts of the Bible, such as the poem of Judges 5, to the tenth or eleventh century B.C.E. It is also during the period of monarchy that the Israelite inscriptions begin appearing in the archaeological record. Again, that does not imply that the Israelites wrote nothing prior to this. It only means that of the material we have preserved in our Bibles today the oldest *written form* comes from this period.

Unfortunately, the archaeological spade has not (yet?) turned up library shelves (royal, temple, or other) from ancient Jerusalem so that when we speak of this ancient library we cannot point to the physical remains. It remains a historical construct most naturally associated with royalty and the priesthood, especially in the Persian (539–332) and Greek (beginning in 332) periods B.C.E., when the priesthood was more and more associated with political power. But such collection activity is in keeping with other nations of Israel's cultural world and the textual evidence of the growing importance of written documents among the Jews. Evidence also includes the sixth and fifth century Persian requirement of written "laws of God and the king" for Judah (Ezra 7:26), the credible report of a Ptolemaic request in the third century B.C.E. to the Jerusalem high priest for a copy of the Torah for the Alexandrian library,[21] and the collection activity of the Maccabees (2 Macc. 2:14). Certainly the Jerusalem priestly establishment must have played a central role in the formation of what became the sacred library of Judaism. It is also historically

credible that different groups produced, preserved, and collected different scrolls in accord with their interests as scribes, priest, or prophets,
and only later were collections merged.

It is within the context of stability of the kingdom of united Israel
(ca. 1000–931 B.C.E.) and even the divided kingdoms of north (Israel,
931–722 B.C.E.) and South (Judah, ca. 931–586 B.C.E.) that many important documents were likely produced by royal, priestly, and other scribes.
A clue to this activity is provided by the many documents mentioned in
Kings and Chronicles as historical sources (e.g., "the Book of the Acts of
Solomon," 1 Kings 11:41). The division of the kingdoms would have
resulted in a natural division between writings from a northern perspective and those of a southern perspective. Indeed, such distinctions
in the origin of sources can be observed in narratives such as 1 Kings
15:29–21:30 (north) and most of 2 Kings (south) and in the names of
sources such as "the Book of the Chronicles of the Kings of Israel"
(1 Kgs. 14:19) and "the Book of the Annals of the Kings of Judah" (1 Kgs.
14:29). Scholars have reasonably speculated that when the Northern
Kingdom of Israel fell to Assyrian forces in 722, some persons with access to such writings must have escaped to the south, Judah, bringing
many scrolls with them.

The growing importance of the written tradition is observed in the
late seventh-century reforms of Josiah (ca. 621 B.C.E.). A scroll is said to
have been found in the temple, which, after being interpreted by the
prophetess Huldah (note the continuing importance of orality), became
the basis of Josiah's reform. Many scholars believe this text was a version of what we know as Deuteronomy, since Josiah's reforms were in
accord with that book. The prophet Jeremiah was a supporter of Josiah's
reforms,[22] and the book bearing his name is a fascinating portrayal of
the last desperate decades before Jerusalem's fall to Babylon (586). In
that book the writings of scribes, priests, and other prophets (Jer. 7:22;
8:8–9; 29:24–31), the written scrolls of Jeremiah and his scribe Baruch
(Jer. 29:1–31; 36:1–32), the oral proclamations of Jeremiah (Jer. 37–38),
and oracles of other prophets (Jer. 23:16–32; 29:8–9) are all pleading and
jostling for a hearing among kings and people. When Judah was
destroyed by Nebuchadnezzar and his Babylonian forces in 586,
undoubtedly many documents were forever lost to the flames. But others,
including those of Jeremiah, were rescued and transferred to Babylon
with the Judean exiles. Many scholars think that those years of exile
produced a drive to preserve in a stable written form the legal, cultic,
narrative, and prophetic traditions.[23] In any case, Ezekiel, a prophet of
the sixth-century exile, was certainly aware of material now contained
in the books of Exodus and Leviticus.[24]

When the Jews were allowed to return to their homeland (538 B.C.E.)
under the more liberally minded Persian empire, the Persian-appointed

Jewish governors were charged with shaping the newly constituted, Persian-controlled Jewish state according to ancestral law in a written form, in harmony with Persian policy, and with royal financial support (Ezra 7:11–26).[25] The governor about whom we know the most is the scribe Ezra—usually dated to the middle of the fifth century B.C.E.— and he is frequently credited with codifying and establishing the Torah, the first five books of every Bible, in the basic Hebrew form in which it exists today. It is difficult to prove Ezra's precise role, but there is little doubt that, whoever should get the credit—and Ezra is certainly the best candidate—the Torah had become the central authoritative collection of texts in Judah and Judaism by this time. Thus, the year 400 B.C.E. is a common ballpark figure for the time by which the Torah had gained a reserved place in the sacred library of ancient Judaism. It was in the following century that the Samaritans socially separated from Judaism, taking with them copies of the sacred books, the Torah. These five books remain to this day the only books in the formal sacred library of the Samaritans, and it is a strong indication that no other books of the Bible had yet been firmly established as permanent acquisitions of the library.

But the Torah was not the only literary product of the newly established Jerusalem community and its exilic forebears. Collections of prophetic oracles, from the persons and disciples of Isaiah, Jeremiah, Ezekiel, and others had been compiled, edited, supplemented, copied, and preserved throughout the exile. So also the nation's narratives of its tribal period, monarchies, divisions, and demise, all of which had their oral and/or written forms prior to exile, survived to be edited during and/or after the exile. A selection of prophetic writings came to take its place beside the Torah of Moses. By 180 B.C.E. the collection of "The Twelve," likely those prophets listed in Bibles from Hosea to Malachi, was already a known entity (Sirach 49:10). Some form of the work of Jeremiah is being used as an authoritative source in the middle of the second century B.C.E. by the author of Daniel (9:2). Thus, most scholars hold that the prophetic books of the Bible (Joshua, Judges, Samuel, Kings, Isaiah, Jeremiah, Ezekiel, The Twelve) were a part of the sacred library at least by 200 B.C.E. Even books such as Ruth, Proverbs, and Psalms may have been placed in Israel's book rooms by this time. Certainly liturgical texts such as the Psalms would naturally have been located among the scrolls collected at the temple.

In fact, it is from the second century B.C.E. that we get our first hint of what this growing library might be called. The prologue to the book of Sirach by Ben Sira's grandson (written ca. 130) refers three times to the great written heritage of Israel as "the law, the prophets, and the other writings" (or "the rest of the books"). These designations give evidence of divisions in the library, and their repeated use suggests that for the author they were the preferred way of conceiving of the Jewish literary heritage. From a later vantage point it would seem reasonable that in the "other writings" category Ben Sira's grandson would have placed books such as Psalms and Proverbs. One of the most fascinating documents from among the Dead Sea Scrolls refers to the sacred collection as "the book of Moses, the books of the Prophets and David" (4QMMT C.10). Similarly, Philo, a prolific Jewish philosopher of Alexandria (ca. 20 B.C.E.–40 C.E.) speaks of "laws, oracles through prophets, and hymns and others" (*Contemplative Life* 25). So also Luke, on one occasion refers to the "Law of Moses, the Prophets, and the Psalms" (24:44).

But this tripartite division is not the only form referred to when speaking of the library. New Testament authors, in fact, refer to the collection of sacred texts more often with the phrase "Law and Prophets" (e.g., Matt. 5:17; 7:12; 22:40; Luke 16:16). The Dead Sea Scrolls also use this designation (e.g., 1QS 1.2–3). Furthermore, these categories may not match precisely what we might expect from their use in today's Jewish community. In one Dead Sea Scroll, David is said to have composed all his songs "through prophecy" (11Q5 27.11). Does this mean writings ascribed to him could be in the category of "prophets"?

But none of these designations or groupings imply the crystallization of a canon, or the establishment of an official and formal collection, or an official title for any such collection, or a clear delineation of the books that might be grouped under each heading (law, prophets, other writings), though it seems certain that by this time the Pentateuch stood alone in the grouping "law." What the terms clearly imply is the process of collection and organization. Second Maccabees speaks of Judas the Hasmonean in the second century B.C.E. collecting the "books that had been lost on account of the war" even as Nehemiah (fifth century) was thought to have "founded a library (*bibliotheca*) and collected books (*biblia*) concerning the kings and prophets and books of David, and letters of kings about votive offerings" (2 Macc. 2:13–14). The report of Nehemiah's activity is not corroborated by our older sources about Nehemiah—though it is by no means incredible—but we at least gain a sense of "library building" as conceived in the second century.

Our earlier mention of the Samaritans reminds us that in the last centuries B.C.E. Judaism was not a monolithic entity. Ezra may have established the Torah as the formal authoritative repository of ancestral narrative and law, but in the centuries to come this did not result in an authoritative Judaism centralized in and controlled by a Jerusalem priesthood or governor. For one thing, Jews lived throughout the Near East and Mediterranean world and were not formally beholden to Jerusalem. While the Jerusalem temple priesthood was likely the most powerfully consistent force within Judaism for much of the time, it was in no position to define Judaism for all or to control the multiple developments of what scholars have come to call the "Judaisms" of the culturally fertile Hellenistic world. The designation Jewish must include the separatist *Yahad* community near the Dead Sea (second century B.C.E. to first century C.E.), the military colony on Elephantine with its own Jewish temple (fifth to fourth century B.C.E.), those sympathetic to Greek culture and ideals after the campaigns of Alexander the Great (late fourth century B.C.E.), Essenes, Sadducees, and Pharisees. By the third century B.C.E., with the entire world of Judaism now under the sway of the Hellenistic kingdoms, a large Jewish community flourished in Alexandria, Egypt, and by the first century C.E. Jewish communities thrived—in the hyperbole of Acts 2:5—in "every nation under heaven."

The resulting picture of the last two centuries B.C.E. and the first century C.E., however foggy it is due to the nature of the slight evidence, is that within this diverse and far-flung world of Judaisms there existed a rough-edged central core of a library of sacred texts. The Torah was certainly established at the heart of the library. This is demonstrable from the works of Philo, the Jewish Hellenistic philosopher of Alexandria and indefatigable Torah commentator, along with the Torah-focused community that produced the Dead Sea Scrolls. So also books beyond the first five associated with Moses had gained a solid place in the library of Judaism after the separation of the Samaritans, but not before.

However, even in the first century C.E. it is still too early to speak of the Jewish canon as a solid canon, that is, a precisely defined sacred library with the entrance and exit doors blocked. The Torah-observing community that produced the Dead Sea Scrolls clearly names and/or quotes as authoritative the works we know as *1 Enoch, Jubilees,* and some of their own peculiar writings. At least in practice their sacred library was larger than that of other Jewish groups.

Furthermore, the lack of uniformity in the number of books in the sacred library among various Jewish communities is paralleled by the additions and changes to Greek translations of books such as Daniel and Esther. In both these cases, Greek-speaking Jewish communities produced a book significantly longer than the original Hebrew version and, especially in the case of Esther, a book of a divergent nature. Furthermore, all of the books of the Deuterocanonicals originated in the Jewish community, even though later history would find them only in canons of Christianity.

After the conflagration of 70 C.E. the Jewish historian Josephus (ca. 95) writes in his apologetic work *On the Antiquity of the Jews* (usually called *Against Apion*) that the Jews have not a myriad of books, but rather "just twenty-two properly accredited books." This is our first record of a formal accounting of the entire library of sacred Jewish books. Josephus reveals much about the status of these works. He considers them the product of prophets alone, and their perfection is due to the "inspiration of God" (1:37–38).[26] He also uses a threefold division of Moses (five books), prophetic history (thirteen books), and "hymns to God and advice to men about life" (four books). We can be generally confident about his categorization of most books, but not certain, since he does not list them by name. It should also be noted that Josephus, in his own history of the Jews, utilized the Greek version of Ezra's activity, known today as 1 Esdras, rather than the version found in the Hebrew Bible or the Septuagint. Furthermore, the actual texts of the biblical books used by Josephus were also not identical to those known today, as has been shown by Eugene Ulrich in the case of Samuel.[27] Finally, his list of twenty-two is certainly close to the twenty-four books of rabbinic and modern Judaism.

Another fascinating Jewish work from around 100 C.E. is an apocalyptic writing known as the Fourth Book of Ezra. Of Jewish origin—but used in Christian circles—it refers to the texts of Judaism having been destroyed and requiring that Ezra, by divine inspiration, dictate the words of twenty-four books and seventy other books. Ezra makes the twenty-four public, but seventy were retained for later dissemination (4 Ezra 14:19–48). These twenty-four books are likely the twenty-four books of the Jewish Bible, though the exact identification is impossible since no list is given. The additional seventy, and 4 Ezra, were never regarded as authoritative by rabbinic Judaism. Like Josephus, 4 Ezra seems to have a library much like the Jewish Bible of today.

In the first and second centuries C.E. Jewish revolts in the Roman Empire met with disaster in Palestine (70, 135) and in the diaspora, including Alexandria (115). The result of this period's complicated and tortuous history was the loss of flourishing diversity among Jewish communities and the ascendancy of rabbinic Judaism, in the rich heritage of the Pharisees, under the leadership of gifted and forward-looking rabbis. For this group of Jewish leaders, who laid the foundations for Judaism for centuries to come, the scriptures seem quite clearly defined as twenty-four books, with only a few possible question marks, though we have no list from this early rabbinic period. The great literary product of second-century Judaism was the Mishna, a codification of rabbinic thought and discussion. Nothing is said in this large work directly about the exact books in the library of Judaism, but in one passage (*Yadyim* 3.5) there is an enigmatic report about the sacredness of the Song of Songs and Qohelet (Ecclesiastes), which may be an echo of discussions about their appropriateness for the library of authoritative writings. A roughly contemporary rabbinic work, the Tosefta (*Yadyim* 2.13), similarly discusses Sirach. In any case, what emerges in rabbinic Judaism and comes to dominate the entire Jewish tradition is the twenty-four-scroll library of Hebrew (with a few Aramaic sections) books. By the time of the Babylonian Talmud (ca. 500 C.E.) the three sections (Law, Prophets, Writings) are clearly fixed, and each book is ordered within each section.

The library of sacred scripture for rabbinic Judaism was now complete. We cannot be sure that all these texts were originally housed in the temple prior to its destruction in 70 C.E., though such a scenario is possible. We also cannot demonstrate that the historical process of building this library which resulted in the twenty-four-book canon was an intentional one centered in only one location with a particular end in view. But we can be sure that ancient Israel used sacred texts even as the books of our Bible were being written, that the books of our Bible emerged as sacred scripture beginning at least in the fifth century B.C.E., and that the end result in Judaism (ca. 200 C.E.) was a library of twenty-four books and no more.[28]

In Christianity, which of course flourished independent of rabbinic dominance, the sacred library, though inherited from Judaism, came to look different on several counts, even beyond the obvious inclusion of peculiarly Christian books. Existing primarily in a Greek-speaking environment, Christians naturally used Greek editions of biblical books. These included books that were very literal translations of the Hebrew originals as well as those that were not literal. These Greek editions sometimes contained large additions (e.g., Daniel). So also many Christians used and adopted whole books of Jewish origin composed in Hebrew or Greek that would not be included in the rabbinic library (e.g., Sirach). These works are now contained in what the Roman Catholic and Eastern Orthodox traditions call the Deuterocanonicals, but are not in most Protestant Bibles. While the libraries of Christendom are consistent in their core, there is no universally accepted list of authoritative books among Christians. The first known Christian interest in precisely defining the canon comes with Melito, bishop of Sardis, who in ca. 180 made a trip to Palestine and inquired about which books were considered sacred for the Old Testament. Not surprisingly, the list of books he gives, as reported by the fourth-century Christian historian Eusebius (*Ecclesiastical History* 26.5), generally reflects the view of Palestine where rabbinic Judaism flourished, except that Esther is not listed, and it is unclear exactly which text is meant by Melito's "Esdras." Later Christian lists, however, would include more books, and church leaders would be divided as to whether a handful of books should rightly be considered canonical. Looking at early Christian lists, perhaps the most striking feature is their lack of unanimity regarding the books of the inherited Jewish library.[29] This diversity suggests that Christianity in general did not follow a single canonical tradition from any single Jewish community, whether in Palestine or outside. Though there were attempts to define the canon precisely, looking at Christianity as a whole in any period of the canonical history, the canon remained a cloud, a bit fuzzy at the edges, but dense and uncontroversial at its broad center. Since the time of Jerome (342–420) some church leaders and bodies have acknowledged this imprecision by creating a category of books that are deemed good, but not as good; that is, good for reading and moral building but not for the establishment of doctrine. In this tradition stand the early editions of the *King James Version* (first edition, 1611) that included the books of the Apocrypha but in a separate section. In any case, the cloud is the Christian heritage to this day, as shown by the comparison of the differing libraries of Roman Catholics, Protestants, Eastern Orthodox, and other groups.[30]

Naming the Library

Instead of "Bible," Jews and Christians in antiquity used other terms to refer to their special books. We have already mentioned some names used in antiquity, such as Torah, Prophets, and others. For those writing in Greek, probably the closest to the modern term Bible, was *graphé*, "writing" (*graphai*, plural). Josephus, the Jewish historian of the late first century C.E., refers to the books (*bibloi*) as *hierai graphai*, "sacred scriptures" (*Against Apion* 2.45). But *graphai* could also be used without an adjective to refer to Jewish (and now Christian) sacred texts (e.g., Mt. 21:42) and, though the plural form is more common when speaking of more than one scroll, occasionally the singular is used as a collective plural for the group (e.g., 2 Tim. 3:16; 2 Pet. 1:20). *Graphé* was translated literally into Latin as *scriptura* and eventually into English as the word "scripture," which to this day may be used as singular or plural in reference to the collection of Jewish and Christian sacred texts.

Another common and plural designation was *hiera gramata*, "sacred writings." This term was used for the sacred writings of any people; already in the fifth century B.C.E. the famed Greek historian Herodotus speaks of the hiera gramata of the Egyptians (2.36). Five centuries later a Christian epistle (2 Tim. 3:15) uses hiera gramata to refer to hallowed Jewish writings, and Josephus uses *grammata* alone (without *hiera*, "sacred") to refer to Jewish holy texts (*Against Apion* 1.42). In Hebrew the equivalent of sacred writings, *kitvé ha-qodesh*, "writings of holiness, holy writings" is found in the Mishna (ca. 200 C.E.) to refer to a collection of Jewish Scriptures (*Yadayim* 3.5). The term *bibliotheca*, "collection of books," was used in the early first century B.C.E. by the author of 2 Maccabees (2:13) in reference to the book-gathering activity of Nehemiah. Centuries later, the Christian scholar Jerome would use this same term to refer to the sacred library.

A specifically Jewish designation is *Miqra*, a Hebrew word literally meaning "reading" or "calling," which has been used as a rubric for the collection of scriptures at least since talmudic times (ca. 500 C.E., see *Babylonian Talmud Taanit* 68a).[31] Another term used within Judaism is *Tanakh* (or *Tanak*). This name is an acronym (T-N-K) of the ancient title <u>T</u>orah (Law), <u>N</u>eviim (Prophets), <u>K</u>etuvim (Writings) and is still used today.

The terms Old Testament and New Testament arose in Christian circles and are intrinsically Christian. Today there is an ongoing discussion, especially within the Christian community, about the usefulness of these terms and there are suggestions of alternative titles.[32] Regardless of one's position, the origin of the terms is instructive. Neither Jesus nor Paul dubbed Jewish sacred writings as "Old Testament." It was not until the late second century C.E. that Christian writers began using these terms, and the purpose in doing so is perhaps surprising. A Christian teacher named Marcion was so convinced that the Christian message of love was contrary to the message of Jewish scriptures that he advocated the rejection of the Jewish scriptures and even of some Christian writings that he thought were corrupted by their Jewish forebears.[33] Marcion went so far as to teach that the God of Jewish scriptures was not the same God as the God of Jesus. In protest against the ideas of Marcion, Irenaeus (130–200), Bishop of Lyons, began to use the terms "Old Testament" and "New Testament" to signify and stress the continuity of the more ancient (Jewish) scriptures with the younger (Christian) writings (*Against Heresies* 4.9.1). At about this same time, Melito (ca. 180), Bishop of Sardis, also used the term "Old Testament" (Eusebius *Ecclesiastical History* 4.26.14). It should now be clear that, if the titles Old and New Testament have been used to disparage the Old (read: "dry, irrelevant, superseded") Testament, it is not in keeping with the purpose of Irenaeus and certainly not reflective of the attitude of Jesus or Paul; it is more akin to the thought of Marcion! It is indisputable that the titles Old and New Testament are theologically Christian (though not necessarily sacroscant), but their original use was not part of an anti-Jewish polemic. Instead it was part of an anti-Marcion argument.[34]

The Books and the Story

The Bible is the oldest source we have for the stories of the relationship between the God of Abraham and the community of faith as described in the Introduction to this book. Yet the Bible's relation to those great stories is not as straightforward as one might imagine. The books of the Bible do not proceed like chapters in a historical narrative, each one telling of successive events.[35] Instead—and here is where the term *library* again proves helpful and more accurate—the various books of the Bible form a library of writings that are related in rather diverse ways to the story. What they all have in common are not topics or themes or piety or perspective or genre or historical information; in all of these areas this collection is highly diverse. What they share is a valuation by a religious community as sacred and important for the community. In this valuation of a diverse and complex library, with all its intrinsic richness and complications, the communities of Israel and the church are united. How the library is ordered and arranged and how individual texts are valued vis-à-vis other books varies dramatically among communities, even within the same faith. But the remarkable fact, despite the religious differences, is the shared vision of a multifaceted and beautifully textured anthology of sacred writings. Perhaps anything less would not be worthy of the complex and diverse discourse with the God of Abraham the library is meant to preserve and foster.

Islam, for its part, has not figured much into this essay because the valuation of the Qur'ān in Islam is so superlative that the libraries of Jews and Christians are not usually encountered directly, though the story and stories of the Bible are the backdrop to much of the Qur'ān itself.[36]

By now the reader should be well aware of the complexity of the history and the issues surrounding the writing and collecting of the scriptures. The living and dynamic nature of that growth should also be clear. Each faith community has established its sacred library in order to unite the values of the past with the needs of the present in its ongoing and unfinished story of relationship to the God of Abraham. People of faith, who see themselves in dialogue with the God of Abraham, believe that God has worked through individual authors, editors, copyists, and through whole communities to preserve a discourse between God and God's people still going on in many media. With the beginnings of these sacred libraries now traced and the vitality of each community now substantiated, we are prepared for the more specific discussions to follow.

Suggestions for Further Reading

Barton, John. *Holy Writings, Sacred Text: The Canon in Early Christianity.* Louisville, Ky.: Westminster John Knox, 1997.

Davies, Philip R. *Scribes and Schools: The Canonization of Hebrew Scriptures.* Library of Ancient Israel. Louisville, Ky.: Westminster John Knox, 1998.

Kugel, James, and Rowan Greer. *Early Biblical Interpretation.* Library of Early Christianity. Philadelphia: Westminster, 1986.

Lampe, G. W., ed. *The Cambridge History of the Bible.* Three volumes. Cambridge: Cambridge University Press, 1970.

McDonald, Lee. *The Formation of the Christian Biblical Canon.* Peabody, Mass.: Hendrickson, 1995.

Sæbø, Magne, ed. *Hebrew Bible/Old Testament: The History of Its Interpretation,1.1.* Göttingen: Vandenhoeck & Ruprecht, 1996.

Sanders, James. *From Sacred Story to Sacred Text.* Philadelphia: Fortress, 1987.

VanderKam, James. *The Dead Sea Scrolls Today.* Grand Rapids: Eerdmans, 1994.

[1]Consider the fine distinction drawn by renowned church historian Jaroslav Pelikan: "Tradition is the living faith of the dead; traditionalism is the dead faith of the living" (*The Christian Tradition*, vol. 1, *The Emergence of the Catholic Tradition, 100–600* [Chicago: University of Chicago Press, 1971], 9).

[2]James Kugel and Rowan Greer, *Early Biblical Interpretation* (Philadephia: Westminster, 1986), 34–39.

[3]Ibid., 13–19.

[4]The oldest extant Hebrew inscription discovered is the Gezer Calendar of the tenth century B.C.E. It comes approximately two and a half centuries after the earliest known reference to Israel, on the stele of the Egyptian king Merneptah, from ca. 1220. References to Israelite scribes are found in 2 Samuel 8:16; 2 Kings 18:37; 22:3; Jeremiah 36:4.

[5]Reported by the early fourth-century historian Eusebius, *Ecclesiastical History*, 3.39.4.

[6]M. Black in vol. 3 of *Cambridge History of the Bible*, ed. S. Greenslade (Cambridge: University Press, 1963), 3:442.

[7]"Bible," *Oxford English Dictionary*, 2d ed. (OED2 on CD-ROM ver.1.01; Oxford: University Press, 1992).

[8]For more on book-making in antiquity see chapter 4 below by Professor Metzger.

[9]There is an example of such a scroll, probably dating to the first century C.E., found in the Judean desert (*Les Grottes de Murabba'ât*, in *Discoveries in the Judaean Desert II*, ed. P. Benoit [Oxford: Clarendon Press, 1961], 181–210). See Sirach 49:10 for what is likely the earliest reference to such a grouping.

[10]Protestant Bibles, especially in the sixteenth through eighteenth centuries, frequently included books of the Deuterocanonicals, usually in a separate section between the testaments. This is true occasionally today also.

[11]Even Deuteronomy, which contains first-person narrative in the name of Moses, is still presented at beginning and end (and several places in between) as the work of an anonymous narrator. Exodus and Numbers associate Moses with recording (e.g., Ex. 17:14; 24:4–8; Num. 33:2) but make no claims for the books' authorship. Genesis, on the other hand, has no Mosaic association whatsoever.

[12]Compare Ezra 1:1–3 with 2 Chronicles 36:22–23; 1 Chronicles 18:1–14 with 2 Samuel 8:1–14; Isaiah 36:1—37:20 with 2 Kings 18:13–27; 2 Samuel 22:1–51 with Psalm 18:1–50; Matthew 4:24—5:12 with Luke 6:17–23.

[13]A great deal can be learned about the Chronicler by noting what he omitted. Compare, for example, 1 Chronicles 20:1–3 with 2 Samuel 11:1—12:26.

[14]See the works of Emanuel Tov ("Some Aspects of the Textual and Literary History of the Book of Jeremiah," in *Le livre de Jérémie*, ed. P.-M. Bogaert, [Leuven: University Press, 1981], 145–167), and Eugene Ulrich ("The Canonical Process, Textual Criticism, and Latter Stages in the Composition of the Bible," in *Sha'arei Talmon*, ed. M. Fishbane and E. Tov [Winona Lake, Ind.: Eisenbrauns, 1992], 267–91).

[15]The Qur'ān also speaks of books by Abraham. See 53:37; 87:19.

[16]See *Babylonian Talmud, Sanhedrin* 99a and *Qur'ān* 2:87–121; 3:64–80; 32:23; 40:53.

[17]Robert van Voorst, *Anthology of World Scriptures* (Belmont, Calif.: Wadsworth, 1994), 7–8.

[18]See the curious situation of Paul's explicit disclaimer of divine impetus in 1 Corinthians 7:10–12.

[19]Recently, Philip R. Davies (*Scribes and Schools* [Louisville: Westminster John Knox, 1998], 50) has stressed the role of a scribal elite over against the "believing community," stressed by James Sanders in his works *Canon and Community* (Philadelphia: Fortress, 1984), and *From Sacred Story to Sacred Text* (Philadelphia: Fortress, 1987). In fact, in ancient Israel the two were inextricably linked. This does not imply the historical caricature of scribes going to "the people" for democratic approval of texts.

[20]For a history of the term, see Appendix 1 of Metzger's *The Canon of the New Testament* (Oxford: Clarendon Press, 1987).

[21]*Letter of Aristaeas* 1–3, 29–46. See the next chapter (2) by Professor Kamesar for more on this episode.

[22]Richard Elliott Friedman (*Who Wrote the Bible?* [New York: Harper & Row, 1987], 125–30) argues that Jeremiah, a levitical priest, was the author of Deuteronomy, composed from the literary traditions of priests.

[23]E.g., David Freedman, "The Earliest Bible," in *Backgrounds for the Bible*, ed. M. O'Connor and D. Freedman (Winona Lake, Ind.: Eisenbrauns, 1987), 29–37.

[24]Friedman, *Who Wrote the Bible?* 161–73.

[25]Jon L. Berquist, *Judaism in Persia's Shadow* (Minneapolis: Fortress, 1995), 131–44.

[26]Josephus clearly understands prophecy in this context as the authoring of inspired and authoritative books.

[27]"Josephus' Biblical text for the Books of Samuel," in *Josephus, the Bible and History*, ed. L. Feldman and G. Hata (Detroit: Wayne State, 1989), 89–96.

[28]For more on the form and use of the Bible in rabbinic Judaism see chapter 3 below by Professor Reeves.

[29]Jack Lewis, "Some Aspects of the Problem of Inclusion of the Apocrypha," in *The Apocrypha in Ecumenical Perspective*, ed. S. Meurer (New York: United Bible Society, 1991), 168.

[30]For more on the differences in Christian canons see the chapters by Professors Constantelos (chap. 6), Fitzmyer (chap. 7), and Steinmetz (chap. 8).

[31]On the significance of this term in contemporary Judaism see chapter 10 below by Professor Meyer.

[32]See *Hebrew Bible or Old Testament*, ed. R. Brooks and J. Collins (South Bend, Ind.: University of Notre Dame, 1990).

[33]Marcion limited the collection of sacred writings to ten letters of Paul and a highly edited version of Luke's Gospel.

[34]See Kugel and Greer, *Early Biblical Interpretation*, 115–25.

[35]On the story theme in contemporary Protestantism see the essay of Professor McClanahan in chapter 9 below.

[36]Chapter 5 below by Professor Johnson considers in detail Islam's relation to the Bible.

2

The Bible Comes to the West: The Text and Interpretation of the Bible in Its Greek and Latin Forms*

Adam Kamesar

In the contemporary world, there is a much greater awareness about the cultural differences between the Western world and the non-Western world than there was a century ago. This is partially due to political changes following the two world wars, and the breakup of the colonial empires. With the fall of those empires, we have seen a greater cultural assertiveness on the part of many newly independent non-Western countries. At the same time, improvements in international communications have given us greater knowledge of the cultural

---

* This chapter was first presented as part of the course offered by James Bowley to undergraduates at King College in the spring semester of 1997, on the "Living Traditions of the Bible." The guest lectures were also open to the general community in Bristol, Tennessee. This setting has determined the general tone and intent of the chapter. The lecture has been revised for publication, but it retains some of the flavor of oral delivery. The aim of the chapter is to provide an accessible and coherent account of the topics under discussion. Accordingly, the presentation of some issues has been simplified for the sake of clarity, and annotation has been kept to a minimum. The bibliography should provide a guide to more detailed treatments of many of the subjects covered here. While I have often simply summarized widely shared scholarly opinion, the chapter, of course, reflects my own general point of view. Where I have relied more specifically on my own published work, I have indicated this in the notes.

traditions of the non-Western world. In addition, there has been significant immigration from many of these countries to Western countries,
which has put us in direct contact with representatives of non-Western
cultures. One of the benefits of this awareness of non-Western culture is
that it provides us with greater insight into Western culture, for it allows
us to understand what is specific to it. And when we consider the Bible
in this context, we see it as something specific to, and intimately
connected with, Western civilization. If we read Western history, philosophy, or literature, or look at Western art, we will easily see how important the Bible has been over the course of the past 2,000 years. We
will appreciate this fact even more when we begin to explore more deeply
some of the Eastern civilizations.

In view of the fact that the Bible has been a characteristic part of the
Western cultural legacy for so long, we sometimes forget that this was
not always the case. In the time of Jesus, Western or European civilization was dominated by the cultures of Greece and Rome, and the Bible,
that is, the Old Testament, was a foreign book in that world. The New
Testament as well, even though it was written in Greek, constituted a
body of literature not immediately comprehensible in the Greco-Roman
context. What follows is a survey and exploration of how that situation
changed, and how the Bible came to be a part of Western civilization.
After a brief historical introduction, our survey will be set forth in two
parts. First we must consider how the Bible came to exist in Greek and
Latin form. For if the Bible had not been translated into the languages of
the West, it could not, in the concrete sense, have become part of Western civilization. Secondly, we will provide a brief history of Greek biblical interpretation and attempt to describe how, in those early centuries,
the Bible was viewed and understood from the Greco-Latin perspective.

Historical Introduction

We may conveniently take the year 500 B.C. as the beginning of this
brief sketch. At that time, as illustrated in diagram 1, the Jewish, Greek,
and Roman civilizations were all existing separately. There was little or
no contact between them. Over the course of the next 500 years, however, up to the time of the birth of Christ, we find that all three of these
civilizations came to be linked.

Around the year 500 B.C., important events took place in all of the
three civilizations under consideration. In Judea, the rebuilding of the
temple (destroyed in 587) was completed in 515, marking the beginning
of the Second Temple period. In Greece, the year 508 witnesses the reforms of Cleisthenes, and the stabilization of Athenian democracy. The
traditional date for the foundation of the Roman republic is 509. The
fifth century itself was an extremely significant one, especially in Judea
and Greece. In Judea, the reforms of Ezra and Nehemiah, traditionally
dated to the years 458–432, ushered in a new society, founded on the

Diagram 1: Roman, Greek, and Jewish Civilizations

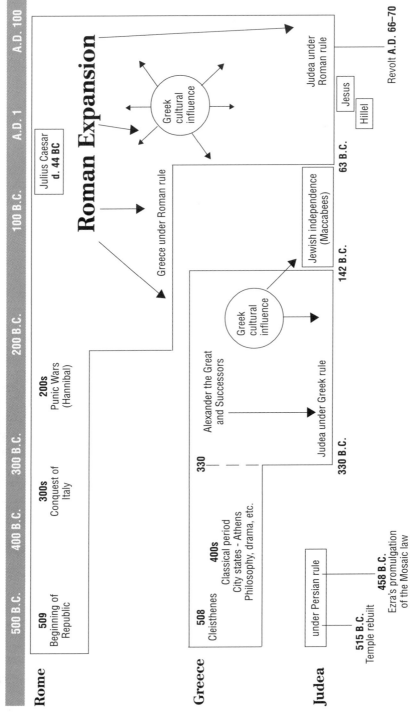

legislation of the Torah, or Pentateuch. In Greece, the fifth century was the golden age of the city-states Athens and Sparta. The city-states existed as sovereign units and, at different times, controlled large "empires" within the Greek world. Athens was characterized by an extremely sophisticated democratic government and an open society within which cultural life flourished. Indeed, the cultural achievements of fifth -century Athens remain unparalleled in world history. This was the age of Socrates, of the dramatists Aeschylus, Sophocles, Euripides, Aristophanes, and of the historians Herodotus and Thucydides. Pericles, the great Athenian statesman, called his city the "school of Hellas" (Thucydides, *Peloponnesian War* 2.41). This same period in Roman history is somewhat less "golden," and scholars are also less confident about the reliability of the historical tradition. Nevertheless, important events did occur in fifth-century Rome, such as the promulgation of the Twelve Tables, the first Roman law code. None of these developments, however, in Judea, Greece, and Rome, were related to one another. So while Nehemiah, Pericles, and the ten commissioners who drew up the Twelve Tables were more or less contemporary individuals, they probably had never heard of each other.

However, over the next 400 years or so there is a change in this situation. All three of these civilizations come into contact. In stage 2 on diagram 1, we observe the end of isolation between Greek and Jewish civilization. This came about through the agency of Alexander the Great. Alexander was from Macedonia, a semi-Greek state in the northern part of Greece. His father, Philip, had put an end to the great age of the Greek city-states by placing them under the hegemony of the kingdom of Macedonia. Alexander inherited his father's position and led an army of both Macedonians and Greeks against the Persians. Alexander conquered the entire Persian Empire, and the separation of West and East, and of Greek and Jew, came to an end. This is because the conquest of Alexander was not only military but cultural. He began the process of what we call the Hellenization of the East. When Alexander went on his expedition, in his footsteps followed many Greek colonists. These colonists established cities, or Greek *poleis*. These poleis were not just places to live, but focal points of Greek civilization. Although they did not possess de facto sovereignty, as the poleis had in the golden age, they were organized internally along classical Greek lines and had sophisticated forms of government, highly developed educational institutions, and an advanced cultural life. The Greek polis was the primary means by which the East became Hellenized, or shall we say, the upper echelons of society became Hellenized.

Upon the death of Alexander his empire became divided among his officers, but the resulting kingdoms were ruled by Macedonian families who encouraged Hellenization, some to a lesser, some to a greater extent.

The Greek language and Greek culture continued to spread in the areas conquered by Alexander. So strong, in fact, was the process of Hellenization in the lands of the Near East, that one cannot really talk about the end of Greek cultural influence in that region until the Arab conquest, which took place in the seventh century of the common era.

While the Jewish and Greek worlds converge at the time of Alexander, the Romans enter the picture somewhat later. As diagram 1 indicates, for the first part of the Hellenistic period the Romans lived apart from the Greeks. In the fourth and early third centuries B.C., the Romans were busy with the conquest of Italy. The famous Punic Wars, which were fought during the years 264–241 and 218–201, pitted the Romans against the Carthaginians and Hannibal. These wars were about control over the western Mediterranean region. However, after the defeat of Hannibal, the Romans turned their attention to the East and became involved in wars with some of the major Hellenistic kingdoms. The Romans established their dominance over these kingdoms in a series of wars fought in the first half of the second century B.C., but the Romans were very slow to move toward annexation and were content to play the role of superpower for a long time. Gradually, however, over the course of about 170 years, they did convert all of the major Hellenistic kingdoms into Roman provinces. The final act in this drama came in the year 30 B.C., when, with the death of Cleopatra, the Ptolemaic kingdom of Egypt became a Roman province. This marks the end of the Hellenistic period from the political point of view and the end of the separate development of the Jewish, Greek, and Roman civilizations. By the time of the birth of Christ, the three civilizations that had existed separately 500 years earlier were now in full and constant contact.

Regarding the Roman conquest of the East, we would do well to remember that it was not a cultural conquest. That is to say, there was no Latinization of the eastern part of the empire as there had been a Hellenization previously. The Romans did not force or even encourage the spread of the Latin language or the adoption of Latin culture on the part of the inhabitants of the old Hellenistic kingdoms. Rather, the Romans left the Greek culture in place, learned Greek themselves, and in many ways Hellenized their own culture. Why? Because the civilization of the Greek polis, and Greek culture generally, were so respected by the Romans that they left the machinery of Hellenistic civilization intact and adopted Greek culture for themselves as a second culture. As the Roman poet Horace put it, Greece, the captive, made the Roman conqueror her own captive (*Epistles* 2.1.156–7). That is why one often hears the expression "Greco-Roman" civilization, but not, say, "Greco-Persian" or "Romano-Islamic" civilization.

It is this historical phenomenon that allowed Christianity to advance as fast as it did in the early centuries. For the new religion spread easily through the unified political realm that was the Roman Empire, and its message was communicated via the Greek language, which was known not only in the East, but was also widely used in the West, especially in the city of Rome itself. Indeed, the early Church Fathers viewed both the translation of the Old Testament into Greek and the establishment of the Roman Empire in the East before the birth of Christ as providential events. By providing the conditions for the spread of the gospel message, they paved the way for the advance of Christianity.

The Origins of the Greek and Latin Versions of the Bible

We may turn now to the origin of Bible in its Greek form. Employing the perspective of the Church Fathers, who are the most important witnesses to the transmission of the Greek Bible, we may distinguish two different traditions of Greek Bible translation, which are shown on diagram 2. One may be termed the Septuagintal tradition, the other, for want of a better term, may be called the "non-Septuagintal" tradition. The Septuagint was the first translation of the Bible into any language. It was produced in the city of Alexandria, in the Ptolemaic kingdom of Egypt, in the time of Ptolemy II, who reigned in the years 283/2–246 B.C. According to the traditional account, the origin of this translation is connected with the great library of Alexandria, which was also established by Ptolemy II, or perhaps by his father Ptolemy I. The library of Alexandria was one of the wonders of the ancient world and was the first large-scale library in the history of Western civilization.

The phenomenon of the library of Alexandria is best understood as an expression of tendencies in Greek culture that came about as a result of or were reinforced by certain events in the age of Alexander to which we have alluded above. First, the Hellenistic period represents an end to the age of the city-states, an end of what the Greeks called liberty or sovereignty. Second, the conquests of Alexander and his successors brought the whole Persian Empire under Greek control. On the one hand, the loss of the sovereignty of the city-states led to the feeling that a great age had finished. The classical age of Athens was over, and the environment in which tragedy, comedy, philosophy, and historiography had flourished was gone. Looking back, it seemed that it was the time to preserve and maintain the memory of this great age, and the formation of a library would allow for the collection of its literary legacy. On the other hand, the conquest of the Persian Empire led to a different kind of phenomenon, or rather strengthened a tendency just developing, namely, that of a broader and more systematic empirical science and scholarship. While in the school of Plato there was much interest in mathematics and theoretical sorts of problems, Aristotle was more of a scientist and scholar and carried out practical research in areas as diverse as biology and constitutional history. Alexander's conquest gave a boost to the

Diagram 2: Traditions of Greek Bible Translation

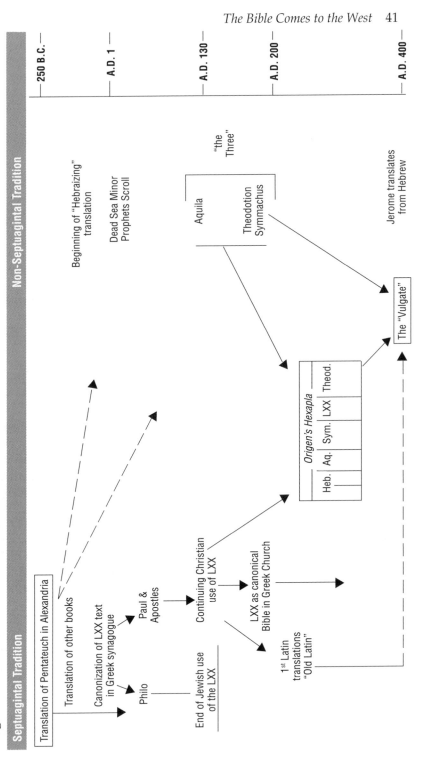

| Septuagintal Tradition | | Non-Septuagintal Tradition |

250 B.C. —
A.D. 1 —
A.D. 130 —
A.D. 200 —
A.D. 400 —

Translation of Pentateuch in Alexandria

Translation of other books

Canonization of LXX text in Greek synagogue

Paul & Apostles

Philo

End of Jewish use of the LXX

Continuing Christian use of LXX

LXX as canonical Bible in Greek Church

1st Latin translations "Old Latin"

Beginning of "Hebraizing" translation

Dead Sea Minor Prophets Scroll

"the Three"

Aquila

Theodotion

Symmachus

Origen's Hexapla

Heb. | Aq. | Sym. | LXX | Theod.

Jerome translates from Hebrew

The "Vulgate"

Aristotelian type of approach. One did not have to debate or write imaginary dialogues about the far places of the earth. One could actually go and visit such places. What were the largest mountains? Where were the largest fish? It was a sort of age of exploration, and there was tremendous energy given to research, cataloging, and systematic description of all kinds of different phenomena. The Alexandrian library, and the sort of scholarship that is associated with it, are in part an expression of this tendency in the field of literature.

How does the translation of the Bible into Greek fit into this picture? The traditional account of the translation is found in a text called the *Letter of Aristeas*, which was probably written in the second century B.C. In this text, it is said that Demetrius of Phalerum, the head of the library of Alexandria, was given large amounts of money to collect all of the books in the world. At a certain point Ptolemy II, the king, asked him about the number of volumes in the library. Demetrius responded that he had over 200,000, but hoped to move toward about 500,000. He also said that the books containing the Jewish laws were missing. The king indicated to Demetrius that he should not worry about budget, and that he should spare no expense in making acquisitions. But at that point Demetrius raised a different sort of problem. He said that the Jewish laws would require translation. So the king and his men arranged to write to the high priest in Jerusalem, and asked him to send them copies of the books and also scholars capable of translating them into Greek. So, according to the *Letter of Aristeas*, seventy-two scholars came to Alexandria. They were welcomed by the king, given a banquet, and then led to isolated quarters on the island of Pharos to do the work. The seventy-two men, according to the account, apparently sat down, much like Bible revision commissions of our time, and made a translation. For this reason, the translation came to be called (that of) the "Seventy-two," or simply, "Seventy," that is, *Septuaginta* in Latin. In later times, this term was applied to the Greek translation of the entire Bible, but it should be remembered that the *Letter of Aristeas* speaks only about the translation of the Pentateuch. In any case, when the translation was completed, it was read first to the Jewish community of Alexandria, which asked if it could also have a copy, and then to the king, who expressed great admiration of its contents (*Letter of Aristeas* 9–11, 28–51, 172–86, 301–12).

This is our traditional account. Many modern scholars have attacked this source, however, claiming that the story is not historical. They think that it is not logical that the librarians of Alexandria would take an interest in an obscure Hebrew text that they probably had not even heard of before. For if one looks at Greek literature before that time, and even for a number of centuries later, one will find almost no mention of or interest in the Bible.[1] In place of the traditional story, an alternative explanation of the origin of the Greek translation of the Bible is proposed.

The initiative is attributed to the Jewish community in Alexandria, which had grown rapidly in the first decades of the third century B.C. The community had become Hellenized quickly, and many of its members did not know Hebrew. It was the community that sponsored the translation, even though it has only the role of an observer in the traditional account. As time went by, the story attested in the *Letter of Aristeas* arose and was embellished out of a desire to glorify the origin of the translation by connecting it with the famous library of Alexandria.

However, this modern reconstruction fails to take into account the specific nature of Alexandrian scholarship at the time. As I indicated above, that scholarship was characterized by various factors. The librarians would not have sought to obtain the books of the Pentateuch on the assumption that it ranked alongside Greek literature of a great bygone age. In this sense, implied associations of the Pentateuch with classical works or works belonging to the classical tradition that are present in the *Letter of Aristeas* may indeed represent later embellishment or wishful thinking (§§ 31, 312–16). On the other hand, as I mentioned, there was another characteristic of Alexandrian scholarship that would entail interest in a work such as the Pentateuch. This was the scientific or empirical tendency. This led to an attempt to collect all kinds of different books, whether they had literary value or not. Today we have fragments from some of the early catalogs of the library of Alexandria, and they mention even a book of etiquette to be observed at banquets with courtesans and cookbooks.[2] So if works such as these were cataloged, then certainly one can accept the notion that there would have been interest in acquiring a copy of the laws of a people within the vicinity. In fact, there is evidence that there were Alexandrian scholars who had a special scholarly interest in the laws of non-Greek peoples.[3] So it would seem that the fundamental basis of the story of the translation of the Pentateuch can stand. Not that every word in the *Letter of Aristeas* is historically accurate, but the general presentation and the linkage of the first translation of the Pentateuch with the library of Alexandria would appear to be legitimate.

Over the course of the next 200 or 250 years, some important developments took place in the history of the Greek Bible (see diagram 2). In the first place, the other books of the Old Testament came to be translated into Greek. We do not know the specific dates, but we know that more or less by the time of the birth of Jesus, not only the Pentateuch, but most of the Prophets and the Writings also existed in Greek. Secondly, we know that the translation, and in particular that of the Pentateuch (the other books to a lesser extent), acquired an almost canonical status in the Greek synagogue. By canonical we mean that the text was viewed as the official Bible of the Greek synagogue. This is particularly clear from the writings of Philo, a Jewish philosopher who was active in the Jewish community of Alexandria during the lifetime of Jesus. He proclaimed that the Greek text of the Pentateuch was the exact equivalent of the Hebrew text, with the implication that use of the Hebrew text was not necessary (*Life of Moses* 2:38–40). Indeed, he does not use the Hebrew text in his voluminous commentary, and his exegesis is carried out by means of a very close reading of the Greek text. In other words, the Hebrew text is not relevant for Philo, neither in theory nor in practice. The Greek text is the text of the Bible, period. In a similar, though not quite as absolute, fashion, Paul relied on the Greek text of the Septuagint when he went on his missions in the middle of the first century C.E. Reading the Acts of the Apostles, one readily notes that Paul almost always starts out in the local synagogue, and most of the synagogues that he visited in Asia Minor or Greece were Greek-speaking. In his theological argumentation based on the Old Testament, Paul operated on the assumption that the Bible was known and used in its Greek form. In short, both Philo and Paul show us the significance and the place of the Septuagint translation in the synagogue.

The position of the Septuagint in the church is based on its importance in the early development of the Christian movement and, in particular, on the phenomenon to which we have just referred. The Septuagint was the means by which the gospel could be preached successfully to "Hellenists" inside Judea (cf. Acts 6:1) and outside Judea generally. The success of the apostles' message that Jesus fulfilled the Old Testament prophecies depended on the availability of an Old Testament which could be understood by Greek-speaking persons. For one cannot understand how Jesus fulfilled prophecies without understanding those prophecies. And if one does not know Hebrew, the prophecies must be read in the Septuagint version. Consequently, as Christianity gradually evolved from being a primarily Aramaic/Hebrew-speaking movement inside Judea to being a primarily Greek-speaking movement outside Judea, it was only natural that the Bible in its Greek form would attain greater authority than the Bible in its Hebrew form. Such authority would only increase as Jewish, Aramaic/Hebrew-speaking Christians not only became a minority, but became alienated from mainstream Christianity.

During the first four centuries of the common era, the position of the Septuagint as the official Bible of the church was consolidated and maintained. It was largely a growing awareness on the part of Christians themselves of the circumstance that I have described in the preceding paragraph, that is, the role of the Septuagint in the spread of the gospel message, that reinforced the authority of the Greek text. Indeed, when the existence and different substance of the Hebrew text became better known to Christians, after the rise of Christian biblical scholarship in the third century (to which I shall return shortly in greater detail), the expression of this idea was further elaborated. The Septuagint attained the preeminent status of "Bible of the Gentiles." For it was believed that if the Greek translation was the primary means by which the Gentiles had come to know Christ, an event ordained by Providence, then that translation itself must be endowed with authority that is equal to or even goes beyond that of the Hebrew original. In the eyes of most of the Church Fathers, the Hebrew Bible was irrelevant, as it had been for Philo, or only had an auxiliary role. In general, the Greek Bible was *the* Old Testament of the early Christian communities. It retained that position among Greek-speaking Christians throughout the medieval period and into modern times. On the other hand, most Greek-speaking Jewish communities stopped using the Septuagint translation, probably during the second century C.E. It is sometimes thought that the Jews abandoned the Septuagint precisely because it was adopted by Christians. This may be partially correct, but the situation is somewhat more complex. In order to understand it, we must now turn to what I have called the "non-Septuagintal" tradition of translation. A discussion of this tradition is also necessary for our treatment of the Latin Bible, which is still to come.

Different factors led to the rise of a rival movement of Greek Bible translation. In the first place, it must be remembered that textual transmission in antiquity was different from what it has become in the age of printing. Anyone who sits down and tries to copy word-for-word even a few pages of text will notice that the new copy has many errors or changes. Before the invention of the printing press, this was the standard method of reproducing texts. Consequently, in the course of a few generations, many differences between copies of the same text were common. If the Pentateuch was translated into Greek in 250 B.C., the form of the text will have evolved somewhat by 50 B.C. At the same time, copies of the Hebrew text circulating in 50 B.C. will have been different from the one used by the translators 200 years earlier. Moreover, the Greek and the Hebrew texts developed for the most part independently of one another from 250 B.C. onward, that is, changes occurring in the Greek did not necessarily influence the Hebrew or vice versa. In short, by 50 B.C. the actual Hebrew and Greek texts would have exhibited some serious differences.

The second point to be made is that the interpretation of the two texts also developed differently. While readers of the Greek text developed their own way of reading the text in a Greek cultural milieu, the interpretation of the Hebrew text developed in its own way in an Aramaic or Hebrew-speaking environment. For example, the meaning and ulterior connotations of a Greek word might evolve otherwise than those of the Hebrew word that it translated in 250 B.C. This may be observed easily by comparing, say, Philo's interpretation of a given Pentateuchal verse with an interpretation of that same verse in a Hebrew text from the Dead Sea Scrolls. So not only was there a separate development in terms of texts, but there was also separate development in terms of textual study and textual understanding.

Alongside these two factors was a third. This relates to a growing awareness of the "canonicity" of the text. As the centuries passed, the Jewish communities developed a more intense reverence for the written text of Scripture, a common development in the evolution of most religious communities. Every "jot and tittle" in the text came to be pregnant with meaning. Any differences in wording, even tiny, were thought to be important. What this meant was that the two developments that I described in the two preceding paragraphs, namely, the real differences between the Greek and the Hebrew texts in wording and meaning, were noticed by those who were aware of both texts. Needless to say, this would constitute a serious problem, for how could God's revelation have two distinct forms?

It was this problem that led to a new movement in Greek Bible translation. In a word, there was an attempt to bring the Greek translation into greater accord with the Hebrew text as it was read and understood in the first century B.C./C.E. Moreover, the greater reverence for the precise text of Scripture led to a method of translation that was different from that used by the Seventy-two. The new movement was about more careful and more literal translation, with greater respect for the precise letter of the text. While the Seventy-two did attempt to be literal, their literalism was somewhat liberal. The new translators tried to render nearly every single word in the Hebrew with a precise equivalent in the Greek. The result was, of course, a translation that contained an even more "Hebraic" Greek style than that of the Septuagint. But this was apparently a small price to pay for a version that was much closer to the Hebrew original.

While one finds evidence of this new movement already in some papyrus fragments from the second or early first century B.C., it comes more clearly to light in the Greek scroll of the Minor Prophets found near the Dead Sea, at Nahal Hever. While the most famous Dead Sea Scrolls are in Hebrew and Aramaic, some are in Greek, and the *Dodecapropheton*, indicated by the siglum 8HevXIIgr, is among the most important. The translation cannot be dated precisely, but the most authoritative opinions place it sometime between 50 B.C. and A.D. 50. Unfortunately, it carries no indication of who the translator was. However, the text is the most significant evidence of an early "Hebraizing" trend in Greek biblical translation, which signals the beginning, for practical purposes, of the non-Septuagintal tradition. It is noteworthy that this movement is pre-Christian, because it means that the movement away from the Septuagint on the part of Jewish communities began earlier than was previously thought and was not determined, at least originally, by Christian use of that version.

I should repeat here that in using the word "non-Septuagintal" to describe this second movement in Greek Bible translation, I am reflecting the perspective of the Church Fathers rather than being strictly accurate. The new movement often does not involve as much translation *de novo* as it does *revision* of the old version. This is indicated in diagram 2 by the broken lines pointing from left to right. In any case, the movement toward more literal translation of the Hebrew gained steam and really came into its own in the second century C.E. In this century we find a group of three translators who came to be known as "the Three." The first is Aquila, who produced a very systematic translation of the Bible in the days of Rabbi Akiba and the Roman emperor Hadrian, that is, in the 130s. Some fifty to seventy years after him came Theodotion and Symmachus. The version of Theodotion comes the closest to being simply a revision of the Septuagint, while Symmachus has the honor of having produced the most "elegant" of the translations, as far as the quality of the Greek is concerned. It was the version of Aquila, however, that came to be most favored by the Jewish communities. At this point, one might have expected Jews and Christians to go their separate ways, the Christians using the Septuagint and the Jews using the version of Aquila. It did not happen quite this way, however, and the versions of "the Three" came to attain their influence among Christians rather than among Jews, and indeed owe their preservation, albeit partial, to the church.

What is the explanation of this phenomenon? It is to be sought in the rise of Christian biblical scholarship. The advent of Christian biblical scholarship should not be confused with Christian use and study of Scripture, because this goes back, of course, to the New Testament itself. This use of Scripture, however, does not qualify as "biblical scholarship," nor for the most part do the writings of the first and second century Christians. Rather, Christian biblical scholarship begins with Origen, whose dates are approximately A.D. 185–255. Origen was a systematic scholar of Greek schooling, and he attempted in his biblical study to employ methods of scholarship that have been discussed above in connection with the Alexandrian library. Origen attempted to reach a comprehensive knowledge of the Bible, "cataloging" its different textual forms and reaching toward a full understanding of its "system of meaning." In the textual sphere Origen's greatest achievement was his six-columned Bible or *Hexapla*, a representation of which is seen in diagram 2. He was interested in what the actual text of the Bible was, so he brought together the available evidence in a scientific fashion. The evidence, for Origen, was the Hebrew text and the Greek versions that he had available. These texts were placed in parallel columns. The number of columns was usually six, thus the name *Hexapla*, although sometimes the number may have been different for different books of the Bible. The first column contained the actual Hebrew text in Hebrew letters, and in the second column Origen placed a transliteration of the Hebrew text in Greek letters. The remaining columns contained, in the following order, four different Greek translations: Aquila, Symmachus, the Septuagint, and Theodotion, although there is some debate about the presence and placement of the version of Theodotion. This layout, in parallel columns, allowed one to compare word by word exactly how the Hebrew was rendered in each translation.

Origen's *Hexapla* exercised considerable influence on the text of the Septuagint, as well as on biblical scholarship in the Greek world. Subsequent scribes sometimes employed the other Greek versions to "correct" apparent errors in the traditional version. Biblical scholars became more aware of the fact that the Hebrew text was the original text of the Scriptures, and did not hesitate to employ the versions of Aquila, Symmachus, and Theodotion in their commentaries. However, the *Hexapla* also led to what could be called a backlash, in that the position of the Septuagint as the Bible of the church was perceived to be under threat from the "non-Septuagintal tradition," specifically, "the Three." This led to the development of some very sophisticated thinking in defense of the traditional translation. The arguments that were put forward as a result of that thinking, one of which we have touched on above (pp. 44–45), in combination with the normal conservatism that tends to accompany any religious institution, allowed the Septuagint to maintain its position as the official Bible of the church in the Greek world.[4] It was rather in the Latin world, to which we now turn, that the implications of Origen's *Hexapla* were carried to their logical terminus, and the "non-Septuagintal" tradition made its real mark.

Before we consider this phenomenon, we must step back a moment chronologically and consider the first Latin translations of the Bible. There are no surviving Latin translations made by the Jewish community. Whether there even were written versions, at least of the sort that were widely copied and transmitted, is questionable. The earliest Latin versions of the Bible that we know come from Christian hands. Now, when Christianity began to have success as a missionary movement, it did so in its Greek form. Many of Paul's successors may not even have known Hebrew. Moreover, Greek was widely known and used in Rome, the major Christian center of the West. Therefore, it was only natural that the first translations of the Old Testament into Latin were made directly from the Septuagint. The origin of these translations is probably to be set in the second half of the second century. These versions were not the result of any official initiative, but came into existence in a rather haphazard manner, probably on an "as needed" basis. According to the view of Saint Augustine, anyone who got hold of a Greek text and thought he had some facility in both Greek and Latin ventured to translate it (*On Christian Instruction* 2.11.16). These first Latin translations, made from the Septuagint, are know as the *Vetus Latina,* or "Old Latin."

The Old Latin version, or better, versions, continued to be used over the course of several centuries. In the late fourth century, however, a new development took place. This was largely the result of the efforts of one man, Saint Jerome (ca. 347–420). Jerome was a born scholar and spent much time in the East, where he gained an outstanding knowledge of Greek and a good knowledge of Hebrew. In 384, he was asked by Pope Damasus to revise the Latin text of the gospels, which, through continuous copying, existed in multiple forms. One thing led to another, and in 391, Jerome began to produce an entirely new Latin translation of the Old Testament on the basis of the original Hebrew. If it was his own instinct and scholarly sense that led him to understand the need for such a project, it was Origen's *Hexapla* that allowed him to justify it to his contemporaries and actually execute it. For by comparing the Greek versions with the original Hebrew in a systematic fashion, he could show that the translations of "the Three" were much closer to the Hebrew text than the Septuagint. He also pointed to the fact that Greeks themselves were sometimes "correcting" the Septuagint on the basis of "the Three," thus implicitly acknowledging the legitimacy of those versions. But whereas the Greeks were unwilling to discard the Septuagint in favor of the "non-Septuagintal" tradition, this ultimately proved not to be the case with the Latins. Greek was not their language, and they probably did not have as much "emotional commitment" to it. And why should they settle for the Old Latin, which, as Jerome put it, "had been poured into the third jar," that is, it was a translation of a translation (*Preface to the Books of Solomon*)? Now, one might be curious as to why it took some 150 years after the death of Origen for a Latin scholar to realize the necessity of this project. The reason is probably to be found in the fact that Latin biblical scholarship, just as the Greek, needed some time to develop and reach maturity. It also needed the self-confidence to bypass the Bible of the church and set a course toward the Hebrew original. Such audacity met with some opposition at first, notably from Saint Augustine and from Jerome's friend-turned-enemy Rufinus, who accused Jerome of replacing the Bible of the church with a Jewish Bible (*Apology against Jerome* 2.39, 41). But Jerome's version of the Old Testament "according to the Hebrew" ultimately became part of the Vulgate, the official Bible of Latin Christianity.[5]

A careful study of Jerome's Latin translation reveals that in most cases, it is very close to the versions of Aquila, Symmachus, or Theodotion. Jerome knew these texts directly and from Origen's *Hexapla*, and they served as his primary guide to the meaning of Hebrew text.

The result is that the Vulgate, while it still maintains features of the Septuagint/Old Latin translation, may be regarded in general as a sort of representative of what I have called the "non-Septuagintal" tradition of Greek translation. The lines of influence are shown in diagram 2.

As we look back on the history of Greco-Latin biblical translation, we note the importance of two different traditions extending from Judaism into Christianity. A longer view reveals that the perspective of Rufinus was not correct. The Septuagintal tradition was not "Christian," nor was the "non-Septuagintal" tradition ultimately an exclusively Jewish legacy. Rather, both originated within Greek-speaking Jewish communities, and the Septuagintal tradition was adopted by the Greek Christian community, and the "non-Septuagintal" tradition was adopted by the Latin Christian community. What we should rather emphasize is the continuity of each tradition as it progresses from Judaism into Christianity.

The Beginnings of Western Biblical Interpretation

The early history of Greek (and Latin) interpretation of the Bible cannot be understood apart from the history of interpretation of secular or "pagan" Greek and Latin literature in antiquity. In fact, the interpretation of the classical patristic age, that is, from Origen to Theodoret (died 466), when Greek and Latin biblical exegesis reached its highest point of development, is to be understood primarily within the context of classical culture and not with reference to Jewish methods of interpretation, although the latter were not without influence.

So what are the major phases and the major moments in the history of Western biblical interpretation? Certainly biblical interpretation in its Greek form must postdate the first Greek translation of ca. 250 B.C. But again one must backtrack into the classical age of Greece to understand some of the approaches that came to be employed in Greek and Latin Bible exegesis. More specifically, when we look at classical interpretation, we need to consider the study of Homer, whose poems are often said to have been the Bible of the Greeks. What this means is that, in the classical world, the Homeric poems come closest to attaining a place similar to the one that the Bible has in Jewish and Christian culture. The early Greeks did have a belief in the inspiration of the ancient poets, although it was not as strong and not as strict as the one that we find in Jewish and Christian tradition. But certainly the Greeks did hold that the poets had some connection with the Muses, if not with the gods. Moreover, one must stress the tremendous role that the Homeric poems played in early Greek education. Homer was regarded by Plato as the "educator of Greece" (*Republic* 10, 606e). The poems were regularly used in primary instruction, and the underlying assumption was that Homer was of great value. This assumption was shared by most of Greek society in the classical period.

Leaving aside the many debates about Homer's date, let us place him around 900 B.C. Some three hundred years later, from about 600 B.C. onward, Greek philosophy began to develop in Ionia and Asia Minor. The early pre-Socratic philosophers, as they are called, attempted to move beyond the mythical worldview that is found in Homer and other early Greek poets such as Hesiod. They objected to many things in Homer, and it was in the wake of their attacks on the poet that literary criticism was born. The attacks focused on two major issues. One was Homer's theology, because he represented the gods in human form. The philosopher Xenophanes rebuked this sort of anthropomorphism, saying that if cattle and horses could draw, they would represent the gods as cattle or horses.[6] The second aspect of the Homeric poems that became subject to attack was their morality. The gods were represented as engaging in adultery, fighting among themselves, tying up other gods, and so on. Such behavior was hardly seen as worthy of emulation by the philosophers.[7] Similarly, some of the Homeric heroes were not viewed as good role models. Achilles, for example, was often prone to anger. Odysseus sometimes used deception to accomplish his aims. Much later, Dante would place him and his pal Diomedes in one of the lowest levels of hell for their trickery and abuse of reason (*Inferno*, canto 26). Problems such as these came to the fore early and ultimately led to the development of highly sophisticated forms of literary criticism.

In a very good summary of the ancient interpretation of literature, J. A. Coulter has distinguished three "streams" or approaches.[8] Coulter's classification can also be applied with profit to Judeo-Hellenistic and Christian biblical interpretation, and it appears in the middle of diagram 3. The approaches are most clearly visible from the Hellenistic period onward, but the allegorical approach and the ethical approach have been set under the name of Plato, whereas the literalist approach has been set under the name of Aristotle. In the case of Plato, this is not because these types of criticism were practiced by him, but rather because they are based on an assumption about the nature of literature that is well represented in Plato, although it is not uniquely Platonic. That assumption is that literature is to be judged on the basis of the broader effects that it has on the individual and on society. On the other hand, the link between the literary criticism practiced by Aristotle, who took the view that literature should be judged in its own right, and the later practitioners of what I have called the "literalist" approach is somewhat stronger. This is because Aristotle made more "positive" contributions to literary criticism than did Plato.

Let us begin with the ethical or "rhetorical" approach. In this sort of criticism the objective is primarily to draw a moral lesson from the text. In the Judeo-Christian context, this approach could easily have been designated "homiletical." When dealing with narrative literature such as the Homeric poems or many books of the Bible, the rhetorical critic is

Diagram 3: Ancient Approaches to the Interpretation of Literature

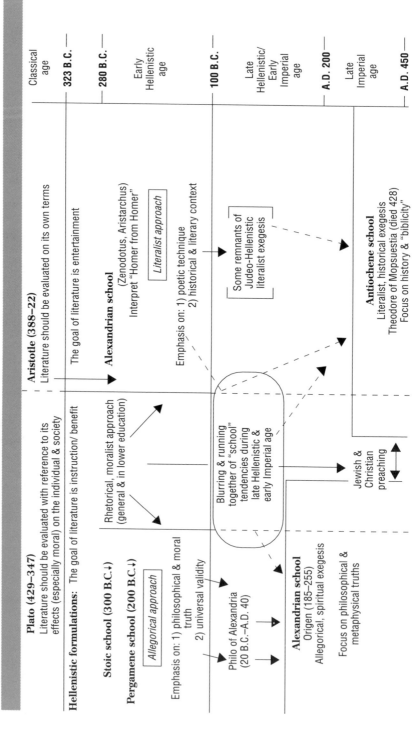

concerned primarily with the characters and how they behave. Ideally, the critic is able to use texts that present characters worthy of emulation. So when one finds characters such as the gods or Odysseus behaving in a reprehensible manner, how can these stories be used in education? How can one point to such characters as moral role models to be emulated?

There were different ways in which the ancient critics dealt with such issues from a moralistic perspective. One way, advocated by Plato, was negative in nature. This was to simply get rid of the problematic literature altogether. In the educational system set up in Plato's *Republic*, the poet of the Homeric type is simply banished from the state (*Republic* 3, 398a–b). Today, similarly, books might be censored or removed from college libraries. A more nuanced approach, which came to be preferred by the majority, involves a moralist reading of literature without censorship. It becomes the role of the teacher or preacher to guide the reader to the proper understanding of these literary works. So for example, in the *Iliad*, if Achilles shows anger on various occasions, one shows how he made ethical progress and that he was able to curb his anger.[9] One may also take examples of reprehensible behavior and hold them up as something not to do. This sort of guided ethical reading of literature is often found in ancient Jewish and Christian preaching and is common in the kind of preaching that goes on today. The preacher reads a portion of the Bible and attempts to elicit from it some moral lesson, even when reading stories that contain material that could be objectionable from the moral standpoint. In pagan antiquity, this method of interpretation was extremely common, especially in the lower levels of education, and did not become the property of any particular philosophical or literary-critical school. It was an approach shared by everyone to some degree.

The second approach, represented on the far left side of diagram 3, is the "allegorical" approach. It came to be associated in the Hellenistic world with the Stoics, although there are antecedents of this sort of interpretation among some pre-Socratic philosophers. The allegorical approach does not involve an attempt to extract moral lessons from the characters or the events of a story. Rather, it sees the characters or events as symbolic of other realities. In fact, the etymological meaning of the word "allegory" is "speaking other things." For example, in the *Iliad* when Zeus throws Hephaestus, the god of fire, to the earth, this symbolizes the fact that in the beginning fire came to man from the sky. For man used the sun's rays to create fire. Similarly, when Zeus punishes his wife Hera by hanging her up in midair with two anvils tied to her feet, this symbolizes the ordering of the physical elements of the cosmos, for Zeus represents ether, Hera the air (the name *Hera* means "air"), and the two anvils the heavy elements, earth and water.[10] Many of the stories of the gods were interpreted in this cosmic or "physical" sense. While allegories could also point to moral truths, they tended to represent more abstract truths in the realm of physics or metaphysics. The allegorical approach was dependent on a more advanced sort of learning, so it is not surprising that it was generally practiced in higher educational settings, such as philosophical schools. In the Hellenistic period, allegorical interpretation was employed not only by the Stoics, but also by the literary critics at Pergamum. Pergamum, a city in Asia Minor, became a center of literary or philological scholarship in the second century B.C. and had its own library. It was a sort of rival to Alexandria, and the scholars working there are thought to have been inspired by a Stoic worldview, although some have denied that Pergamum should be viewed as a "school." In any case, the Pergamenes were the ones who really "sold" the allegorical approach and made it popular.

As is shown on the left side of diagram 3 from Plato downward, the ethical and the allegorical approaches share a common assumption. That assumption, as formulated in the Hellenistic period, was that the primary goal of literature is instruction and benefit. The writer or poet might "teach" by presenting ethical role models, or by employing allegories. Accordingly, one should read literature in order to become a better person or to learn philosophical truths. This view was certainly the more widespread, although the appeal of the allegorical method specifically was less so.

Finally, we may turn to what I have called, perhaps somewhat anachronistically, the "literalist" approach.[11] This approach was definitely that of a minority of ancient critics and was based on the teaching of Aristotle. Aristotle thought, as diagram 3 shows, that poetry or literature should be evaluated on its own terms, and it should not be seen primarily as a medium of moral or philosophical instruction. If one wants moral or philosophical instruction, one should read didactic writings or philosophy; literature should be viewed as literature. In the Hellenistic period, Aristotle's views were taken up and further developed by the Alexandrian school, that is, the school connected with the library of Alexandria. The Hellenistic formulation of the basic Aristotelian position was that the goal of poetry or literature is entertainment or pleasure.[12] This is not exactly what Aristotle had said, but it is close enough, and was certainly inspired by his literary theory.

This basic view had implications for the way in which the interpretation of literature was to be conducted. In the first place, the study of literature is a field in its own right. It is not a part of ethics or of philosophy, but a separate science. Indeed, it is significant that this science, termed *grammatikē* (literally, "grammar") by the ancients, was thought to have originated with Aristotle.[13] As practiced by the Alexandrians, the essence of this science was to "explain Homer from

Homer," as the ancient maxim goes.[14] One should not evaluate Homer on the basis of the moral assumptions of the fifth century B.C., or of the "physics" of the pre-Socratics or Stoics. One must enter Homer's own society. So the emphasis of the school of Alexandria tended to be very scientific. Its practitioners looked at things such as the language and meter of Homer, the historical context and customs of the Homeric world, and Homer's poetic technique. They were concerned not with whether Homer preached a good or a bad morality, or whether he was philosophically correct or incorrect, but whether he was a good poet. For them this was the question on which one should focus when reading the Homeric poems.

Since, as I indicated, the "ethical" approach was widely shared, the primary contrast to be noted in the first part of the Hellenistic period is that between the Pergamene school in Asia Minor and the Alexandrian school located in Egypt. The philosophical tendencies of the Pergamenes were Stoic, whereas those of the Alexandrians were Peripatetic, that is, Aristotelian. The Pergamenes practiced allegorical interpretation, whereas the Alexandrians did not. From around 100 B.C., however, such distinctions begin to break down. While the general tendencies are still present, it is harder to locate such tendencies in specific cities or geographical areas. There is a trend toward combining and mixing the different approaches, and the earlier "school" distinctions are less visible. I have tried to depict this phenomenon graphically on diagram 3. This Hellenistic background is extremely important for the understanding of Greek and Latin biblical interpretation because similar issues are involved, and, indeed, a similar "school conflict" comes to the fore in the classical patristic age.

The origins of Greek biblical interpretation are obviously to be sought in Alexandria in the third century B.C., since that is where the Greek translation was produced. For this reason, one might have expected that Judeo-Hellenistic biblical interpretation would have been shaped by Alexandrian models. This, however, is not the case. When we look at Jewish-Hellenistic interpretation as a whole, we see that, for the most part, it was under the influence of Pergamene tendencies (diagram 3), even though Philo, the great Jewish interpreter, lived in Alexandria. This is probably to be explained by a number of factors. In the first place, the Jewish interpreters will not have shared the basic Alexandrian assumption that "literature is for the purpose of entertainment." Secondly, one could appeal to the phenomenon that I mentioned in the previous paragraph, namely that toward the later part of the Hellenistic period, the school distinctions were less connected to geographical factors. On the other hand, however, one should note that evidence of Alexandrian influence is visible in some Judeo-Hellenistic interpretation, which is preserved in fragmentary form. Such influence is particularly discernible in Demetrius the Chronographer.[15] Moreover, when one reads the writings of Philo closely, one finds that he occasionally cites interpretations of his "literalist" predecessors without a great deal of elaboration, or uses "literalist" techniques. Yet it is sometimes possible to reconstruct from these statements and usages a Judeo-Hellenistic exegesis that seems to have a stronger connection with the Alexandrian school.[16]

Generally, however, one must say that Jewish biblical interpretation in its Hellenistic form is heavily characterized by the allegorical method. This may be seen already in the *Letter of Aristeas*, a text that we have discussed above. In one passage, the author deals with the biblical food laws and interprets them allegorically. He says that it was not out of real concern for food that Moses prohibited certain foods. Rather, he prohibited the consumption of birds of prey, for example, to show that men should not imitate the behavior of such creatures in their dealings with their neighbors (§§ 144–9). By the time of Philo, we find a very elaborate system of allegorical interpretation applied to entire episodes of the Bible. For instance, Philo talks about the migration of Abraham from Ur of the Chaldeans in Mesopotamia to Haran and the land of Canaan as Abraham's progress from the admiration and study of the natural, physical world to the recognition of the immaterial world and a transcendent, Platonic God. Philo reads Genesis 11—12 as a Platonist, treating it not as a story about a man moving from one land to another, but intellectually advancing from the study of "physics," as the ancient philosophers called it, to the study of metaphysics and incorporeal realities (*On Abraham* 68–88).

Philo is the major representative of Judeo-Hellenistic biblical interpretation. The historian Josephus, who lived after Philo, during the years A.D. 37–ca. 100, may also be regarded as a biblical interpreter, but not in the same explicit sense. Josephus used the Bible as a historical source, and his interpretation is of a more indirect form. After the death of Josephus, the age of Jewish-Hellenistic literature, which begins with the translation of the Septuagint in 250 B.C., essentially comes to an end. The continuity of Greek biblical interpretation is maintained, however, as one passes on to Christian exegetes. This is particularly the case if one defines exegesis somewhat more narrowly as "biblical scholarship," as practiced by Origen, and anticipated to a certain extent by his predecessor, Clement of Alexandria.

Origen, besides being a great textual scholar, as noted above, was also the first of the Church Fathers to put forward a systematic approach to the interpretation of Scripture. He was highly influential for many centuries. As Jerome put it, he was the greatest teacher of the church after the apostles.[17] Although Origen was an outstanding interpreter of the literal meaning of Scripture according to the methods of Alexandrian *grammatikē*, more characteristic was his application of the allegorical method. For he took the position, offensive to many Christians, that there were passages in the Bible that had no literal meaning, but could only be taken allegorically (*On First Principles* 4.2.5, 4.3.10). On the one hand, this was a continuation of the Philonic legacy, although Philo had not stated it in such an emphatic theoretical fashion. The literal meaning of the Bible was discarded or simply neglected in favor of Platonic truths. In fact, not long after Origen's death, Porphyry, the pagan critic of Christianity, said in effect that Origen was inserting Platonic ideas into the biblical text by means of the Stoic allegorical method.[18] On the other hand, Origen's approach was further determined by his view that the Old Testament was a prophecy of Christ, and this necessitated a somewhat creative reading of many passages in the Old Testament. In Origen's own eyes, however, he was not reading into the text that which was not there. Rather, he was simply deciphering the often obscure and encoded message of Scripture. He himself employed a simile known to him from Jewish sources, according to which Scripture is to be compared to a building with many locked rooms. By each room there is a key, but not the key to that particular room. The goal of the interpreter is to match the right key with the right room and thus open the closed or obscure parts of Scripture (*Philocalia* 2.3). The Bible contained great hidden truths; one merely needed to discover them.

A famous example of Origen's use of the allegorical method, which caused much controversy a century later, is his interpretation of the "garments of skins" in Genesis 3:21. According to the biblical text, after Adam and Eve had eaten of the forbidden fruit, God made "garments of skins" for them to wear and expelled them from the garden of Eden. For Origen, this passage was rather crass and anthropomorphic. It simply could not be accepted that God would make clothes for Adam and Eve. So he interpreted the text along Platonic lines to the effect that originally everything was pure essence, without material existence. Platonism stressed the existence of a transcendent, nonphysical world of forms and ultimate realities beyond the material. Originally, in that mode, humans were just souls. The making of the "garments of skins" is an allegory that indicates that at a certain point humans took on bodily form, covered by skin. Origen rejected the literal sense of Scripture in that particular verse and favored an allegorical interpretation.[19]

The allegorical method of Alexandrian scholars such as Philo and Origen allowed Jews and Christians to find Greek philosophy in the Bible. This was significant, because Greek philosophy was the most respected and scientifically advanced system of thought at the time. Origen went beyond Philo in his construction of a more elaborate system, and in his application of the allegorical method to the entirety of Scripture, not just to the Pentateuch. He of course also added the Christian dimension, or the "christocentric" approach, to the Old Testament. But from the point of view of method and general spiritual orientation, Philo and Origen belong to the same tradition.

Within Christianity, however, there was a major reaction against Origen's approach. But it took nearly a century for this reaction to come into its own, that is, to find its most sophisticated form of expression. The center of this countermovement was Antioch in Syria, another very important city in early Christian history. One often reads of an "Antiochene school," though many scholars have questioned whether it is correct to speak of a school in the formal sense. While there has been recent acknowledgment of the importance of the figure of Eusebius of Emesa (ca. 300–359),[20] the most famous members of the "school" are Diodore of Tarsus (died ca. 390) and Theodore of Mopsuestia (ca. 350–428).

Diodore and Theodore formulated two main criticisms of Origen and his allegorical method. First, they said that Origen did away with the literal meaning of the text when he incorporated allegory. That is, when he brought in an allegorical meaning, it would, in their eyes, entail the rejection of the literal sense of Scripture, as it did in the case of the coats of skin in Genesis 3:21. The Antiochenes recognized that Origen's allegorism had been derived from Philo and had its roots in Greek literary scholarship. They therefore interpreted it, legitimately to a large extent, on the basis of what they knew of the mechanics of Greek allegorism. Specifically, they knew that allegorism had been applied by the Greeks primarily to mythical material, such as the stories of the gods in the Homeric poems, as we saw above. Accordingly, if Origen allegorized Scripture in the same way that the Greek philosophers had allegorized myth, this must mean that he had set Scripture on the same level with Greek myth. Origen, they said, by using this Greek method on the Bible, had essentially Hellenized or mythologized a text that should not be mythologized. According to the Antiochene school, Scripture was something that was fundamentally different from Greek myth, and could not be set alongside of it.

The second criticism which the Antiochenes put forward concerned the content of Origen's allegorical interpretations. In their view, he had introduced "alien subject matter" into the biblical text. By this, they clearly meant that one should not read Platonic philosophy into the biblical message by application of the allegorical method. Abraham's migration to the promised land is not about a movement from "physics" to "metaphysics," but a historical event reflecting God's plan for Israel. Platonic philosophy is not part of the biblical message.[21] These Antiochene criticisms may owe something to Porphyry's comments which we have cited above. In essence, they seem to have been saying that Origen was wrong about the form of Scripture by assimilating it to Greek myth; and wrong about the meaning of Scripture by assimilating it to Greek philosophy; a very powerful indictment of the "greatest teacher of the Church after the apostles."

We have seen that on the one hand the Antiochene method came about as a direct reaction to the Philonic-Origenian tradition. On the other hand, however, and this is perhaps a more interesting point, there seems to have been a connection between the classical scholarship of Alexandria and the methods of the Antiochene school. It must be emphasized that the Antiochenes did not accept the basic Alexandrian/ Peripatetic assumption that the goal of literature is entertainment. The Antiochenes clearly belong to the Jewish and Christian tradition, according to which, as expressed in classical terms, the Bible was written for the purpose of instruction and benefit. However, some of the methods that the Antiochenes used do follow the principles of pagan Alexandrian scholarship. There was an attempt to read the Bible on its own terms and not introduce Greek philosophy into it. One may consider, for example, the way in which the Antiochenes interpreted the psalms. The psalms, of course, are very difficult to understand because of their figurative language and because of the problems that often arise in determining their context. Many psalms had come to be interpreted in Christian tradition either from the allegorical perspective, as indicating philosophical realities, or from a typological perspective, as pointing forward to certain events in the life of Christ or the life of the church. But the Antiochenes were willing to read very few psalms in a christological sense. Instead, their method involved an attempt to situate the psalms in the context of Israelite history. It was believed that almost all of the psalms were by David, but sometimes David would speak, because of his gift of prophecy, "in the person of" another individual in the history of ancient Israel. The Antiochenes studied very closely the historical narrative in the books of Samuel, Kings, Chronicles, and so forth., and other sources, such as the *Histories* of Herodotus, that might shed some light on the history of biblical Israel. In short, they tried to interpret almost all psalms within an Old Testament context, without viewing them as prophecies of Christ. This is an almost modern perspective, but it also follows the old Alexandrian maxim, "to explain Homer from Homer," or in this instance, the "Old Testament from the Old Testament."[22]

But if the Antiochenes were indeed inspired by pagan Alexandrian methods, we are confronted with a question. Why in the pagan world does the "literalism" of Alexandria stand in contrast to the allegorism of Pergamum (in Asia Minor), whereas in the Jewish/Christian world of interpretation the geography is reversed, and Alexandria represents allegorism and Antioch literalism? How did this reversal come about? Part of the answer may lie in the blurring of geographically determined "school" distinctions, to which I referred above, in late Hellenistic and

early imperial times (i.e., the period between the age of classical Hellenistic interpretation and the emergence of a scientific Christian biblical
scholarship). However, the problem has not yet been completely solved.
I suspect that there may be some lines of connection between Philo's
"literalist" predecessors and the later Antiochene school that have yet
to be fully elucidated. I have taken the liberty of indicating this on diagram 3, although the proposition remains to be demonstrated. It would,
however, be in conformity with what I have been trying to say in these
pages. There is a great continuity in Greek and Latin biblical scholarship, and we should not create thick walls of separation between Jewish
and Christian interpretation, so long as we remain in the Greco-Latin
orbit. Both traditions make better sense when considered in light of each
other and in light of pagan literary scholarship. One must be concerned
with all three of these traditions, and understand their interaction.[23]

Suggestions for Further Reading

The following two works contain survey articles, with extensive bib-
liographies, about many aspects of both the Greek and Latin versions,
and Greek and Latin biblical exegesis:

Mulder, M. J., ed. *Mikra: Text, Translation, Reading and Interpretation of the
Hebrew Bible in Ancient Judaism and Early Christianity.* Compendia
Rerum Iudaicarum ad Novum Testamentum II.1; Assen:Van
Gorcum, 1988.

Sæbø, M., ed. *Hebrew Bible/Old Testament: The History of Its Interpretation,*
I.1. Göttingen: Vandenhoeck and Ruprecht, 1996.

The standard book-length English introductions to the Bible in Greek,
which also contain material on the Bible in Latin:

Jellicoe, S. *The Septuagint and Modern Study.* Oxford: Oxford University
Press, 1968.

Swete, H. B. *An Introduction to the Old Testament in Greek.* 2d ed.
Cambridge: Cambridge University Press, 1914.

Introductory guides to classical Greek and Latin literary scholarship:

Grube, G. M. A. *The Greek and Roman Critics* London: Methuen, 1965.

Russell, D. A. *Criticism in Antiquity.* London: Duckworth, 1981.

A good short survey of Judeo-Hellenistic and patristic interpretation:

Grant, R. M. *The Letter and the Spirit.* London: SPCK, 1957.

---

[1]The first citation of the Greek Bible in a pagan text may be found in Ps.-Longinus,
On the Sublime 9.9. This text is generally dated to the first century C.E.

[2]See R. Pfeiffer's edition of the works of Callimachus, vol. 1 (Oxford: Oxford University
Press, 1949), fragments 433, 435.

[3]For further information about this evidence, see my remarks in the *Journal of the American Oriental Society* 110 (1990): 576–77.

[4]For a more detailed discussion of the position of the Greek Bible in the church in the period after Origen, see my *Jerome, Greek Scholarship, and the Hebrew Bible* (Oxford: Oxford University Press, 1993), 28–40.

[5]For a fuller account of Jerome's "discovery" of the Hebrew text and his arguments in favor of his new version, see my *Jerome* (above, n. 4), 41–72.

[6]For this statement of Xenophanes, see J. M. Robinson, *An Introduction to Early Greek Philosophy* (Boston: Houghton Mifflin, 1968), 52.

[7]See again the criticism of Xenophanes as given in Robinson, op. cit., 55.

[8]*The Literary Microcosm* (Leiden: E. J. Brill, 1976), 5–30.

[9]For this technique, see Plutarch, *On Listening to Poetry* 8, 26A–E.

[10]For these two allegorical interpretations, see Heraclitus, *Homeric Allegories* 26, 40. This text may be as late as the first century C.E., but it probably contains earlier material.

[11]Coulter, (n. 8), 7–9, calls this "genre criticism," which is less satisfactory in the present context.

[12]The most famous statement to this effect is that of Eratosthenes (275–194 B.C.), preserved by Strabo, *Geography* 1.2.3.

[13]See the testimony of Dio Chrysostom (A.D. 40–112), *Oration* 53.1.

[14]For this maxim, see R. Pfeiffer, *History of Classical Scholarship* [i] (Oxford: Oxford University Press, 1968), 225–27.

[15]On Demetrius, see my article "Philo, *Grammatikē*, and the Narrative Aggada," in *Pursuing the Text: Studies in Honor of Ben Zion Wacholder* ed., J. C. Reeves and J. Kampen (Sheffield: Sheffield Academic Press, 1994), 219–22.

[16]For an attempted reconstruction of this sort, see my article, "The Literary Genres of the Pentateuch as Seen from the Greek Perspective: The Testimony of Philo of Alexandria," *The Studia Philonica Annual* 9 (1997): 143–89.

[17]*Preface to Origen's Homilies on Ezekiel.* Jerome here cites the testimony of Didymus the Blind (A.D. 313–98).

[18]Porphyry's criticisms of Origen are transmitted by Eusebius, *Ecclesiastical History* 6.19. This characterization of Origen's exegesis would be equally valid for Philo.

[19]This interpretation goes back to Philo, *Questions on Genesis* 1.53. I have somewhat oversimplified the problem of Origen's interpretation of this verse on the basis of later sources, especially the unfriendly Epiphanius (*Panarion* 64.4.5–9), but also the friendly Didymus the Blind (*Commentary on Genesis* 3:21; presumably drawing on Origen). For a detailed discussion of the problem, see M. Simonetti, "Alcune osservazioni sull'interpretazione origeniana di Genesi 2,7 e 3,21," *Aevum* 36 (1962): 370–81.

[20]See esp. the recent work of R. B. ter Haar Romeny, *A Syrian in Greek Dress* (Louvain: Peeters, 1997).

[21]The Antiochene criticisms of allegorism may be read in extracts from Diodore's *Commentary on the Psalms*, found in translation in K. Froehlich, *Biblical Interpretation in the Early Church* (Philadelphia: Fortress, 1984), 82–94, and in Theodore's comments on Psalm 118, now available in D. T. Runia, *Philo in Early Christian Literature* (Assen: Van Gorcum, 1993), 267.

[22]In general, the maxim "to explain Homer from Homer" is viewed as expressing a principle inimical to allegorical interpretation; see Pfeiffer loc. cit. (n. 14). However, the decipherment of the obscure mysteries of Scripture by means of the allegorical method was also thought to be dependent on indicators or "keys" present in the body of Scripture itself. This idea may be present in Origen's use of the Jewish tradition about the locked rooms of a building discussed earlier, and Scripture could be thought to "explain itself" allegorically. See further N. R. M. de Lange, *Origen and the Jews* (Cambridge: Cambridge University Press, 1976), 111; J. Pépin, *La tradition de l'allégorie*, 2 (Paris: Etudes Augustiniennes, 1987), 187–97 (esp. 195–97).

[23]I would like to thank James Bowley, the editor of this volume, for his invitation to participate in the original course and for his encouragement and good counsel in the preparation of this chapter of the volume. His assistance at every stage has been most essential.

3

Scriptural Authority in Early Judaism

John C. Reeves

What constitutes "Sacred scripture" for the varieties of early Judaism attested during the Hellenistic and Roman periods of ancient Near Eastern history?[1] Does the concept of "Bible," at least in terms of how that title is customarily understood by modern readers, exist for any of the religious groups found in *Eretz Israel* or the Diaspora? How should we conceptualize the demarcation—if any—between what is "canonical" literature and what is, by contrast, "apocryphal" or "spurious"? Please note that these initial queries deliberately feature special nomenclature—certain words or phrases framed by quotation marks—which is intelligible to modern readers, but which is gradually coming to be recognized as anachronistic by informed scholars of early Judaism. What are these inaccurate, allegedly inappropriate, terms? They are quite frankly expressions like "Bible," "Sacred Scripture," and "canon."

An essential thesis of this essay can be expressed in a sentence-length assertion; namely, that the concept of "scripture" in early Judaism was not consonant with what moderns term "the Bible." One can, in fact, go even further and say that the notion of "Bible" in the form of a fixed list of written texts that are foundational for the behavior and ideology of a

63

particular community of people, a group of scriptures whose composition and individual contents could not be altered in any way, or in other words a *canon* of authoritative scriptures—was probably not operative among *any* of the religious parties in *Eretz Israel* until the final decades of the first century or perhaps even the initial decades of the second century of the Common Era.[2]

In order to construct support for these statements, which many readers will recognize run directly counter to the widely accepted wisdom of established textbooks and commentaries, we will need to rehearse several topics of fundamental importance. These are, in the order of their appearance: (1) a brief discussion of both the traditional and pre-Dead Sea Scrolls understandings of the development of the biblical canon; (2) a summation of the evidence from the Dead Sea Scrolls that pertains to this issue; and (3) the presentation of a new proposal, one whose aim is not only to reconstruct the conceptual ideology undergirding the production of what comes to be termed "Bible," but that also intends to shed light on the process of the preservation and transmission of writings and the history of the Abrahamic religions throughout the Near East during the first millennium of the Common Era.

Traditional Understanding of the History of the Canon

Up until the rise of modern critical methods for the study of the Bible, it was widely assumed by Jewish and Christian scholars alike that the Bible achieved its final canonical form sometime during the career of Ezra the scribe,[3] who is depicted in the biblical book bearing his name as "a scribe learned in the law of Moses which the LORD, the God of Israel, presented" (7:6). Officially commissioned by the Persian monarch Artaxerxes as a special governmental emissary, he is dispatched from the royal court in order "to inspect [the province of] Yehud and [the city of] Jerusalem [to determine their concordance] with the law of your God which you possess" (7:14). He also bears financial subsidies contributed by both the Persian administration and the Jewish inhabitants of Babylon for the material support of the temple service. Moreover, Ezra is granted full authority to appoint magistrates and judges to insure compliance with "the law of your God" and "the law of the king" (7:25–26).

The key recurrent phrases—"the law of [your] God," or sometimes "the law of Moses"[4]—have traditionally been interpreted as the earliest extant references to what eventually becomes, at the minimum, the first five books of the Bible—the so-called "books of Moses" or the Torah—or at the maximum, the entire contents of what we now term "Bible," or what Christians call "the Old Testament." Modern critical scholars tend to prefer a minimalist view,[5] recognizing that our present Bible does indeed include material that dates well after the purported time period of

Ezra (fifth or fourth century B.C.E.),[6] whereas maximalist interpretations are the norm in some of the earliest external sources that we possess for the process of canonization. For example, the first-century Jewish historian Josephus has this to say about what appears to be the Bible:

> [thanks to the authorial activity of the prophets]…we do not possess myriads of inconsistent books, conflicting with each other. Our books, those that are justly accredited, are but two and twenty, and contain the record of all time. Of these, five are the books of Moses, comprising the laws and the tradi- tional history from the birth of humanity down to the death of the lawgiver…From the death of Moses until Artaxerxes, who succeeded Xerxes as king of Persia, the prophets subsequent to Moses wrote the history of the events of their own times in thirteen books. The remaining four books contain hymns to God and precepts for the conduct of human life.

Josephus continues his presentation with the following intriguing no- tice: "From Artaxerxes to our own time the complete history has been written, but has not been deemed worthy of equal credit with the earlier records, because of the failure of the exact succession of the prophets."[7]

The careful reader discerns in the testimony of Josephus two useful principles for determining where the boundaries of the scriptural canon were drawn for that particular writer, who is perhaps our most impor- tant source for the reconstruction of first-century Jewish history. Accord- ing to Josephus, a writing is "justly accredited" if it (1) was authored by someone belonging to the period stretching from Moses to Artaxerxes, inclusive, and (2) that someone also enjoyed the status of "prophet." Twenty-two books reportedly satisfy these criteria, and they are grouped under three headings: laws and ancestral traditions, histories, and hymns and precepts. Josephus' generic arrangement, coupled with his trifold numerical grouping (5+13+4), is usually viewed as a primitive expres- sion of what eventually became the standard tripartite mode of describ- ing the contents of the Bible within classical Judaism; namely, as *Tanakh*, an acronym signaling the three components of *Torah, Nevi'im, and Ketuvim*.[8] The sum total of twenty-two books diverges from the rabbinic reckoning of twenty-four, but this is not a grave discrepancy; it is likely that Josephus may have counted certain books as a single work that later tradents treated as two separate compositions; for example, count- ing Jeremiah and Lamentations as one book due to their alleged com- mon authorship.[9]

Of especial interest, though, for our present purposes are his im- plicit requirements for membership within the approved roster of Jew- ish scriptures. One credential is chronological, while the other is built on reputation. The chronological parameters, as mentioned above, are

Moses and Artaxerxes, the Persian monarch of that name "who suc-
ceeded Xerxes as king of Persia" (1.40). A quick glance at the roster of
Achaemenid royal succession permits us to identify this particular
Artaxerxes (there were three!) as Artaxerxes I Longimanus, who ruled
464–423 B.C.E.[10] Why does Josephus employ the name of this foreign
ruler as a chronological marker? According to the exposition of biblical
history contained in his *Antiquities*, Artaxerxes is identical with
Ahasuerus, the royal husband of Esther (Esth. 1:1–2).[11] Furthermore, as
we have seen above, the Bible itself associates an otherwise unqualified
"Artaxerxes" with the period of Ezra the scribe (Ezra 7:1). It would thus
appear that Josephus has roughly synchronized the final production of
"justly accredited" records and the demise of prophecy with the era associated with the events depicted in the biblical books of Esther (explicitly) and Ezra-Nehemiah (implicitly).[12] Sacred Scripture thus emanates
from authors situated between the boundaries of Moses and Ezra.

The other principle utilized by Josephus for the identification of a
"justly accredited" work is its reputed publication by a "prophet." A
close reading of this passage in conjunction with the remainder of
Josephus' surviving corpus of works demonstrates that he did not re-
serve this title for only the authors of the thirteen "histories" mentioned
in *Contra Apionem* 1.40, but intended the label to be applied to all the
"scriptural authors."[13] Hence "Scripture"—in order to be "Scripture"—
required a prophetic imprimatur.

Is this an accurate understanding of Josephus' scheme? We can test
our reading of Josephus by comparing his portrayal to that found in the
Babylonian Talmud, another Jewish source whose final redaction occurs over half a millennium after the time of Josephus, but whose oral
roots reach back into the final years of the Second Temple period of Jewish history, or in other words, to the period when Josephus was active.
Therein we read the following interesting material:

> Who wrote the Scriptures? Moses wrote his own book and…
> Job. Joshua wrote the book which bears his name and (the
> last) eight verses of the Pentateuch. Samuel wrote the book
> which bears his name and the book of Judges and Ruth. David
> wrote the book of Psalms…Jeremiah wrote the book which
> bears his name, the book of Kings, and Lamentations.
> Hezekiah and his colleagues wrote Isaiah, Proverbs, Song of
> Songs, and Ecclesiastes. The Men of the Great Assembly wrote
> Ezekiel, the Twelve Minor Prophets, Daniel, and Esther. Ezra
> wrote the book which bears his name and the genealogies of
> Chronicles up to his own time (i.e., up to 2 Chron. 21:2)…who
> finished (the book of Chronicles)? Nehemiah b. Hachaliah (*b.
> B. Bat.* 15a).[14]

This talmudic witness allows us to confirm the information supplied by the statements of Josephus. Here too biblical authorship is held to begin with Moses, but instead of culminating in the production of the book of Esther, we discover instead that the scribal activity of Ezra and Nehemiah completes the scriptural period for the Sages. Moreover, the book of Esther is mentioned immediately *prior* to the invocation of Ezra and Nehemiah, whereas in Josephus the events associated with that novella are situated *after* the missions of Ezra and Nehemiah. Thus the Sages—like Josephus—consider the material featured in the books of Esther and Ezra-Nehemiah to be roughly contemporaneous.

A comparative examination of the Bible and Josephus' *Antiquities* reveals that Josephus has artificially synchronized Ezra with Xerxes, the predecessor of Artaxerxes I (*Antiquities* 11.120–58), and assigns to the latter ruler the events associated with the production of the book of Esther (*Antiquities* 11.184–296). Both the biblical book of Ezra and the Greek 1 Esdras—probably Josephus' primary source for this period—feature an otherwise unidentified "Artaxerxes, king of Persia" as the ruler who commissions Ezra and dispatches him to Judea with "the law of God" (7:1–28; cf. *1 Esdras* 8:1–27). Hence the names "Artaxerxes" and "Ezra" interplay as narrative contemporaries within biblical discourse, regardless of the actual historical identity of the ruler (Xerxes? Artaxerxes I? II?) intended by the biblical author. This is the historiographic model followed by the rabbinic schema—for the Sages, an Ezra/Artaxerxes nexus clearly postdates the marriage of Esther and Ahasuerus. Note too that since Josephus is addressing his exposition in *Contra Apionem* to an educated pagan readership, it makes rhetorical sense for him to use chronological markers that such an audience could readily identify. Moses enjoyed an international fame thanks to his reputation as an early lawgiver and powerful magician,[15] but Esther, Mordecai, and even Ezra remained unknown outside of Jewish circles. By contrast, given the frequent encounters and hostilities between the Greek and Persian cultural spheres, the names of the Achaemenid monarchs, as well as their relative dates, were familiar to an audience schooled in the histories of Herodotus, Ktesias, and Xenophon.

Can the systems of Josephus and the Sages be reconciled? Provided we group the events associated with the biblical books of Esther and Ezra-Nehemiah around the common rubric "Artaxerxes," we can read Josephus' use of the name Artaxerxes as a type of transcultural code for "Ezra" and understand him to be stating that "justly accredited books" within Jewish culture can be placed on a continuum between the biblical figures of Moses and Ezra. Moses and his era mark the beginning point; Ezra and his era mark the termination point, and by implication, the closing of the scriptural canon. Any writing ascribed to a figure who preceded Moses in the traditional history—for example, Enoch, Noah, or

Abraham—is not "justly accredited." Neither can one be that is ascribed to a figure who postdates Ezra—for example, Ben Sira, or R. Judah ha-Nasi.

Such an articulation of the chronological principle is clearly at work in the talmudic citation quoted above. Everyone else credited with authoring, or perhaps better, "finishing," a biblical book falls somewhere between the two narrative boundaries of Moses and Ezra. Moreover, all of the names occurring in that citation are explicitly identified as prophets, or otherwise associated with prophetic activity, in other places within rabbinic tradition.[16] The Men of the Great Assembly, the legendary governing body bridging the temporal gap between the return from exile and the Hellenistic era,[17] is often linked with certain alleged aspects of Ezra's activity, such as his supposed identity with the pseudonymous prophet Malachi.[18] So as in the testimony of Josephus, the Talmud too would seem to hold that scriptural production—that is, the authoring of books that we find in our Bible—ceases in the time of Ezra, broadly construed. This period also coincides with the alleged disappearance of prophecy from Israel.[19]

The rabbinic estimation of the significance of Ezra for the existence of the Bible is more explicitly stated in other sources.[20] Consider, for example, the following opinions: "Ezra and the Torah are more important than the rebuilding of the Temple" (*b. Meg.* 16b), or "R. Yose said: Ezra would have been worthy of receiving the Torah had Moses not preceded him" (*t. Sanh.* 4.7; *b. Sanh.* 21b). A multitude of similar sentiments could be cited. The high evaluation of Ezra's role in the written codification of Jewish scriptures finds its most picturesque depiction in the apocryphal book of 4 Ezra, a Jewish work whose composition was roughly contemporary with the activity of Josephus.[21] Therein the character Ezra is deliberately cloaked in the Mosaic mantle: He is addressed by God from a bush in the wilderness (4 Ezra 14:1–2) and spends forty days and nights dictating a fresh revelation of God's Law to a five-man secretarial pool (14:37–44).[22] Once this task is completed, Ezra receives the following instructions from God:

> The twenty-four books that thou hast written publish, that the
> worthy and unworthy may read (therein): but the seventy last
> thou shalt keep, to deliver them to the wise among thy
> people. For in them is the spring of understanding, the
> fountain of wisdom, and the stream of knowledge. And I did
> so. (2 Esdras 14:45–48)[23]

Here too Ezra is portrayed as being the one responsible for the promulgation of the entire Bible: This is the only viable explanation for the precise sum of twenty-four books, a sum that matches the standard enumeration in later Jewish sources.[24] What is perhaps more intriguing though is the mention of "seventy" additional writings that are also of divinely inspired authorship and that appear to be more valuable than the contents of the Bible itself. In order to appreciate fully the significance of this particular datum, we should gain some familiarity with the contents of what is probably the most important archaeological discovery of this century—the Dead Sea Scrolls.

The Contribution of the Dead Sea Scrolls

The discovery of the Dead Sea Scrolls approximately fifty years ago has now put us in a position to reassess the nature of what we call the Bible during an era not far removed from the periods of Josephus, 4 Ezra, and the rabbinic Sages. In order to facilitate this task, we must carefully consider both the contents of the Scrolls themselves and the ways by which those works we now term "biblical" were transmitted and referenced.

According to archaeological estimates, had the texts been preserved entirely intact for us, there would have been over eight hundred separate scrolls surviving from Qumran caves 1–11.[25] As is well known, almost all of these writings have suffered damage, most of them to the extent that they have to be painstakingly pieced together from numerous smaller fragments in order to restore some semblance of an intelligible text. Of the over eight hundred scrolls, a significant proportion, about 25–30 percent, were copies of biblical texts, with every book in the present-day Hebrew canon being represented except Esther and Nehemiah. The remaining 70–75 percent are grouped by modern scholars under the label "nonbiblical literature," a rubric that encompasses a wide variety of what were undoubtedly important literary works. Within this category are multiple copies of documents that contain rules and regulations governing the communal life of those thought responsible for authoring and/or copying the scrolls. There are collections of hymnic compositions that presumably played some role in liturgical life. There are commentaries on certain works deemed "prophetic" by the community—books like Isaiah, Habakkuk, and Nahum. There are copies of books that never achieved canonical status within Judaism or classical Christianity, but which featured teachings or apocalyptic motifs that were treasured by certain groups in Second Temple Judaism—books like those of *Enoch, Jubilees*, and the Aramaic predecessor to the *Testament of Levi*. In fact, an interest in eschatology is well attested among the scrolls. One work, the famous "War Scroll," describes the final forty-year conflict that will culminate with the expulsion of the Gentiles from the land of Israel and the reestablishment of home rule. Another complementary text, the equally famous "Temple Scroll," depicts the new sanctuary that God will build at that time to replace the polluted second temple and prescribes the rituals to be celebrated there. A number of smaller texts outline the procedures to be followed in the determination of festival dates, the order of priestly service, and the proper interpretations to follow in resolving purity disputes.[26]

We therefore are in possession of a veritable treasure trove of Jewish literature emanating from the last three centuries before the Common Era and the first half of the first century of the Common Era, a period of time immediately preceding that of Josephus, 4 Ezra, and the Sages. The question that must now be asked is whether the new data supplied by the caves at Qumran confirm, discredit, or hopelessly complicate the picture created by the traditional authorities.

We might begin by considering the manuscript remains of the biblical books that have been recovered from Qumran—books like Genesis, Deuteronomy, Jeremiah, or Psalms. Almost all of the biblical books attested at Qumran are present in multiple copies,[27] and one is tempted to conclude that such statistical significance was directly proportional to their religious importance, or at least popularity, at that time. Problems arise, however, when we begin closely comparing the numerous separate copies of portions of the Pentateuch—the books of Genesis, Exodus, Leviticus, Numbers, and Deuteronomy—with one another. There are manuscripts of these works that closely mirror their counterparts in the best medieval manuscripts and modern printed editions of the Hebrew Bible, the so-called Masoretic tradition, upon which our modern English translations are based. Yet there are also manuscripts that present the text in forms which vary from that of the Masoretic tradition, for instance, that of the Samaritan Pentateuchal tradition, an early version of the five books of Moses which differs from that of the Masoretes in a number of places.[28] Still others reproduce a form of the Hebrew text of the Pentateuch that is very close to the one underlying the Greek translation of the Pentateuch, the so-called Septuagint. Which manuscript tradition was considered to be "Bible" at Qumran? One of these? All of these? Some combination of these traditions? Or even none of these?[29]

The situation does not improve when we move to other examples of what we characteristically term "biblical books." Among the extant copies of portions of the book of Jeremiah at Qumran are the manuscript remains of two distinct editions of this work, one of which is represented in our Bibles, and the other in the Greek or Septuagint translation of that prophet. These two different editions of the book of Jeremiah diverge markedly in length and in the order of the book's contents.[30] Or consider the case of the book of Psalms: The largest psalms scroll recovered from Qumran includes many of the psalms now found in the last third of the canonical Psalter, but they are arranged in a very different order and sporadically interspersed with apocryphal Davidic hymnic works.[31]

Moreover, there are a significant group of Qumran texts that scholars typically refer to as "parabiblical texts"; that is to say, they imitate the style and, at times, even the verbiage of biblical texts, but render a product that does not correspond to the form of the Hebrew text of the Bible that we employ today.[32] Examples of this type of work would be manuscripts that conflate portions of the two versions of the Ten Commandments found in the books of Exodus and Deuteronomy, or manuscripts that collect in one narrative locale the various biblical regulations pertaining to certain cultic or purity rules. A clarifying word or phrase might be added in order to prevent misunderstandings of the rule's intent. The precepts themselves might be rearranged to accord with what was perceived to be a more logical order or schema. In short, what is on prominent display in such parabiblical texts, when viewed from the perspective of what we know as "Bible," is a "rewriting" of the Bible itself. This particular practice—interpreting the Bible by rewriting the Bible—is a very significant piece of cultural information that possesses far-reaching implications for tracing the authority of what we call "Bible" in early Judaism.[33]

When we turn to the other so-called "nonbiblical" works preserved at Qumran, we soon discover that a tentative working principle of "multiplicity of copies indicates a more authoritative status" can be a two-edged sword. The *Book of Jubilees*, essentially a rival version of the book of Genesis and the early chapters of the book of Exodus, is represented among the Dead Sea Scrolls by sixteen different copies,[34] a number that is higher than that for the majority of the so-called "biblical books." More than a dozen copies of portions of works associated with the forefather Enoch are present at Qumran.[35] Does this mean that works like *1 Enoch* and *Jubilees* were "Bible" at Qumran or other locales in the land of Israel or elsewhere during this time? One is tempted to answer affirmatively. Consider the following quotation, taken from one of the most important Qumran writings, the so-called Damascus Document:

> Therefore let one resolve to return to the Law of Moses, for in
> it everything is specified. And regarding the exposition of the
> times when Israel was blind to all these (precepts), behold,
> one finds precise explanation in the Book of the Divisions of
> Time into Jubilees and Weeks. (CD 16:1–4)[36]

This sectarian treatise explicitly places the *Book of Jubilees* on the same plane of authority as the "law of Moses," whatever *that* may mean in its present context (we could ask which version of the law? Masoretic? Samaritan? proto-LXX? some parabiblical compilation like the Temple Scroll?).

So perhaps now one can appreciate some of the reasons why it was stated at the outset of the present essay that the concept of "Bible," as we customarily employ it, did not seem to exist for the Dead Sea Scroll community. Does that realization mean, then, that there was no scriptural authority whatsoever, whether at Qumran or anywhere else? Obviously there was some notion of a piece of literature enjoying some measure of respect, for we just observed an instance of such wherein the *Book of Jubilees* was recommended as an excellent guide for gaining understanding about the past transgressions of Israel. So clearly there are "scriptures" broadly construed;[37] the quandary comes when we try to construct a *fixed list* or *canon* of such writings along with their contents. How can we distinguish what was scriptural from what was non-scriptural at Qumran?

The information culled from our previous consideration of the testimonies of Josephus, 4 Ezra, and the Sages may be of some utility at this point. We observed above that two principles seem to govern the bestowal of "scriptural" status upon a particular piece of literature. The first tenet was a chronological one—the Moses-Ezra authorial continuum; viz., all "scriptures" were authored (or in the case of 4 Ezra restored)[38] by personages whose literary contexts fall between the inclusive narratological brackets of Moses and Ezra. Upon examination of the non-biblical (from the later perspective) remains recovered from Qumran, one notes a demonstrable interest in literature associated with Moses at Qumran,[39] but there is also considerable fascination with literary texts purportedly authored by biblical figures who antedate Moses—characters like Enoch, Noah, and Abraham.[40] Moreover, the figure of Ezra does not seem to have attracted much interest among the groups responsible for the production and/or the preservation of the Scrolls. It would thus appear that a Moses-Ezra continuum was not operative at Qumran.

The second principle enunciated by Josephus, presumed by the Sages, and symbolically articulated by the author of 4 Ezra was the "prophetic" status of all "scriptural" authors. It is clear from the Qumran evidence that "all the words of His servants the prophets"[41] are of paramount importance for this group, enjoying a standing that is equivalent to that of the Torah of Moses. Given that Moses is explicitly recognized as the greatest of the prophets (Deut. 34:10),[42] we may be justified in concluding that the designation "prophet" holds the key to the resolution of the problem of "scriptural identity." In fact, the title of "prophet" may be the essential credential for widespread recognition as a "scriptural" author.

Prophetization and Scripturalization

There is a curious phenomenon at work in the religious ideologies of late antique Near Eastern religious communities that one might tentatively designate "prophetization." What is meant by this term is fairly simple to recognize: It is the seemingly arbitrary bestowal of prophetic rank upon a number of literary or even historical figures who do not normally enjoy such status within the traditional scriptures. An important national hero like David, for example, is portrayed within the Hebrew Bible as a monarch, warrior, and skilled musician, but he is never credited therein as a "prophet"; instead, he receives counsel from professional soothsayers like Gad (1 Sam. 22:5) and Nathan (2 Sam. 7). Postbiblical literature, however, "prophetizes" David: His alleged writings or pronouncements (e.g., the book of Psalms) are now scrutinized for the possible light they can shed upon questions affecting the present or future ages.[43] Insofar as David gradually achieves recognition as a prophet, attention is increasingly devoted by scribal circles to the identification, preservation, and transmission of writings that he supposedly authored. Similar projects of prophetization—not all of which are Jewish in their final form—focus upon figures like Adam, Seth, Enoch, Noah, Abraham (note Gen. 20:7!), Jacob and his family, Aaron, Joshua, Solomon, Baruch, Zerubbabel, Ezra, Mordecai, and Daniel. Even Gentile figures like Jethro, Balaam, the Sibylls, and Zoroaster attract attention in this regard. By the end of late antiquity, the eventual result of this process is the generation of approved "lists" of "trustworthy prophets" who serve as a chain of authority for the faithful mediation and transmission of the teachings that define a particular religious tradition.[44] The list of biblical authors recited in *b. B. Bathra* 15a above—each of whom, recall, is also a "prophet"—represents a classical Jewish articulation of this concept.

"Prophetization," metamorphosing a cultural tradition's heroes and heroines into "prophets," and "scripturalization," encoding that same tradition in written format, appear to be closely related phenomena. Great "prophets" of past generations—Moses, Isaiah, Jeremiah—are inexorably connected with "books." Perhaps under the influence of this classical prophetic paradigm that associates one or more "books" with each prophet, every potential candidate for the title of "prophet" had to exhibit some tangible evidence of their oracular prowess, the best proof of which would be a book transmitting their revelatory message to subsequent generations. This conceptual necessity helps explain the remarkable eruption of pseudepigraphic works attributed to biblical characters during the Second Temple period of Jewish history and the continuing popularity of this style of publication within early Christian and gnostic circles. Those figures dubbed prophets must, if they are to be credible candidates for this title, have a "book."

A "book" however, is not equivalent to scripture. The authority of what functions as scripture within a textually-centered religious community is based on a public recognition that this particular writing expresses the core values of the tradition; moreover, it enunciates them in such a way that its narrative structure, syntax, and vocabulary elicit continual discussion, comment, and exegesis by subsequent generations of readers. Given this stricture, it may prove more useful to approach the issue of scriptural authority in early Judaism by paying closer attention to *literary* signposts and signals than to *theological* abstractions. The advantage in such an approach is that it is inherently more concrete: It utilizes the tangible structural elements present within the texts themselves.

In order to perform this operation, let us borrow and adapt a classificatory scheme originally proposed by the Israeli biblical scholar Devorah Dimant as a description of the primary forms of biblical interpretation practiced during the Second Temple period of Jewish history.[45] Dimant observes that this interpretive literature basically falls into two categories or genres of texts, compositional and expositional. A "compositional" work, according to Dimant, is one that freely weaves portions of what we know as biblical text with other, nonbiblical, material in order to create or further develop a continuous narrative line. Furthermore, compositional works contain no formal markers within them that distinguish what is later recognized as biblical from those elements that are later considered nonbiblical. An author or an editor appears to enjoy complete freedom in adjusting, expanding, rearranging, or deleting words, sentences, and even entire narrative episodes from what Dimant assumes to be the "base" text: namely, our Bible. Examples of compositional works include at least one work that eventually won canonical status in its own right, the biblical book of Chronicles, but also works like *Jubilees*, the Temple Scroll and other parabiblical texts, portions of *1 Enoch*, and the Genesis Apocryphon, yet another rewritten version of portions of what we know as the book of Genesis. Practically every work that scholars have placed under the label "the rewritten Bible" falls into this category of interpretive composition.

By contrast, Dimant describes an "expositional" work as one where the biblical elements are explicitly presented as an integral unit, with clear formal markers distinguishing what is Bible from what is not Bible, that is, commentary or expansive gloss. Examples of expositional works would be writings like the Qumran *pesharim*, wherein quotations from biblical books like those of Habakkuk or Nahum are linguistically distinguished from the later interpretations by the insertion of the phrase "its meaning [*pesher*] is…" Another formal marker of this type would be the occurrence of a phrase like "as it is written…," which is then immediately followed by a textual quotation. In an expositional work, in other words, there is no way that the attentive reader (or listener) could confuse text and interpretation. Each occupies its own place on the page and is carefully distinguished as if each had been printed using a different typeface.

Dimant intended her classificatory scheme to be descriptive of the primary forms of biblical exegesis practiced during Second Temple Judaism. However, her insights also possess great potential for reconceptualizing the problem of scriptural authority in early Judaism, especially if we expand her self-imposed chronological boundaries to encompass the literary history of the varieties of Judaism attested in the Near East for over a millennium. Let us therefore superimpose on Dimant's scheme another formula for describing the history of Jewish literary activity from approximately 500 B.C.E. to approximately 600 C.E. To judge from the extant evidence, there appear to be three distinct stages through which all written Jewish literature can potentially progress during this period: (1) publication, (2) scripturalization, and (3) canonization. A few words of explanation are required for the definition of each stage.

By "publication" is meant a process by which literature shifts from an oral to a written format, or alternatively, moves from the mind of an author to the inscribed page. Having been "published," the work is now encoded in a written format, and as such is no longer necessarily dependent upon its author or tradent for its physical survival. It has become a corporeal object. Once having achieved this format, the work is potentially available for inspection and utilization by any literate individual or group within society. Authors may of course amend, alter, or withdraw their publications; similarly, readers are free to use or ignore them as they see fit.

"Scripturalization" labels a subsequent stage in literary history where a publication, due to its presumed antiquity, alleged authorship, or wide social appeal, manages to achieve a certain cultural authority and status. Whenever precedent or justification for a particular action of collective import is required, a "scripture" might be cited in order to support or criticize a certain decision or activity. Similarly, texts that are "scriptural" continually receive close study and exposition from various scribal circles for the purpose of enhancing and extending their utility in a world that, culturally speaking, is far removed from that of their original composition and publication. Often a concrete result of such intensive study and exposition is the issuance of new editions of the scripture, editions that physically incorporate within them the various glosses, explanations, and interpretations that have been produced and come to be accepted by generations of exegetes.

Finally, by "canonization" is meant the compilation of a fixed list of scriptures, the whole of which is deemed to be literarily inviolable. The text of a canonized writing cannot be altered in any way, for better or for worse, even if a blatant error is demonstrably present. Similarly, the list of scriptures that advance to the rank of "canon" is often conceived as a closed corpus, with no provision granted for addition to or subtraction from this list.

When we approach early Jewish literature using Dimant's scheme in tandem with the superimposed developmental formula, we immediately notice some very interesting things. First, the evidence from the Dead Sea Scrolls indicates that the Qumran community possessed, used, and even respected a large number of writings that fall into the categories of publication and scripture. The evidence is largely negative, however, with regard to their recognition of a canon, whether viewed from the later perspectives of classical Judaism and Christianity, or from the community's own sectarian documents. Texts like the books of Genesis, Exodus, Deuteronomy, Isaiah, and the Psalms are clearly scriptural. The cultural authority of such books is attested by the inordinate attention devoted to their reproduction, expansion, abbreviation, and elucidation, as well as by the occurrence of quotations from them with explicitly marked citation formulae like "as it is written" or "as the prophet NN says." But *also* scripture are nonbiblical texts like *Jubilees*, the Enochic cycle of books, and the Aramaic predecessor of the *Testament of Levi*, works that are treated exactly the same way as those biblical books mentioned above. None of these works, though, are canonical; their precise linguistic formulation, the way the words are arranged on the page, is demonstrably still in flux. There apparently remains considerable freedom for scribes to revise and manipulate the wording of any scripture. Nor does there appear to be any evidence for a fixed list of acceptable scriptures.

In fact, the very production of Dimant's compositional genre of literature indicates that the material that such works incorporate and manipulate cannot be canonical.[46] While texts like the book of Chronicles or *Jubilees* or the Temple Scroll may use materials that we recognize as biblical, nothing qualitatively distinguishes their treatment of biblical passages from materials and traditions that are manifestly nonbiblical. Nevertheless, within compositional works a certain level of authority is beginning to become visible in that the author or editor consciously chose to develop, expand, adapt, or adjust this particular scripture, namely, something that is discernibly Bible, as opposed to some other mythological tradition. This level of attention and intellectual effort would only be expended on a writing that contained material that already had won some level of authority in the community, even if its exact verbal expression had not yet been determined.[47]

An additional degree of authority becomes visible in those texts that belong to Dimant's "expositional" category. Here the base text—in most cases (but not *all*) what we term "Bible"—is physically distinguished from other phrases and sentences supplied by the later interpreters. No attempt is made to conflate or combine text and commentary; each remain discrete textual units. It would seem that expositional works offer our first concrete evidence of the promotion of a scripture to something approaching canonical status.[48] The author cites an authoritative passage from an earlier text and then proceeds to record an accepted interpretation for that passage. Such works do not alter their transcription of the base text, even when their interpretations feature a wordplay or pun that would facilitate such tampering. It is, moreover, probably no accident that the Dead Sea Scrolls expositional texts—works like the *pesharim*—appear to be among the youngest of the scrolls as determined by palaeographic and empirical methods of analysis, whereas the compositional texts predominate among the older scrolls found at Qumran. This relative dating of interpretational form implies that the notion of canon, a qualitative difference among scriptures, is only beginning to emerge during the middle decades of the first century C.E.[49]

By the time of the early rabbinic midrashim (second to fourth centuries C.E.), we witness an almost exclusive production of expositional texts: A clear distinction is constantly maintained between Bible and what is often a variety of authoritative interpretation(s). But by this time we are already clearly in possession of a formal canon—the *torah shebiktav* or "Written Torah." Classical Judaism would, in fact, go on to recognize a supplementary "canon," the *torah sheba'al peh* or "Oral Torah," via a parallel process of publication and scripturalization that mirrors the dynamic outlined above.

Addendum: A Brief Introduction to Rabbinic Exegesis of the Bible

In order to illustrate some of the ways whereby the Sages interact with a literary corpus that has finally achieved canonical status, that is, the Bible, a few words should be said about the exegetical process termed "midrash." The Hebrew word *midrash*, often mislabeled a distinct literary genre, is better understood as a type of interpretative activity—the English word "exposition" perhaps best captures its essential meaning. There are, broadly speaking, two kinds of midrash: (1) *midrash halakhah*, or halakhic midrash, wherein explicit precepts or guidelines for conducting one's life in accordance with God's mandates are deduced from biblical discourse; and (2) *midrash haggadah*, or haggadic (or aggadic) midrash, wherein explanatory comments, expansive additions, illustrative anecdotes, and legendary stories are generated from what are perceived to be pregnant, yet silent, aspects of the biblical text. Common to both categories of midrashic activity—halakhic and haggadic—is its bibliocentric basis: Midrash does not transpire in a textual vacuum; the Bible always serves as the point of origin or the ultimate court of appeal for midrashic formulation and argumentation. Hence, midrash necessarily presupposes the concept of an authoritative text.

Some actual examples of how midrash works may prove useful here. An excellent illustration of halakhic midrash occurs in the initial discussions of the Mishnah[50] in tractate *Berakhot* regarding the mechanics of prayer, a topic upon which the Bible provides almost no guidance, even though it is a form of pious behavior clearly valued by God.[51] In *m. Ber.* 1:3, we read: "The School of Shammai taught that everyone should stretch out (prone) and recite (the *Shema*)[52] in the evening, but should stand (and recite the *Shema*) in the morning, for Scripture says: 'in your lying down and in your rising up' (Deut. 6:7)." Since the Bible refers to these two bodily postures in the very portion of Scripture that serves as the first part of the *Shema* recitation, the School of Shammai concluded that the Bible was hinting how the recitation was to be physically performed: One assumed a prone position in the evening ("in your lying down") and an upright stance in the morning ("in your rising up"). A behavioral norm is thereby deduced from the literal wording of the biblical text.

The very same mishnah demonstrates, however, that the Shammaite deduction is in fact flawed: "The School of Hillel responded, (If your interpretative logic is followed), everyone may recite (the *Shema*) in whatever posture (lit. 'way') they happen to be in, for (the same) Scripture says, 'in your proceeding on the way' (Deut. 6:7)." In other words, if at least two phrases of the referenced clause in the verse signify the physical posture to be assumed when engaging in the recitation, it is reasonable to conclude that the other syntactic components of that clause ("while you sit in your house and during your proceeding on the way") also encode a similar message. But the messages are in fact contradictory—therefore the opinion of the School of Shammai must in this instance be wrong. "If so," the mishnah continues, "why would the Bible use the language of 'in your lying down' and 'in your rising up'? (It actually means) *at the time* of your lying down, *and at the time* of your rising up." The Shammaite attempt to generate halakhic midrash from this verse, although undermined at the level of an overly literal understanding, is in fact affirmed by the Hillelites. The verse, however, does not teach about bodily posture, but instead uses this language metaphorically to serve simply as temporal markers for the occasions of the *Shema*'s recitation—at the time one normally goes to bed and at the time one normally gets up.

Haggadic midrash, like halakhic midrash, also displays a heightened sensitivity to the various interpretational nuances of the biblical text. The goal of haggadic midrash, however, is not the derivation of behavioral guidelines; rather, it seeks to probe certain intriguing aspects of the biblical text in order to uncover hidden cultural "data." For example, in *b. Hag.* 12a we read: "Why (did God name the firmament) 'heavens' (*šamayim*; see Gen. 1:8)? R. Jose bar Hanina taught '(the word *šamayim* means) for there (*šam*) was water (*mayim*).'" According to this Sage, God's phonetic articulation of the word for "heavens" embeds within it the biblical teaching regarding its original function; viz., to serve as a barrier for separating and restraining the primeval chaos-waters (Gen. 1:6). The same source continues: "A *baraita*[53] teaches that the Holy One, blessed be He, brought fire (*eš*) and water (*mayim*) and mixed them together and thereby made the firmament."[54] This is an alternative haggadic explanation for the vocable "heavens," observing that the primal elements from which the "heavens" were apparently made (fire and water) are still visible as separate vocalic components of the divine designation (Gen. 1:8: "and God named the firmament '*šamayim*'"). According to this latter midrash, a careful study of God's language, as recorded in the Written Torah, may possibly shed unexpected light upon the elemental structure of the created order, a point further underscored by God's very use of the spoken word to fabricate the physical universe (Gen. 1, *passim*).

A lengthier example of haggadic midrash can be illustrated from the *Mekhilta de R. Ishmael*, a Tannaitic midrash keyed to a large portion of the biblical book of Exodus. Therein we read:

> R. Nathan taught: From where (i.e., from what Scriptural passage) can one learn that God showed Abraham our ancestor (the future events of) Gehenna, the revelation of the Torah, and the splitting of the Sea of Reeds? Scripture states: "when the sun set and it was very dark, there appeared a smoking *oven*..." Gen. 15:17)—this was Gehenna, for Scripture confirms: "(the Lord) has an *oven* in Jerusalem" (Isa. 31:9; cf. 30:33)—"... and a flaming *torch*..."(Gen. 15:17)—this was the revelation of the Torah, for Scripture confirms: "all the people witnessed the thunderings and the *torches*" (Exod. 20:15)—"... which passed between those *pieces*" (Gen. 15:17)—this was the miracle at the Sea of Reeds, for Scripture confirms: "who split the Sea of Reeds into *pieces*" (Ps. 136:13). He (also) showed him the Temple and the sacrificial service, as Scripture indicates: "He (God) answered, Bring me a three-year old heifer, a three-year old she-goat, a three-year old ram, etc." (Gen. 15:9). He (also) showed him the four empires who were destined to enslave his descendants, for Scripture says: "As the sun was setting, a deep sleep fell upon Abram, and a *great dark dread fell* upon him" (Gen. 15:12). "Dread"—this is the empire of Babylon; "dark"—this is the empire of the Medes (and Persians); "great"—this is the empire of the Greeks; "fell"— this is the fourth empire, wicked Rome.[55] But there are some who reverse the interpretation: "fell"—this is the empire of Babylon, for it is written "*Fallen* is Babylon" (Isa. 21:9); "great"—this is the empire of the Medes (and Persians), for it is written "King Ahasuerus *made great* (Haman)" (Esth. 3:1); "dark"—this is the empire of the Greeks, for they darkened the eyes of Israel with fasting; "dread"—this is the fourth kingdom, for Scripture says "fearsome and *dreadful* and very powerful." (Dan. 7:7)[56]

This passage succinctly illustrates the primary way by which the Sages extracted additional levels of meaning from what was ostensibly a straightforward narrative recounting of the cementing of Abraham's covenantal relationship with God, the so-called "covenant of the pieces" (Gen. 15). As the ceremony unfolds in its biblical telling, Abraham falls into a trance, wherein God reveals to the patriarch the future Egyptian subjection and eventual liberation from that bondage of his descendants (Gen. 15:13–16). But just how much of the future did God actually display before Abraham? Surely he did not limit himself to just the exodus experience? Since he revealed to Abraham the event of the Exodus, is it not reasonable to assume that he would also reveal his miraculous acts associated with that event, especially the crossing of the sea and the gift of the Torah? And would God not also show Abraham the eventual fate of those who rejected this gift; namely, the fires of Gehenna? Would God not show the ancestor of Israel the glories of the future temple on Zion? And if the Egyptian oppression was explicitly signaled, a misfortune that transpires while Israel is absent from her land, what about the other equally grievous experiences of subjection and exploitation that Israel was destined to endure while dwelling in her promised inheritance when she would be ruled by successive world empires? The quoted midrash demonstrates that such "cultural data" is indeed encoded within the biblical text of Genesis 15, provided the reader possesses the biblical literacy and exegetical ingenuity required to detect it. Certain terms and locutions can be correlated with identical or analogous expressions in the other biblical books to establish a conceptual identification.[57] In other words, an essential presupposition of midrash is the notion that biblical terminology is never arbitrary; it is deliberately polyvalent and consciously intertextual. Any biblical book can be used to interpret any other biblical book, regardless of age, genre, or authorial intention.

The examples of midrash provided above thus demonstrate that rabbinic midrash, generally speaking, is an expositional enterprise: There is normally a clear internal distinction made between the text being exposited (the Bible) and the exposition itself (the midrash). This holds true even for later midrashic compilations that appear at first glance to be compositional enterprises—works like *Pirqe de-Rabbi Eli'ezer* or *Sefer ha-Yashar*, whose flowing narrative styles exhibit a relatively seamless movement between canonical text and midrash, but without casting suspicion upon the primacy of the canonical scriptures. This sort of narrative structure may be indebted in part to that of the Targum, the expansive Aramaic rendition of the biblical text, particularly as exhibited among the so-called Palestinian versions such as *Pseudo-Jonathan*.

Suggestions for Further Reading

In addition to the works cited in the footnotes, one should consult the following items:

Sæbø, M., ed. *Hebrew Bible/Old Testament: The History of its Interpretation*
Göttingen: Vandenhoeck & Ruprecht, 1996. Many illuminating articles on a variety of historical and exegetical issues.

Strack, H. L., and G. Stemberger. *Introduction to the Talmud and Midrash.*
Minneapolis: Fortress Press, 1992. Indispensable navigational aid
for students seeking guidance while traversing the "sea of Talmud."

VanderKam, James C. *The Dead Sea Scrolls Today.* Grand Rapids:
Eerdmans, 1994. Probably the best introduction to date on this vola-
tile corpus.

---

[1]The present essay represents a conflation of lectures presented at King College (Feb-
ruary 17, 1997) and UNC Charlotte (September 29, 1997). Unless otherwise indicated, all
abbreviations follow the style guide of the *Journal of Biblical Literature*.

[2]Cf. the following strident statement "...we should probably not think of a 'Bible' in
the first century B.C.E. or the first century C.E., at Qumran or elsewhere. There were col-
lections of Sacred Scripture, of course, but no Bible in our developed sense of the term."
Quotation is from E. Ulrich, "The Bible in the Making: The Scriptures at Qumran," in *The
Community of the Renewed Covenant: The Notre Dame Symposium on the Dead Sea Scrolls*, ed.
E. Ulrich and J. VanderKam (Notre Dame: University of Notre Dame, 1994), 77.

[3]An old but still valuable discussion of this issue is W. Robertson Smith, *The Old
Testament in the Jewish Church: A Course of Lectures on Biblical Criticism*, 2d ed. (New York: D.
Appleton and Co., 1892), 149–87. See also S. R. Driver, *An Introduction to the Literature of the
Old Testament* (repr. New York: Meridian, 1956), i–xi; E. Sellin and G. Fohrer, *Introduction to
the Old Testament*, 10th ed. (Nashville: Abingdon, 1968), 482; O. Eissfeldt, *The Old Testa-
ment: An Introduction* (New York: Harper and Row, 1965), 562–64.

[4]In addition to the verses cited above, see also Ezra 3:2; 7:6, 10; Nehemiah 8:1, 8, 18;
9:3; 10:29–30.

[5]"...there is no doubt that the law of Ezra was the whole Pentateuch..." So J.
Wellhausen, *Prolegomena to the History of Ancient Israel* (repr. Cleveland and New York:
Meridian, 1957), 408. Note also Eissfeldt, *The Old Testament: An Introduction* (New York:
Harper and Row, 1965), 556–57.

[6]I will not attempt to resolve here the thorny problem regarding the chronology of
the textually interwoven missions of Ezra and Nehemiah. For bibliographic guidance with
regard to this issue, consult L. L. Grabbe, *Judaism From Cyrus to Hadrian*, 2 vols. (Minneapolis: Fortress, 1992), 1.27–42, 88–98.

[7]Josephus, *Contra Apionem* 1.37–41. Translation is that of H. St. J. Thackeray in the
Loeb Classical Library edition *Josephus*, 10 vols. (repr. Cambridge: Harvard University
Press, 1976), 1.179. For recent thorough discussions of this passage and its significance, see
J. Barton, *Oracles of God: Perceptions of Ancient Prophecy in Israel after the Exile* (New York
and Oxford: Oxford University Press, 1988), 25–27, 35–50, 58–60; S. Mason and R. A. Kraft,
"Josephus on Canon and Scriptures," in *Hebrew Bible/Old Testament: The History of its Inter-
pretation*, 1.1; ed. M. Sæbø (Göttingen: Vandenhoeck & Ruprecht, 1996), 217–35.

[8]Note however Barton, *Oracles*, 48: "The impression one gets is not that Josephus is
attempting to describe how the Jewish canon is officially or usually divided by the Jews
themselves, but that he is analysing the sacred books of the Jews in a way that will make
them comprehensible (and convincing) to Gentile readers." Mason and Kraft ("Josephus
on Canon and Scriptures," 221–22, 234–35) similarly object to this common interpretation,
but the numerical sequencing (5+13+4) would seem to indicate that some type of tripartite division is indeed envisioned. For other early testimonies to a bipartite or tripartite
canon, see H. M. Orlinsky, "Some Terms in the Prologue to Ben Sira and the Hebrew Canon,"
Journal of Biblical Literature 110 (1991): 483–90.

[9]As is done by Origen; see the list of biblical books excerpted from Origen by Eusebius,
Ecclesiastical History, 6.25.2 for this very practice. A number of relevant testimonia have
been collected by S. Z. Leiman, *The Canonization of Hebrew Scripture: The Talmudic and*

Midrashic Evidence, 2d ed. (New Haven: The Connecticut Academy of Arts and Sciences, 1991), 41–50.

[10]A sequential list of the Achaemenian line can be found in R. G. Kent, *Old Persian: Grammar, Texts, Lexicon*, 2d ed., AOS vol. 33 (New Haven: American Oriental Society, 1953), 158; also E. J. Bickerman, *Chronology of the Ancient World*, 2d ed. (Ithaca: Cornell University Press, 1980), 127–28.

[11]Josephus, *Antiquities* 11.184–296 (LCL 6.402–57).

[12]Compare, however, Josephus, *Bellum* 1.18 (LCL 2.10–11), wherein he states that the "prophets conclude" their histories immediately prior to the advent of Antiochus IV (175–164 B.C.E.).

[13]Note especially *Contra Apionem* 1.37, as well as the remarks of Barton, *Oracles*, 35–95; Mason and Kraft ("Josephus on Canon and Scriptures," 221): "all of the authors are prophets."

[14]Translation cited from Leiman, *Canonization*, 52–53.

[15]J. G. Gager, *Moses in Greco-Roman Paganism*, SBLMS 16 (Nashville: Abingdon, 1972).

[16]See *b. Meg.* 14a; *Seder 'Olam Rabbah* 20–21. According to these sources, forty-eight prophets and seven prophetesses were active during Israelite history.

[17]*Targum Canticles* 7:3 synchronizes the careers of Ezra, Mordecai, Zerubbabel, Jeshua, and Nehemiah, naming them as members of the Great Assembly. For a comprehensive discussion of this legendary group and its activities, see L. Ginzberg, *The Legends of the Jews*, 7 vols. (Philadelphia: The Jewish Publication Society, 1909–1938), 6.447–49 n. 56.

[18]See *b. (Meg.* 15a; *Tg. Mal* 1:1. For the progressive prophetization of Ezra, see R. A. Kraft, "Ezra Materials in Judaism and Christianity," in *Aufstieg und Niedergang der römischen Welt*, 19.1 (Berlin and New York: W. de Gruyter, 1979), 127–29. An illuminating intercultural presentation of the postbiblical image of Ezra can be found in H. Lazarus-Yafeh, *Intertwined Worlds: Medieval Islam and Bible Criticism* (Princeton: Princeton University Press, 1992), 50–74.

[19]See *t. Sota* 13.2; *b. Sanh.* 11a. An excellently nuanced discussion of this issue is F. E. Greenspahn, "Why Prophecy Ceased," *Journal of Biblical Literature* 108 (1989): 37–49.

[20]See the discussion and sources provided by D. W. Halivni, *Peshat and Derash: Plain and Applied Meaning in Rabbinic Exegesis* (New York and Oxford: Oxford University Press, 1991), 134–54.

[21]G. H. Box, "4 Ezra," in *Apocrypha and Pseudepigrapha of the Old Testament*, 2 vols. ed. R. Charles (Oxford: Clarendon, 1913), 2.542–624; B. M. Metzger, "The Fourth Book of Ezra," in *Old Testament Pseudepigrapha*, ed. J. Charlesworth (Garden City, N. Y.: Doubleday, 1983), 1.516–59. See now the Hermeneia commentary of M. E. Stone, *Fourth Ezra: A Commentary on the Book of Fourth Ezra* (Minneapolis: Fortress, 1990).

[22]In addition to the obvious correspondences with the revelation(s) vouchsafed to Moses, there are echoes of the prophetic experiences of Jeremiah (15:16) and Ezekiel (2:8–3:4) within this chapter.

[23]"4 Ezra," in *Apocrypha and Pseudepigrapha of the Old Testament*, 2.624.

[24]See the sources conveniently collected by Leiman, *Canonization*, 53–56. He considers 4 Ezra 14:45 to be the earliest allusion to the twenty-four book scheme. Note, however, the *Gospel of Thomas* 52: "His disciples said to him, 'Twenty-four prophets spoke in Israel, and all of them spoke in you.'" If the *Gospel of Thomas* is indeed a mid-first-century sayings source, as a number of scholars advocate, it would supplant 4 Ezra as the earliest reference to a twenty-four book biblical canon. The *Gospel of Thomas* logion is cited from *The Nag Hammadi Library in English*, 3d ed., ed. J. M. Robinson (San Francisco: Harper & Row, 1988), 132.

[25]Ulrich, "Bible in the Making," 78; J. C. VanderKam, *The Dead Sea Scrolls Today* (Grand Rapids: Eerdmans, 1994), 29.

[26]For an authoritative survey of the contents of the Scrolls, see VanderKam, *Dead Sea Scrolls*, 29–70.

[27]A list of all the Qumran manuscripts is contained in *Companion Volume to the Dead Sea Scrolls Microfiche Edition*, 2d ed., ed. E. Tov and S. J. Pfann (Leiden: Brill, 1995). For a discussion of the biblical texts found at Qumran, with copious bibliographical documentation, see E. Tov, *Textual Criticism of the Hebrew Bible* (Minneapolis and Assen/Maastricht: Fortress and Van Gorcum, 1992), 100–117.

[28]For a brief overview of the chief differences, see E. Tov, "Proto-Samaritan Texts and the Samaritan Pentateuch," in *The Samaritans*, ed. A. D. Crown (Tübingen: J. C. B. Mohr, 1989), 397–407.

[29]For a clear exposition of these issues, see Ulrich, "Bible in the Making," 77–93.

[30]See especially E. Tov, "The Literary History of the Book of Jeremiah in the Light of its Textual History," in *Empirical Models for Biblical Criticism*, ed. J. H. Tigay (Philadelphia: University of Pennsylvania Press, 1985), 211–37.

[31]Namely 11QPs^a. See J. A. Sanders, *The Psalms Scroll of Qumran Cave 11 (11QPs^a)*, Discoveries in the Judaean Desert 4 (Oxford: Clarendon, 1965).

[32]See E. Tov, "Biblical Texts as Reworked in Some Qumran Manuscripts with Special Attention to 4QRP and 4QparaGen-Exod," in *Community of the Renewed Covenant* (see n. 1 above), 111–34.

[33]The term "rewritten Bible" was apparently first introduced in the seminal researches contained in G. Vermes, *Scripture and Tradition in Judaism: Haggadic Studies*, 2d ed. (Leiden: Brill, 1973), 67–126.

[34]VanderKam, *Dead Sea Scrolls Today*, 40. The Cave 4 manuscripts of *Jubilees* have now been published in *Qumran Cave 4, VIII: Parabiblical Texts, Part I*, Discoveries in the Judaean Desert 13; ed. J. C. VanderKam, et al. (Oxford: Clarendon, 1994), 1–185. For the remaining manuscript evidence, see the references supplied by M. E. Stone, "The Dead Sea Scrolls and the Pseudepigrapha," *Dead Sea Discoveries* 3 (1996): 278, nn. 22–23.

[35]J. T. Milik, *The Books of Enoch: Aramaic Fragments of Qumrân Cave 4* (Oxford: Clarendon, 1976).

[36]*The Dead Sea Scrolls: Hebrew, Aramaic, and Greek Texts with English Translations, Volume 2: Damascus Document, War Scroll, and Related Documents*, ed. J. H. Charlesworth (Tübingen and Louisville: J. C. B. Mohr and Westminster John Knox, 1995), 38.

[37]One should note the occasional references to the authoritative status of the "law of Moses" and the exhortations associated with the "prophets" within various Qumran texts; e.g., CD 7:14–18; 1QS 1:2–3, 8:15–16; 4QMMT C 10–11. For this last text, see E. Qimron and J. Strugnell, *Qumran Cave 4, V: Miqsat Ma'ase ha-Torah*, Discoveries in the Judaean Desert 10 (Oxford: Clarendon, 1994), 58.

[38]Note *b. Sukk.* 20a: "Formerly when all Israel had forgotten the Torah, Ezra came up from Babylon and reestablished it."

[39]"There seem to have been a number of pseudo-Mosaic writings at Qumran…" (Stone, "Scrolls and the Pseudepigrapha," 293). *Jubilees* and the Temple Scroll are obvious examples. See especially the discussions of J. Strugnell, "Moses-Pseudepigrapha at Qumran: 4Q375, 4Q376, and Similar Works," in *Archaeology and History in the Dead Sea Scrolls: The New York University Conference in Memory of Yigael Yadin*, Journal for the Study of the Pseudepigrapha Supplement 8, ed. L. H. Schiffman (Sheffield: Sheffield Academic Press, 1990), 221–56; D. Dimant, "New Light from Qumran on the Jewish Pseudepigrapha— 4Q390," in *The Madrid Qumran Congress: Proceedings of the International Congress on the Dead Sea Scrolls, Madrid 18–21 March, 1991*, 2 vols., ed. J. Trebolle Barrera and L. Vegas Montaner (Leiden: Brill, 1992), 2.405–48.

[40]See especially Stone, "Scrolls and the Pseudepigrapha," 277–88.

[41]1QpHab 2:8–9; cf. 7:4–5; 1QS 1:3; CD 7:17; 4QpHos (4Q166) 2:5.

[42]Note also *Leviticus Rabbah*, 1.14; *b. Yebam.* 49b.

[43]David is explicitly accorded prophetic status within certain Qumran manuscripts, Josephus, early Christian literature, and rabbinic tradition. For an illuminating discussion of the prophetization of David, see J. L. Kugel, "David the Prophet," in *Poetry and Prophecy: The Beginnings of a Literary Tradition*, ed. J. L. Kugel (Ithaca: Cornell University Press, 1990), 45–55.

[44]Such lists of "true prophets" are extraordinarily important for certain Jewish Christian sects, classical gnosis, Manichaeism, Mandaeism, and Islam. For extended discussions, see J. E. Fossum, "The Apostle Concept in the Qur'an and Pre-Islamic Near Eastern Literature," in *Literary Heritage of Classical Islam: Arabic and Islamic Studies in Honor of James A. Bellamy*, ed. M. Mir and J. E. Fossum (Princeton: Darwin Press, 1993), 149–67; J. C. Reeves, *Heralds of That Good Realm: Syro-Mesopotamian Gnosis and Jewish Traditions*, Nag Hammadi and Manichaean Studies 41 (Leiden: Brill, 1996); idem, "Exploring the Afterlife of Jewish Pseudepigrapha in Medieval Near Eastern Traditions: Some Initial Soundings," *Journal for the Study of Judaism* 30 (1999): 148–77.

[45]D. Dimant, "Use and Interpretation of Mikra in the Apocrypha and Pseudepigrapha,"in *Mikra: Text, Translation, Reading and Interpretation of the Hebrew Bible in Ancient Judaism and Early Christianity,* Compendia rerum iudaicarum ad novum testamentum 2.1, ed. M. J. Mulder (Assen/Maastricht & Philadelphia: Van Gorcum & Fortress, 1988), 381–84.

[46]An analogue may exist in early Muslim literature and its usage of the Qur'ān. In the ninth-century chronicle of al-Ya'qubi, "he [al-Ya'qubi] makes no attempt to identify a Qur'ān verse through formal language, but rather weaves the words of Scripture into his own commentary…some have considered this to be evidence for a late date for the [canonical status of] Qur'ān." Citations from R. Firestone, *Journeys in Holy Lands: The Evolution of the Abraham-Ishmael Legends in Islamic Exegesis* (Albany: State University of New York Press, 1990), 54, 200, n. 11.

[47]Or, as David Kraemer has bluntly observed, "People do not publish comments on texts that they deem unimportant." Quotation is from his *The Mind of the Talmud: An Intellectual History of the Bavli* (New York: Oxford University Press, 1990), 65.

[48]"[The canonization of scripture] meant that new explanatory or expansive understandings of the Hebrew Bible could no longer be folded into the text." Quotation is from J. M. Harris, "From Inner-Biblical Interpretation to Early Rabbinic Exegesis," in *Hebrew Bible/Old Testament* (see n. 7 above), 258.

[49]According to Meir Sternberg, "…form has no value or meaning apart from communicative (historical, ideological, aesthetic) function." If this is so, the expositional form of biblical commentary communicates volumes about the perceived authority of the scriptural text. Quotation taken from M. Sternberg, *The Poetics of Biblical Narrative* (Bloomington: Indiana University Press, 1985), xii.

[50]The Mishnah is the earliest formal collection of oral Torah. According to tradition, it was compiled by R. Judah ha-Nasi around 200 C.E. This date also marks (roughly) the division between the Tannaitic and the Amoraic eras of Sages.

[51]Nowhere does the Bible issue practical instructions regarding how prayer is to be performed. Where can one pray? Can one pray anywhere? Or are certain locales (e.g., a privy) inappropriate? When does one pray? How often should one pray? What sort of physical posture should one assume when praying? What language should one use in prayer? Only Hebrew? Is the local vernacular acceptable? And so on. Questions such as these are the chief motivation for the practice of midrash halakhah.

[52]Three biblical paragraphs (Deut. 6:4–9; 11:13–21; Num. 15:37–41; with preceding and concluding blessings) that encapsulate the basic teachings of Judaism. The name *Shema* stems from the first word ("Listen!") in Deuteronomy 6:4.

[53]A *baraita* (literally, "outside") is a Tannaitic tradition not found in the final edition of the Mishnah.

[54]Compare *Gen. Rab.* 4.7 (Theodor-Albeck 31) where the tradition is attributed to the third-century Amora Rav.

[55]This follows the Hebrew word sequence, not the English.

[56]*Mek., Yitro, Bahodesh* §9 (Horovitz-Rabin 236).

[57]I have marked the key terms above with an italic font.

4

The Context and Development of the Christian Canon

Bruce M. Metzger

The Christian canon refers to the books that the church regards as Holy Scripture. Etymologically the word canon comes from an ancient Semitic root meaning "reed," or "stalk." The word came to be used as something that could be used to measure lengths and make a straight line, and if it had dots along the edge it could measure different lengths. When applied to a group of different literary pieces, a canon of literature is the established critical standard of that material. The canon may be simply drawn up as a list of the titles of several different texts, or the word canon may refer to the assembled texts themselves. So the term canon has both these connotations: It is a list as well as the contents of what is comprised in that list.

Preliminary Considerations

Some preliminaries need our attention before we consider the writing of the books of the New Testament and their collection as the New Testament. There is certain background material that perhaps we take for granted, but don't always appreciate. First of all, after the Holy Spirit, as we believe, inspired a gospel or an epistle or another book of the New Testament, how did people come to know about the book? How was it disseminated throughout the then civilized world? How did the books that were disseminated at different places at different times become collected together?

The first question concerns intercommunication in the Roman Empire. As is true today, people at the beginning of the Christian period also did a great deal of traveling in the then civilized world. These travels would take them to other lands and countries. They traveled either by land or by water. The Mediterranean enabled them to sail to different places in seasons when it was not too stormy. Those who traveled by land had several different modes of locomotion. They could travel either by wheels or in sedan chairs, being carried on beasts of burden, or on foot. Different people made a variety of different trips. There were Roman officers, soldiers, teachers, students—and invalids who traveled elsewhere because they wished to go to some spa and relieve their poor health. There were workmen who went hither and thither in search of jobs. There were merchants who carried things to Palestine and who carried various exports from Palestine.

Focusing briefly on Palestine, a small country, we derive information from various sources as to the different kinds of products that were brought to Palestine. Beans and lentils came from Egypt. Greece sent squashes. The Egyptians sent mustard. Edom was a source for vinegar. Abyssinia sent various cheeses. Cotton came from India. These imports were balanced by various exports. For example, among the exports from Palestine, Lake Tiberias produced salted and pickled fish. Galilee was celebrated for its linen. Judea supplied wool and woolen goods. Jerusalem had its sheep market and its wool market. This brief review shows us that once the books of the New Testament were written, there was ample opportunity for people to carry them to other places and to disseminate the various books that eventually would be brought together in a canon.

Another preliminary consideration has to do with the way in which books were made in ancient times. Nowadays we go to a book shop and choose a book—a Bible, a book of mathematics, and so on. We are able to get copies that are exactly like other copies in a given printing because of the invention of Johannes Gutenberg. In 1456 Gutenberg produced the first printed book in the West from moveable type. (One must say the first printed book in the West, meaning Europe or America, because some forty years earlier than Gutenberg printers in Korea had produced printed books using moveable type. There was, of course, no correspondence between the two; the art was independently developed in both continents.) Prior to moveable type, books were produced by scribes, working painstakingly, line by line, letter by letter.

Books in Antiquity

First we shall consider the material of ancient books and, secondly, their format. There were two chief materials used in making books in antiquity. One was of vegetable origin, papyrus; the other of animal origin, parchment. The papyrus plant belongs to the sedge family of plants. It grows to be about the height of a corn stalk with a tasseled top. It grows best in swampy land, such as the Delta of Egypt. Some papyrus also grew in the swampy lands of Sicily. But it was chiefly Egypt that manufactured and exported large amounts of paper made from papyrus.

Writing material was made as follows. When the papyrus plant was fully mature, it was harvested, and sections of the central part were cut into segments about twelve to fourteen inches in length. Then the outer rind was cut open and the core of pith removed. With a sharp knife this was sliced into thin, tape-like slices that were laid side by side on a flat surface and a second layer put crosswise. Then the two layers were pounded together so that the naturally gelatinous substance of the pith would cause the two layers to adhere even without glue. When it was dried it was a useable piece of paper, a little heavier than our paper is today, but very serviceable. It was already lined on one side because of the horizontal direction of the fibers. On the other side, of course, the fibers were vertical, and this side proved a little more awkward for writing in straight lines across the page. Sheets of papyrus were manufactured and sold in various grades of quality: good quality, medium quality, poor quality.

The other material used in making books was of animal origin—the hide of an antelope, a goat, a sheep, a calf. The hide was prepared after slaughtering the animal by scraping off the hair, applying some sort of substance such as chalk to both sides of the sheet of hide, and then stretching it to dry. The parchment was marked with lines for writing by using a straight-edge and a blunt-pointed instrument and scoring (but not cutting through) on one side, line by line. There were different patterns of this scoring depending on the use to be made of the manuscript. The person making the lines would measure a rectangle within which the writing was to be put, and then prick each of the four corners and finally score the lines from one side. The indentations on one side protruded a bit on the other, and so the opposite side was also prepared at the same time to be used for writing.

Different kinds of ink were used for writing on papyrus or parchment. The ink used for writing on papyrus was made of water, some lampblack, and a gummy substance to give it a little more body. But that kind of ink would easily flake off animal hide. For parchment the ink was made with oak-nut galls and other chemicals that would bite into the surface of the parchment. If the ink was too strong, however, several generations later it would be discovered that the ink of the letter omicron ("o") had eaten through the surface making a hole in the parchment because there was nothing to hold fast the inner part of the circle.

With regard to the format, ancient books were in two kinds. There was the time-honored scroll (or roll) and later the leaved book (or codex). A scroll was made by either gluing or stitching together various sections of the writing material. The maximum length that was handy to use was about thirty to thirty-two feet. Anything longer than that became unwieldy when rolling and unrolling. Reading required both hands, for as one read a scroll it was necessary to unroll with one hand and to roll up with the other hand. When finished reading, if one was considerate, one would roll it back again so that the scroll would be at the beginning for the next person to use.

We find in the Gospel according to Luke (4:16–20) that Jesus, "as was his custom on the Sabbath day," went into the synagogue where he read from the book of Isaiah. He chose to read from chapter 61. Isaiah has sixty-six chapters, and chapter 61 stands near the end of the scroll. So the congregation would wait while he managed carefully to unroll and roll up, unroll and roll up, until he found the place where it was written, "The Spirit of the Lord is upon me" (Isa. 61:1–2).

Now if someone was awkward and accidentally dropped one of the two rolls, that could be disastrous. We have pictures of that happening. The ancient artists of Greece made use of all kinds of scenes to decorate ordinary, everyday vases. Besides pictures of gods and goddesses, on a few Greek vases we find artistic representation of what happened when somebody was unlucky enough to have dropped one side of the scroll; it started to unravel and eventually encircled the reader!

At first the early Christians worshiped in synagogues and were acquainted with the scroll format. But by the end of the first Christian century a new format of books was adopted by Christian scribes. The leaved book is much more handy. It can be held in one hand, freeing the other hand. It was much less difficult to locate a passage in the middle of a codex simply thumbing through the pages than it was to unroll a scroll. The leaved book was also cheaper because both sides of the material could be used.

The earliest codices were single quire books. A quire is a grouping of leaves folded together. One sheet folded over had four pages. If twenty or thirty sheets were folded together in a single quire, the central leaves would protrude from the open edge and would need to be trimmed off to make a smooth place to thumb through the pages. That was wasteful. So scribes came to prefer making a book of several quires, usually of eight leaves each. Several quires would be bound together at the back so that the outer edge would be even. Hence nothing needed to be cut off from the exposed edges of the central leaves.

One final item by way of preliminaries has to do with various difficulties confronting the ancient scribe. Glasses were invented at Venice in 1374, but astigmatism and myopic conditions no doubt existed among people from time immemorial. Likewise, sometimes it would happen that the copy from which a scribe was making a new copy might be old and worn, and some of the ink might have flaked away. And so, in spite of all the good will in the world, one might not be able to read exactly the letters of the Hebrew or Greek text. It might also happen that the copyist would be interrupted in the task of copying, and upon resuming work, through an oversight, he might not start at the same place where he had stopped. If he started earlier, part of the text would be duplicated; if he started after, some words or sentences would be omitted. These are some of the hazards by which mistakes would occur in the transcription of manuscripts.

Finally, there are also many variations among the manuscripts as to the order of words in Greek. A scribe would look at a copy, retain in his memory the words of a clause, and then write it out. But an imperfect memory could reproduce the words in a different sequence in the new copy. In Greek, however, that is not such a terrible thing to happen. Change of word order is far less disastrous to the sense than it would be in English because, unlike English, Greek is an inflected language; word endings indicate which word functions as subject and which word functions as object.

Special Features of New Testament Greek Manuscripts

There are some specific features of New Testament manuscripts to which we now turn. Words pertaining to Jesus, God, the Holy Spirit, and the title Lord, are written in a special way in New Testament Greek manuscripts. These are the *nomina sacra*, "sacred names." They are identified in Christian manuscripts by being contracted, the scribe using only the first and last letters of the word with a line above to show that it is to be understood as a sacred name. Secondly, chapters and headings for the different chapter divisions were devised for New Testament manuscripts. Thirdly, among the manuscripts, what are called lectionaries were prepared. A lectionary is a book of various scripture readings for appointed days of the ecclesiastical calendar. The Eastern lectionary begins with Easter, and selections are chosen from the gospels for the days after Easter and so on around the calendar, back again through Lent to the next Easter.

To assist the cantillation of the scripture, musical indications were written (usually with a different color of ink) to indicate the pitch as well as other musical features. In the Middle Ages, for a very elegant copy of the gospels, the scribe would provide a picture of Matthew or one of the other evangelists. How did people in the Middle Ages know what Matthew, Mark, Luke, and John looked like? They did not know, but they adopted and adapted the characteristic poses (standing or seated) of classical Greek philosophers and poets of antiquity and used these in developing the representations of Matthew, Mark, Luke, and John. These artists eventually drew up what is called the painter's manual, giving specific instruction so that thereafter, for example, the virgin Mary always would be painted with a blue gown and Judas with a mustard colored or black robe. These and various other requirements were set down in order to provide an unvarying tradition over the generations as to how such pictures must always be represented. Finally, some manuscripts were equipped with commentaries in the margin. Larger script was used for the scripture text itself, and in the margin a narrower column in smaller handwriting provided comments about the meaning of this or that passage on that page.

The New Testament and Other Christian Writings

How did early Christians learn of the existence of the New Testament? These different books were not first gathered together with a title "The New Testament"; each of them originally was separate. How were these various books identified? How were they distinguished from apocryphal writings?

Apocryphal books fall into the same four categories that we have in the New Testament, namely, gospels, acts, epistles, and books of revelation. Imitations in each of these categories were produced in the second, third, fourth, and fifth Christian centuries. Some church people were quite fond of them. How did it eventually come about that only the twenty-seven books that we now accept as the New Testament were recognized? Once we see what is in some of these books, we will perceive that there is a considerable difference between canonical and apocryphal books.

Apocryphal Gospels. First, we may consider the recently discovered Coptic manuscript of the *Gospel of Thomas*, which came to light in the late 1940s and was published in the 1950s. The *Gospel of Thomas* was discovered in Egypt along with about fifty other documents of a Christian gnostic library. The *Gospel of Thomas* contains 114 different sayings attributed to Jesus. Each of these sayings begins with the words, "Jesus says…" Unlike the canonical gospels, there is no narrative framework—only the sayings of Jesus. Several of these sayings resemble what we have in the New Testament. For example, "Jesus says, 'A city that is set on a high hill cannot be hid'" (*logion* 32). That is just like Matthew 5:14b except it adds the word "high." Another saying is, "Render to Caesar the things that are Caesar's, render to God the things that are God's, render to me the things that are mine" (*logion* 100). That last phrase adds

50 percent more to the words found in Mark 12:17 (and Mt. 22:21; Lk. 20:25).

Other statements in the *Gospel of Thomas* are totally unlike anything in the New Testament. For example, "Jesus says,… 'Lift the stone, there am I. Cleave the wood, there am I'" (*logion* 77). This statement is pantheistic and suggests that Jesus is conterminous with material of this world. There are some other unusual things in the *Gospel of Thomas*. The 114th saying, which ends the document, reads as follows: "Simon Peter said to them [the disciples], 'Let Mary go away from us, for women are not worthy of life.' Jesus says, 'Behold, I shall lead her so that I can make her a male so she can enter the kingdom of Heaven.'"

Another specimen of apocryphal gospels is known as an infancy gospel. The New Testament says very little about Jesus as a child. There is only Luke's account (2:41–50) of Jesus when he was twelve years old and his parents took him to Jerusalem where he talked with Jewish teachers in the temple. Early Christian believers were dissatisfied with such a limited account of the early life of Jesus. What else did Jesus do as a child? When people are curious, they usually make an effort to satisfy their curiosity. And so there developed among Christian believers various narratives of what Jesus might have said, or what Jesus could have done as a child.

The infancy narratives include some very bizarre narratives. For example, one story adds to the account of Matthew 2:13–15 where in a dream Joseph was told to flee to Egypt with Mary and Jesus because Herod was about to search for the child, to destroy him. So during the night the family packed up and went south toward Egypt.

The person who expanded this narrative (known today as the *Gospel of Pseudo-Matthew*) had a good imagination. He understood that Mary, having given birth recently, would become tired on the journey, and that is what happened (chap. 20). While resting under a palm tree, she saw some fruit on it and said that she would like to have some. The tree, however, was too high for Joseph to reach the fruit to satisfy her hunger. But the child on her lap commanded the tree to bend over, which it did, so she could pluck some dates. After this, Mary became thirsty. The child again satisfied the need of his mother by commanding that a stream of water should gush out as a spring from near the roots of the tree. Mary quenched her thirst.

Subsequently Mary became very weary, so Jesus shortened the geographical distance between Palestine and Egypt (chap. 22). When the family passed over the border and arrived at Hermopolis, they entered a city called Sotinen. Here they had to lodge in a temple where there were 365 gods. When Mary and the child entered, all the idols fell, a testimony that someone more powerful than they had entered their domain.

Other infancy gospels tell what Jesus did as a boy. When he was five years old, according to the *Infancy Gospel of Thomas*, Jesus was playing with other children on the sabbath day near a brook. Jesus molded twelve sparrows from the soft clay. A Jewish elder, having seen what Jesus did, reported it to his father Joseph, who came and rebuked Jesus for breaking the Sabbath. But Jesus simply clapped his hands, and the clay sparrows took flight and flew away (§ 3).

In the same work the slightly older Jesus was helping his father in the carpenter shop. An order had come from a rich man to make him a bed. Unfortunately one of the two pieces of wood was too short for the bed, and Joseph did not know what to do. So Jesus instructed Joseph, "Lay down the two pieces of wood and make them even at the end next to you." Jesus then stood at the other end and took hold of the shorter beam and stretched it, making it equal with the other (§ 13).

Another incident shows that Jesus could also be something of a bully. Once while going through the village a boy ran and dashed against Jesus' shoulder. Jesus was angered and said to him, "You shall not go farther on your way." Immediately the boy fell down and died (§ 4).

These are some of the more interesting samples from this kind of literature. In all there were about twenty-five apocryphal gospels written in the second and following centuries.

Apocryphal Acts. Books of acts of the apostles were another entertaining narrative form produced by early Christians. A Greek papyrus manuscript of the *Acts of Paul* found in the 1930s was edited and published at Hamburg in 1936 by Professor Carl Schmidt. This text tells about Paul and the baptized lion. Paul was traveling as an evangelist in Asia Minor, and while going through the wilderness he was accosted by a large lion that asked Paul to preach the gospel to it. After Paul preached the gospel, the lion professed faith in Jesus. Then the lion requested baptism, and, once again, Paul obliged. Later the two parted, the lion going back to its native habitat, and Paul going on to Ephesus.

In Ephesus Paul preached the gospel and converted a number of people, mainly women. One was the wife of the governor, and she henceforth paid more attention to Paul than she paid to her husband. Naturally, this triangle did not please her husband, and so he tried to persuade her no longer to sit and listen to Paul expounding the Old Testament, but to no avail. So Paul was arrested, and a day was set for him to fight with a wild beast in the amphitheater. On the appointed day a large crowd was present in the amphitheater; the cage was opened and a lion, exceedingly fierce, the record says, emerged—none other than the lion that Paul had previously baptized! The lion came up and looked at Paul and said in a human voice, "Grace be with thee." Then Paul responded, "Grace be with thee, lion."

This conversation was cut short because the crowd was eager to see some action. The lion was rubbing against Paul's shins like a big over-grown pussycat, and so the governor gave a command that the archers should start shooting arrows at the lion in order to anger the beast so it would turn upon Paul. Just then a huge hail storm broke out, and one of the hail stones struck and tore off the right ear of the governor. There-upon, the gates were opened and the crowd was dispersed, while Paul and the lion left unmolested.[1]

There is also the *Acts of the Apostle John*. This book tells about an episode of John and the obedient bedbugs (§§ 60–61). John was going through Asia Minor preaching at different places. He was elderly now, in his late eighties, and he had younger people with him. They came at nightfall to a house that was empty, so they pushed open the door. In-side was only one bed, so out of deference to the aged John, the others allowed him to sleep in the bed while they stretched out on the floor. John soon discovered that he was not alone in the bed, for many bed-bugs prevented him from falling asleep. The bugs became more and more troublesome to him. After midnight he said to them in the hearing of his companions, "I tell you, you bugs, to behave yourselves, one and all. You must leave your home for tonight and be quiet at one place and keep your distance from the servants of God." Then John fell asleep, undisturbed.

The next morning John's younger associates rose first. They were astounded to see outside at the door a great number of bugs collected together. When John woke up they explained to him what they had seen. John then spoke to the bugs and gave them permission to go back again to their accustomed places.

In another text attributed to pseudo-Abdias, John proved to the high priest at Ephesus, Aristodemus, his authority as an apostle by drinking poison without being harmed by it. Two criminals who were to be ex-ecuted drank the poison and died on the spot. This showed that the potion was really lethal. Then John drank of the poisoned cup himself. When after three hours he remained unharmed, the people called out, "There is but one true God, he whom John worships." Even so, Aristodemus did not yet believe, but demanded that the two poisoned men be first restored to life. John gave his cloak to Aristodemus, in-structing him to lay it first on one criminal and then on the other. This done, the dead men stood up, whereupon Aristodemus was converted and received baptism (§§ 20–21).

Apocryphal Letters. Since it is more difficult to compose entertaining letters than a gospel or a book of acts, it is understandable that fewer apocryphal letters have been produced than apocryphal gospels or apoc-ryphal acts. Fourteen letters of the correspondence of Paul and Seneca, the Stoic philosopher, were composed, as it seems, a couple of centuries after the deaths of Paul and Seneca. They were popular among Roman Christians, and more than 300 Latin manuscripts of the correspondence have survived. The banal content and colorless style of the letters show that they cannot have come from the pen of either the apostle or the moralist.

There is also the spurious letter to the Laodiceans. This was produced by someone who had read Colossians 4:16, where Paul directs the recipients to exchange letters with the church of the Laodiceans. Since Christian believers had the letter of Paul to the Colossians, they wondered about this letter that Paul refers to as being at Laodicea. Where was that letter? Again, curiosity produced an answer. Someone felt able to reproduce the content of the letter in Latin, and in the third or fourth Christian century there emerged the letter that Paul wrote to the Laodiceans! It is very brief—the Latin contains but 247 words—and comprises a cento of short, unconnected phrases, lifted chiefly from Paul's letter to the Galatians and his letter to the Philippians. It is not just a second-rate or third-rate letter; it is at least a fourth- or fifth-rate letter in comparison with Paul's genuine writings. But the curious thing is that it was incorporated amid Paul's letters in many Latin manuscripts of the New Testament. Still more amazing is the fact that the first eighteen German Bibles, which came from the printing press prior to the translation made by Martin Luther from the Greek and Hebrew texts, include in the New Testament this spurious letter to the Laodiceans following the letter to the Galatians.

Apocryphal Apocalypses. In addition to the book of Revelation in the New Testament written by John, there are several apocalypses attributed to other apostles. The earliest of these is the *Apocalypse of Peter* from the first half of the second century, preserved in part in Greek and fully in Ethiopic. Making use of popular beliefs about the afterlife from Homer's *Odyssey*, book 11 and from Vergil's *Aeneid*, book 6, the unknown author tells of the delights of the redeemed in heaven and (at much greater length) the torments of the damned in hell. These ideas were elaborated extensively in the following century by the author of the *Apocalypse of Paul*, who describes how Paul was caught up to paradise (see 2 Cor. 12:1–4) and witnessed the judgment of two souls, one righteous and the other wicked (§§ 14–18). Some of these themes became part of medieval beliefs given wider dissemination through Dante's *Divine Comedy*. With the discovery in 1946 of the Nag Hammadi library in Coptic, the number of apocryphal apocalypses increased: another *Apocalypse of Peter*, another of Paul, the first and second *Apocalypses of James*, and others.

The Recognition of the New Testament Canon

We learn about the recognition of the canon by examining what various writers in the early church have to say about these books and their collection. Already in the New Testament, in 2 Peter (3:15–16), we find that the author speaks of "all of Paul's letters." We do not know how many are covered by "all," but it is a plurality.

An important book for this kind of study is *The New Testament in the Apostolic Fathers*, prepared by a committee of the Oxford Society of Historical Theology (1905). This study lists the quotations and echoes of the New Testament in the documents known as the Apostolic Fathers. The earliest of the Apostolic Fathers is a letter written about A.D. 96 by a Christian named Clement and sent from the church at Rome to the church at Corinth. In it he quotes from the Old Testament and also makes some remarks about Paul's first letter to the Corinthians, quoting some sentences from it. He also alludes to one or two other letters that Paul wrote. These quotations show that the letter that Paul wrote to Corinth was also available in Rome in the year 96.

Another of the texts generally included among the Apostolic Fathers is the *Didaché*, a document that purports to have been written by the twelve apostles. Here we find echoes and allusions from the Synoptic Gospels. We do not know when the *Didaché* was issued in written form—perhaps it was early in the second Christian century, ca. 125.

Another of the dozen or so writings in the corpus known as the Apostolic Fathers is a letter attributed to Barnabas, not the Barnabas who was the companion of Paul, but another who wrote about A.D. 125 from the city of Alexandria concerning the way Christians should interpret the Old Testament. In this letter Barnabas makes use of various parts of the New Testament, though he does not refer by name to any particular book of the New Testament. Another document widely read and appreciated by early Christian believers of the second and third centuries is called *The Shepherd*. Written by a man named Hermas, *The Shepherd* is a long, rambling narrative of parables and visions. Once again, this book is found to contain allusions to several New Testament books, along with references to the Old Testament. Both the letter of *Barnabas* and *The Shepherd of Hermas* were so highly regarded that the famous codex Sinaiticus, a fourth-century copy of the Greek Bible and one of the earliest parchment manuscripts of the Bible, contains both of these writings following the end of the New Testament.

From the middle of the second Christian century come the writings of an important teacher named Justin Martyr. After he was converted, Justin left off his task of being a rhetorician and went to Rome in order to teach Christianity. In Justin's writings he quotes freely from the three

Synoptic Gospels, referring to them as the memoirs of the apostles. Whether he knew the Gospel according to John is not evident from his writings, but he refers by name to the Revelation of John written on the island of Patmos. This is the first time that a church father refers by name to a document that is in our New Testament.

Toward the end of the second century, about 170, a Syrian Christian decided to weave together all four gospels, Matthew, Mark, Luke, and John, into one narrative. This person was Tatian, a student of Justin Martyr at Rome. In his opinion the four gospels, Matthew, Mark, Luke, and John, were far above any other gospels.

These are the beginnings of the slow, steady spread and recognition of the existence of the books of the New Testament by various people, starting in the late first century.

The first major period in the development of the New Testament canon is from about the year 180 to 200. The idea of a Christian canon, along with the Jewish canon of the Old Testament, was reported by Irenaeus, a Christian from Asia Minor who traveled to Rome and from there went on to Gaul, modern France. As bishop in Gaul, he learned the Celtic language and preached in the local dialect. Irenaeus refers by name to the four gospels and also to several Pauline letters, as well as to other books in the New Testament.

Toward the close of the second century in North Africa, in the city of Carthage, was a lawyer who had been converted in midlife; his name was Tertullian. He became a powerful promoter of the Christian religion and a prolific writer. In about the year 200 he wrote several treatises in which he quoted from eighteen of the twenty-seven books of the New Testament. Tertullian also wrote against heretics. One heretic that he went after tooth and nail was Marcion, who lived in the mid-second century. According to the lengthy treatise that Tertullian wrote against him, Marcion had joined an abbreviated Gospel of Luke with several Pauline letters as a kind of modified Christian canon. Tertullian attacks Marcion for having cut out the majority of the books of the New Testament.

Another prominent Christian writer of this period was Titus Flavius Clement. An Athenian by birth and of pagan parentage, in his adult years Clement embraced the Christian religion. After extensive travels in pursuit of learning he came to Alexandria about A.D. 180. Here he worked for the conversion of pagans and the education of Christians. As head of the catechetical school in Alexandria, Clement devoted himself to lecturing to his pupils and to writing many books, the majority of which have disappeared. Three of his major works have survived: The *Protrepticus*, or "Exhortation to the Greeks," was addressed to pagan readers; the *Paedagogos*, on Christian life and morality; and the *Miscellanies*. Throughout his writings Clement makes copious citations of both classical and biblical literature; the total number of citations is about 8,000. Of this number about 1,575 quotations are from the four gospels and about 1,375 from the Pauline epistles. In the course of his several treatises, Clement cites all the books of the New Testament except Philemon, James, 2 Peter, and 2 and 3 John.

From the works of Irenaeus, Tertullian, and Clement during this first period (180–200), we have evidence for the wide-spread recognition of twenty of the twenty-seven books of the New Testament. Seven books are still lacking general recognition, namely, Hebrews, James, 2 Peter, 2 and 3 John, Jude, and Revelation.

The second period of the development of the canon may be reckoned from about the year 200 to about the year 325, the date of the Council of Nicea. During this period, it is the writings of Origen and Eusebius that are particularly instructive. Among ante-Nicene writers of the Eastern Church, the greatest by far was Origen, both as a theologian and as a prolific biblical scholar. Born of Christian parents in Egypt, probably about A.D. 185, he spent most of his life in Alexandria as head of the catechetical school, but he also visited Antioch, Athens, Arabia, Ephesus, and Rome and lived for a rather long period at Caesarea in Palestine. Having traveled widely, he had the opportunity of observing the usage of churches and individual Christians as to the acceptance of books of the New Testament. Origen's witness is clear and forthright, declaring that one must distinguish between the accepted or acknowledged books, which all Christians accepted as scripture, and the disputed books, which some did not accept. As acknowledged books Origen lists the four gospels, fourteen letters of Paul (including Hebrews and the letters to Timothy and Titus), the Acts of the Apostles, 1 Peter, 1 John, and the Revelation of John—twenty-two in all. The disputed books, which he himself accepted as belonging to the New Testament, were James, 2 and 3 John, Jude, and 2 Peter.

Born about A.D. 260, Eusebius became bishop of Caesarea by 315. He wrote his great *Ecclesiastical History* in sections and issued it, with revisions and additions, three times during the first quarter of the fourth century. What renders Eusebius' work most valuable to us is his concern to trace the history of the Christian Bible. He gives a summary in Book 3, chapter 25, where he distinguishes three categories of books: (1) universally acknowledged, (2) disputed, and (3) spurious (i.e., uncanonical). The first two groups are similar to Origen's listing. In the third group Eusebius identifies as spurious the *Acts of Paul*, *The Shepherd of Hermas*, the *Apocalypse of Peter*, and in addition the so-called *Epistle of Barnabas* and the so-called *Teaching of the Apostles* (the *Didaché*). Eusebius lists the Apocalypse of John twice, both among the universally acknowledged and among the spurious books, both times with a qualifying clause "should it seem right." Eusebius' apparent inconsistency arises from the fact that the Apocalypse was acknowledged by those churches whose opinion he valued most, whereas he himself was unhappy about it—he could not reconcile himself to its millennial teaching.

A landmark in the recognition of the canon of the New Testament is the year 367. In that year Athanasius, bishop of Alexandria, for the first time put forth a list of exactly the twenty-seven books that we have today in the New Testament, though they are not in the same sequence—the general epistles precede the Pauline epistles. Now for the first time there is an acknowledgment of which books are in the New Testament by an authoritative Christian leader. Later Christian synods held at Hippo in North Africa in 393 and at Carthage in 397 and 419 acquiesced in the same listing of these twenty-seven books.

Influences Shaping the Canon

It is helpful to consider some of the pressures that were put on the church to identify which books are the canonical books. Among external pressures, there was a custom in early Christian worship of reading apostolic letters in services of Christian worship along with reading Old Testament passages. And so it was natural for people to regard letters by Paul, by Peter, by Jude, and so on as having a certain authority. Secondly, there was an increase of quotations of New Testament documents in the growing Christian literature, beginning, as we saw above, with the Apostolic Fathers. Thirdly, controversies between heretical sects and the great church were instrumental in discriminating between what was heretical and what was authoritative and orthodox. The claims of heretics, such as Marcion and, in the following generation, Montanus, meant that the leaders of the church needed to make certain that people were not led astray by documents that the heretics promoted. Such controversies were therefore a catalyst, but not a constitutive element in the development of the canon—a catalyst that made it imperative for Christians to make up their minds which were the authoritative New Testament books. Fourth, another set of circumstances exerted pressure on individuals to be certain which books were scripture and which were not. During periods of persecution the imperial police would knock at one's door and ask, "Are you a Christian?" and "Do you have any Christian literature?" If the answer to the second question was yes, the Christian writings would have to be turned over to be destroyed. So it became imperative to know which writings could be delivered up without incurring the guilt of sacrilege and which must be protected even at the cost of persecution. These external pressures served as catalysts to make the discrimination as to the identity of biblical books known and acknowledged.

Other criteria (chiefly internal) for determining canonicity are the following three major items: the content of what is written, consideration of authorship, and general acceptance. Put differently, the first criterion for determining canonicity was whether or not the book conformed to the *regula fidei*, or rule of faith. Is this or that document congruous with the general run of what is already accepted as scripture? The second question concerned apostolicity of authorship. Was it written either by an apostle or by a companion of an apostle (such as Mark who accompanied Peter, or Luke who accompanied Paul)? The third test of the authority of a book was its continuous acceptance and usage by the church at large. Different congregations in various parts of the ancient world were in agreement that Matthew, Mark, Luke, and John were authoritative books. But here and there other gospels circulated, the *Gospel of Thomas* in one place, the infancy gospels elsewhere. The continuous acceptance and usage by the church at large was one of the considerations that tested the authority of a given book. Saint Jerome (342–420) declared, "It does not matter who was the author of the Epistle to the Hebrews, for in any case it is the work of a church writer and is constantly read in the churches."[2]

These three criteria, orthodoxy, apostolicity, and consensus, would naturally operate as people became generally aware of what should be accepted and what should be rejected. Which of these criteria was given the chief weight would differ at different places. For some, the chief weight would be given to the criterion of agreement with the rule of faith. Others would have weighed the criteria differently. But in any case it is remarkable that general unanimity was attained during the first two centuries among very diverse and scattered congregations, not only in the Mediterranean world, but also over an area stretching from Britain to Mesopotamia.

The Variety and Order of the Canon

We turn our attention to consider the kinds of books that the early Christians put together: four different gospels, twenty-one different letters, one book of history (Acts), and the book of Revelation. Of twenty-seven books, seven-ninths are in letter format. There is no book of the Old Testament in the form of a letter. The letter format was found by early Christians to be a useful medium that combined the ability of conveying religious truth using the third person with the more intimate nature of the second person. "I say to you," combines the systematic and specific declaration of facts with the warm approach of a personal appeal. Since that is what a letter is able to do, it is not surprising that so many of the books of the New Testament utilize this marriage between the third person and the second person in the epistolary genre.

With regard to the sequence of the books in the New Testament, it seems obvious that the books that pertain to the life of Jesus would stand first. The book of Acts joins the gospels to the following twenty-one letters. We might ask, What is the sequence of the Pauline letters? The sequence is not chronological or alphabetical. The order of these letters in the New Testament is the order of descending length, with Romans, the longest of the Pauline letters to congregations first, and 2 Thessalonians, the shortest of Paul's letters to congregations, last. And then another sequence begins with Paul's letters to individuals, and is again arranged from the longest (1 Timothy) to the shortest (Philemon). The same is true with regard to the general or catholic letters, Hebrews, the longest, is first, and Jude, the shortest, is last. It is interesting that, except for the first *sura*, the Qur'ān similarly arranges the 114 different *suras* according to length.

The Greek manuscripts of the New Testament differ, however, from the order of modern New Testaments. They put the general letters immediately after Acts, followed by the Pauline letters. That is also the order (as we have seen) that Athanasius gives in his listing in A.D. 367. Our way of putting the Pauline letters followed by the general or catholic letters arose in the West in Latin manuscripts. With regard to the order of the gospels, there are manuscripts of the four gospels that have the four gospels in different sequences. A sequence that was very popular was Matthew, John, Luke, and Mark, putting the two apostles together—Matthew and John—followed by the two gospels written by the associates of the apostles.

Conclusion

There are two ways of describing the canon of the New Testament. One can describe the canon as (1) a collection of authoritative books or as (2) an authoritative collection of books. The first means that the books had authority individually before they were collected. The second formulation implies that the books got their authority by being collected at a given time. It seems to the present writer that the books had an intrinsic worth prior to their having been assembled, and that their authority is grounded in their nature and source. There is, one might say, an ontological canon as well as a historical canon. Ideally, the canon existed as soon as the individual books were written, even though it took some time for people to recognize that they had in their hands books of the New Testament.

It is clear that the recognition of the canon was the result of a long process of forces that brought about the expression of the historical canon. What is remarkable is that, even though the fringes of the canon remained unsettled for a time, there was actually a high degree of unanimity concerning the greater part of the New Testament within the first two centuries. And this was true among very diverse congregations scattered over a wide area.

The development of the canon is an example of the survival of the fittest. Arthur Darby Nock used to tell his students at Harvard, "The most traveled roads in Europe are the best roads; that's why they are so heavily traveled." Scottish commentator William Barclay put it this way: "It is the simple truth to say that the New Testament books became canonical because no one could stop them doing so." One often reads or hears it said that various councils excluded this or that book from the canon. That is an imaginary depiction of history. The earliest councils approved what already had come to be generally approved by Christian believers throughout the church. A council or a synod did not sit around a long table on which lay many manuscripts, and then, for the first time, look at a manuscript and say, "This we will put in the New Testament," or "No, we will exclude that one." Before councils were held, the earliest Christian readers themselves detected the voice of the Good Shepherd in the Gospel of John, but heard the voice of the Good Shepherd only in a muffled way in the *Gospel of Thomas*; they did not hear the voice of the Good Shepherd at all in various infancy gospels. Prior to being excluded by any council, the apocryphal books excluded themselves.

Suggestions for Further Reading

Barton, J. *Holy Writings, Sacred Text: The Canon in Early Christianity.* Louisville: Westminster John Knox, 1997.

Bruce, F. F. *The Canon of Scripture.* Downers Grove, Ill.: InterVarsity, 1988.

Metzger, B. M. *The Canon of the New Testament; Its Origin, Development, and Significance.* New York: Oxford University Press, 1987.

For English translations of apocryphal gospels, acts, letters, and apocalypses, reference may be made to the following:

Elliott, J. K. *The Apocryphal New Testament.* Oxford: At the University Press, 1994.

Schneemelcher, W. *New Testament Apocrypha,* vol. 1, *Gospels and Related Writings,* rev. ed. Philadelphia: Westminster Press, 1990; vol. 2, *Writings Related to the Apostles, Apocalypses, and Related Subjects,* rev. ed., 1993.

---

[1]For the first English translation of this episode in the Hamburg papyrus, see my article "St. Paul and the Baptized Lion," *Princeton Seminary Bulletin* 39 (1945): 11–21.

[2]*Epistle* cxxix, written A.D. 414 to a certain patrician, Claudienus Postumus Dardanus.

5

The Lessons of the Garden:
An Examination of the Scriptural
Legacy of Islam

Kathryn Johnson

An audience familiar with Judaism and Christianity will very likely note a number of shared elements between Islam, the third of the major monotheistic traditions, and its two predecessors. Indeed, as Muslims describe their views on the origin of humankind and explain the significance of Islam's required practices and doctrines, the extent of the shared elements of the three religions becomes increasingly apparent. Muslims, like Jews and Christians, refer to a scriptural account that tells of the creation of Adam and Eve and an act of disobedience that resulted in exile from the garden. And when describing the required practices, Muslims frequently make reference to the older traditions. The Five Pillars, or five obligatory practices are, first, that one is to give testimony that there is no god but God, and Muhammad is his messenger. The faithful are also obliged to perform the five ritual prayers daily, fast during the month of Ramadan, give alms, and make the pilgrimage to Mecca if physically and financially able. Several of these required rites focus upon the central shrine of Islam in Mecca, the Ka'aba. And it is the Ka'aba that once again links Islam to the older religions, for it is believed to have been a place of worship of the one God since the time of Adam. After having been destroyed in the flood of Noah, it was rebuilt by Abraham and Ishmael. And after later having fallen in to use as a pagan shrine, the Ka'aba was at last restored to its proper role by the Prophet Muḥammad in 630 C.E. when Mecca fell to the Muslims. The basic doctrines of Islam again confirm its strong connection to the older monotheistic faiths. Muslims are required to affirm God's unity (*tawhid*). God is absolutely transcendent, and although his existence is confirmed by reason, revelation is necessary to understand how to have a successful relationship with him. Thus, Muslims also acknowledge the series of prophets sent by God beginning with Adam and concluding with Muḥammad and the books revealed to humankind that include the Torah, Psalms, Gospel, and Qur'ān. They affirm the role of the angels who are God's servants and acknowledge the existence of predestination. And finally, they believe that all who have been created will ultimately stand before God in a final judgment.[1]

The scriptural content, doctrines, and practices of Islam all give clear indication of a pedigree that links it to Judaism and Christianity. But in what sense are the three traditions related? In this essay we shall explore several aspects of that relationship, beginning with the creation account provided in the Qur'ān, the sacred scripture of Islam. Although the three traditions share the framework story of an ancestral couple who lived in the garden and were cast out after an act of disobedience, each takes its own lessons from the story. We shall then examine the manner in which Muslims themselves have defined the place of their faith among the monotheistic religions. Muslims reject the notion that theirs is an unrelated faith whose followers worship an alien deity called "Allah." Rather, Islam is the final, perfected religion that culminates the series of revelations that includes Judaism and Christianity. Muḥammad is the seal of the prophets, and the Qur'ān is the final scripture that will be revealed to humankind, concluding the cycle of prophets and revelations. Finally, we shall touch upon the challenge raised by modern Western scholarship to the traditional Islamic perspectives. As has been the case with other religious traditions, the methodologies employed by modern scholars have sometimes produced conclusions that contradict the long-held views of the faithful.

The Lessons of the Garden

Jewish discussions of the creation account in Genesis have often emphasized that this is a story about the burden and privilege of being human. Having eaten of the fruit of the tree of knowledge of good and evil, humankind is now in the image of God. As a species we know good and evil, and therefore have the freedom to serve God or deny him. The unfolding of the history of Israel will be the story of the covenant that is offered to a particular people and the consequences that follow when they choose or reject God. The descendants of Adam and Eve can never go back to the garden; humanity has exchanged a perfect existence for knowledge. But knowing good and evil, each individual can truly enter into a relationship with God.

Christian theology has found very different lessons in the same story. If we examine the time line of events from the Christian perspective, this is a story in which a transformation occurs in Adam and Eve because of their act of disobedience. Whether this change is described as the burden of original sin or alienation between God and humanity that is the consequence of the choice made by Adam and Eve, the relationship between God and humankind is different after Eden. To understand the pivotal role of Jesus Christ, one must understand this point. Otherwise we could not understand why the Christian theologian is able to speak of Jesus as the Second Adam and his coming as the beginning of a new creation. It is by accepting the perfect gift offered by Jesus that the Christian restores the relationship with God. And, it is through Jesus that one truly comes to know God. Christ as Savior is critically necessary in the theology of Christianity because humanity is critically in need of redemption and knowledge.

The Muslim story, however, properly begins before the creation of Adam when a primordial covenant (*mithāq*) is established between God and all of the humans who will ever live:

> When the Lord drew forth
> From the Children of Adam
> From their loins—
> Their descendants, and made them
> Testify concerning themselves (saying):
> "Am I not your Lord?"
> They said: "Yea!
> We do testify." (This) lest
> You should say on the Day
> of Judgment: "Of this
> We were never mindful." (Qur'ān 7:172)

Even before creation, Muslims believe that humanity as a whole has recognized God as Lord (*rabb*). It is this covenant relationship to which every man and woman is called during his or her lifetime on earth. Each human being is said to have a *fiṭrah* that is Muslim, a nature that instinctively knows God, although an individual may be distracted by the world and choose to ignore it. This most basic understanding of human nature is reflected in the very name given by God to the religion, Islam, and that of its followers, Muslims. The natural state of humans is to live in submission to God (*islām*); and one who does so is a *muslim*, a "submitter." For this reason, also, English-speaking Muslims often refer to new members of the faith as "reverts" rather than "converts," because they are understood to be returning to their primordial religion rather than exchanging one faith for another.

The account of the creation of Adam from clay (Qur'ān 15:28) and the series of events that occur (Qur'ān 2:30–33) when the angels learn of his existence are to be understood against the backdrop of a relationship that has already been established between humanity as a whole and God. Yet when God announces his intention to create this new being, Adam, who will be given the title of *khalīfah* (vicegerent), a curious event occurs. The angels, God's faithful servants, appear to question him.

> Remember when your Lord said to the angels, "I will place a vicegerent (*khalīfah*) on earth." They said, "Will you place one therein who will work corruption therein shed blood?—while we do celebrate Your praises and glorify Your holy (name)?" He said, "I know what you do not know."
>
> And He taught Adam the names of all things; then He placed them before the angels, and said: "Tell Me the names of these if you are right." They said: "Glory to You; of knowledge we have none, save what You have taught us; In truth it is You Who are perfect in knowledge and wisdom."
>
> He said, "O Adam! tell them their names." When he had told them their names, God said, "Did I not tell you that I know the secrets of heaven and earth, and I know what you reveal and what you conceal."   (Qur'ān 2:30–33)

Now, angels are perfect beings, incapable, by their very nature, of rebellion or mischief. When they appear to question God, they are exhibiting behavior that clearly contradicts Islamic doctrine. Muslim commentators, therefore, must explain their odd behavior since they do not admit the possibility that angels might challenge God. Instead, they offer several alternative explanations for the angels' response. Some exegetes are of the opinion that God must have given the angels an intuitive sense of the future behavior of humanity that led them to ask God's purpose. Others argue that their questions are based upon the angels' knowledge of the period of history that preceded God's announcement. The angels fear humanity's potential for violence because they have previously witnessed the destructive behavior of the *jinn*. The jinn were the first rational species created and, like humans, had the ability to acknowledge and serve God. However, they waged war against one another in a prehistoric conflict that ended when angelic forces were sent against them. The angels, then, are voicing their fear that this second rational being and his descendants will repeat the unfortunate mistakes of his predecessor.[2]

Muslim commentators have also paused to reflect upon the significance of the hidden knowledge to which God alludes and the names taught to Adam. A variety of interpretations have been proposed, depending upon the theological perspective of the author. Shi'i Muslims have found references to the Imams, who are vicegerents by virtue of their perfect ability to interpret the revelation. Mystics perceive allusions to esoteric wisdom. Regardless of the source, however, there is a sense shared by all of the authors that God has great plans for this new species.

Adam is given knowledge of creation that distinguishes him from even the angels. From Adam will come prophets and ordinary folk who will freely choose to worship God. Although formed of clay, he is given the title of *khalīfah*, vicegerent, and is taught the names by God. Implied is a relationship in which humankind is given guardianship over the world and knowledge of it in order to learn. The physical universe is the place in which men and women will be given the opportunity to prepare for the second, eternal portion of life.[3]

Recognizing the high honor that has been bestowed upon Adam, the angels submit to God's command and bow before him—all save Iblīs.

> And remember when We said to the angels, "Prostrate
> yourselves before Adam," they all prostrated themselves
> except Iblīs. He refused to be among those who prostrate.
>
> (Qur'ān 2:24)

Iblīs is obviously a rebel residing in the celestial ranks, and he, like the questioning angels, raises a theological dilemma for the commentators. Who is Iblīs? Angels have been described as perfect servants of God. How could an angel refuse to obey a direct command from God? To identify this being who dwells with the angels, but nonetheless rebels against God, commentators frequently resort to the previously mentioned history of the rebellious *jinn* that had once inhabited earth. Perhaps Iblīs was a *jinni* that had fought in the ranks of the angels who defeated the wicked *jinn* and was then elevated to a celestial office as a reward for his devotion? Or again, perhaps he belonged to a separate species of beings created of fire that resembled the angels yet did not share their pure nature? Such a being might be overly proud and capable of disobedience. Whatever Iblīs' pedigree, of far greater importance is the consequence of his rebellion. For when Iblīs disobeys God, he is cast out.[4]

> It is We Who created you and gave you shape. Then We bade
> the angels to prostrate to Adam, and they prostrated, save
> Iblīs. He refused to be among those who prostrate.
>
> (God) said, "What prevented you from prostrating when I
> commanded you (to bow)?"

He said, "I am better than he. You created me from fire, and him from clay."

(God) said, "Get you down from it! It is not for you to be arrogant. Here, get out, for you are of the meanest (of creatures)."   (Qur'ān 7:11–13)

So, Iblīs is dismissed from the angelic ranks, but his work is not finished. He requests a respite until the Day of Judgment and predicts that he will find many of this new human species ungrateful to their Creator and quite willing to follow the temptations he places before them. Iblīs is the devil, the *shayṭān*. But as we shall see, he has not been given the authority to do more than serve as a tempter. He is the "Cursed Whisperer" who encourages humans to disobey God. He cannot seize one single soul to drag it down to damnation—only we human beings can do that for ourselves. Iblīs simply encourages us to indulge our own worst instincts.

He (Iblīs) said, "Give me respite until the day they are raised up."

He (God) said, "You are among those who have respite."

He (Iblīs) said, "Because you have thrown me out (of the Way), lo! I will lie in wait for them on Your Straight Way."

"Then will I assault them from before and behind, from their right and their left. Nor will You find, in most of them, gratitude (for Your mercies)."

He (God) said, "Get out from this, despised and expelled. If any of them follow you, I will fill Hell with all of you."
                                    (Qur'ān 7:14–18)

In other words, Iblīs has asked God to allow him to tempt humans until the Judgment Day at which time he and those who follow him will be punished. And he anticipates that many humans will willingly follow him. He apparently understands that along with the ability to choose God is the option to ignore that most ancient covenant and all of the mercies that have since been bestowed.

Iblīs' first target will be Adam, who along with his mate, Ḥawwā' (Eve), has been given the garden as a dwelling. They are warned by God to beware of Iblīs' scheme and reminded that everything that they may require is already to be found within their garden home.

We had already, beforehand taken the covenant of Adam, but he forgot; and We found on his part no firm resolve.

When We said to the angels, "Prostrate yourselves to Adam." They prostrated themselves, but not Iblīs. He refused.

The We said, "O Adam! Truly, this is an enemy to you and your wife. Therefore, do not let him get you out of the Garden, so that you land in misery.

There is therein (enough provision) for you not to go
hungry, or naked, or suffer from thirst, or from the sun's
heat."

(Qur'ān 20:116–119)

Even though Adam and Eve have been forewarned that Iblīs is their
declared enemy whose goal is to drive them from their idyllic existence
into misery—when he tempts them, they still disobey God.

And We said, "O Adam! You and your wife dwell in the
Garden; and eat of the bountiful things therein as you will.
But do not approach this tree, or you will become
transgressors."
Then did Satan make them slip from the Garden and get
them out of the state (of felicity) in which they been. And We
said, "Get you down, all, with enmity between yourselves. On
earth will be your dwelling place and your means of
livelihood for a time."   (Qur'ān 2:35–36)

Humans are exiled from the garden; earth will be home for all future
generations, and discord will be ever present. What is the promise, the
sales pitch, that persuaded Adam and Eve to trade paradise for a short
painful lifespan on earth?

But Satan whispered evil to him. He said, "O Adam! Shall I
lead you to a Tree of Eternity and to a kingdom that never
decays?"
In the result, they both ate of the tree, and so their naked-
ness appeared to them; they began to sew leaves from the
Garden together for their covering. Thus did Adam disobey
his Lord and fall into error.   (Qur'ān 20:120–121)

According to one traditional exegesis, Iblīs discovers that which
Adam and Eve fear most. He then tearfully tells the couple how very
sorry he feels for them because they cannot stay in the beautiful garden
and enjoy it forever. They will eventually die. "Eat this fruit and stay
here forever," he promises. Adam and Eve obey. In typical human fashion, they are afraid of risking what they have, the beauty of the here and
now. Adam and Eve make a very human choice—they take what they
know and cling to the lovely garden. They do not trust God's promise to
care for them. They disobey and so lose paradise.[5]

But the conclusion of the Qur'ānic story is quite different from the
biblical text. The Muslim reader understands that there will be no covenant established between God and a particular people; the first primordial covenant remains firm and all-inclusive. Nor will there be any
change in human nature—the potential of every human being to recognize God as Lord was fixed long before the creation of Adam. Instead,

the Qur'ān emphasizes two important points. First, Adam and Eve's actions are personal acts of disobedience. Their foolish choices do not carry over to future generations. In other words, no fundamental change occurs in human nature or in the potential of each human being to respond to God. In addition, the Qur'ān clearly emphasizes that it is Iblīs who is the instigator of the act; Iblīs "made them slip" and "put them out of the state (of felicity) in which they had been" (Qur'ān 2:36).[6]

Humanity must now endure all of the hardships of life on earth, true. But humans have also been made the vicegerents of the earth with the freedom to choose to obey or reject God. As Iblīs predicts, we will often prove forgetful of all that God has given. But we also have been given the ability to seek God's forgiveness, knowing that God may accept our sincere repentance.

> It is He Who has made you the inheritors (vicegerents) of the
> earth; He has raised you in ranks, some above others that He
> may try you in the gifts He has given you. For your Lord is
> quick in punishment; yet He is indeed Oft-Forgiving, Most
> Merciful.   (Qur'ān 6:165)

So it is that Adam and Eve repent in the Qur'ānic account, and God accepts their repentance. The parents of all human beings in this sense set the pattern for their descendants. Men and women become distracted by the pleasures of the world and stray, as did Adam and Eve. And God stands ready to hear their prayers of repentance, just as he once heard those of the exiles from the garden.

> Then Adam learned certain words (of inspiration) from his
> Lord and his Lord turned towards him; for He is the Oft-
> Returning, Most Merciful.
>   We said, "Get down, all of you from here. And if, as is
> sure, guidance comes to you from Me, whosoever follows My
> guidance, they shall have no fear, nor shall they grieve."
>   (Qur'ān 2:37–39)

Adam and Eve realize the necessity of God, for as they now tell him, they are lost without his mercy.

> They said, "Our Lord, we have wronged our own souls; if You
> do not forgive us and bestow Your mercy, we shall certainly
> be lost."
>   He (God) said, "Get down, with enmity between your-
> selves. Your dwelling place will be on earth for a time and
> your means of livelihood, for a time."
>   He (God) said, "Therein you will live, and therein you will
> die; but from it you shall be taken out (at last)." (Qur'ān 7:23–25)

God gives each person an *'ajal*, an allotted lifespan, at the end of which all human beings will, as promised, return to him. In the meantime, each individual must either choose or reject God.

The Muslim understands that God has chosen humanity. That is why he has sent prophets and revelations. And if an individual does make the choice for God, he or she is promised divine guidance—not through an intermediary, because there is no alienation between the human species and God, but from God himself.

But his Lord chose him for (His grace). He turned to him, and gave him guidance.

He (God) said, "Get down, both of you together, from the Garden, with enmity one to another. But if, as is sure, guidance comes to you from Me, whosoever follows My guidance will not lose his way, nor fall into misery."

(Qur'ān 20:122–23)

The story of Adam and Eve's disobedience thus concludes with their departure from the garden, a prayer of sincere repentance, and the promise given by God. Guidance will be offered to humankind; messengers will summon future generations to Him.

O children of Adam! Whenever there comes to you messengers from amongst you, rehearsing My signs unto you—those who are righteous and mend (their lives)—on them shall be no fear nor shall they grieve.

(Qur'ān 7:35)

Issues in Interpretation of the Qur'ān

Readers familiar with Judaism and Christianity might assume upon encountering the Qur'ānic creation story that Muslims must surely recognize the biblical origins of their scripture and, therefore, read the texts of the parent traditions with equal reverence. They might also assume that Muslims readily turn to the older traditions as a source of guidance when explaining the verses of the Qur'ān. In reality, the relationship of the three religions has been more complex. The fact that Muslims see their own tradition as the culmination of the process of revelation that includes those scriptures earlier received by Jews and Christians has shaped its use of their spiritual legacies. We shall discover that, although Muslims have made rather extensive use of the scripture and exegetical materials from the older monotheistic religions, they have customarily been read and judged against the standard of the Qur'ān and then reshaped to conform to its requirements.

Islam's self-definition as the religion that brings to conclusion the cycle of revelation with the coming of the Qur'ān has had a second consequence. Just as Muslims have been hesitant to embrace the Bible as a coequal scripture to the Qur'ān and have rejected accounts that contradict the Qur'ān when composing exegetical literature, so too have they rejected some of the methods and conclusions of modern scholarly analysis. Western scholarship in the nineteenth and twentieth centuries has attempted to delineate the substantial impact of Judaism and Christianity on both the content of the Qur'ān and exegetical literature produced by later generations of Muslims. Today, an enormous gap separates those scholars who employ modern methods of historical criticism and Muslim scholars who continue to rely upon the traditional Islamic methods of analysis. As we shall discover, Western-trained academics and traditionally educated Muslim scholars have often reached contradictory conclusions with regard to the content and dating of the Qur'ān and the influence of Judaism and Christianity upon the development of its exegesis.

While Western scholarship has focused upon discovering the biblical pedigree of the scripture, Muslims have rejected any notion that the Qur'ān was composed by a human agent and therefore reflects both the spiritual legacy of the age and the doctrinal inclinations of its author, Muḥammad. Any similarities in the scriptures are said to exist because of the universal message that the divine Author wished to convey in the revelations granted to all three monotheistic religions. And while modern scholars record the substantial impact of the Jewish and Christian communities upon the content of Qur'ānic exegesis, Muslim scholars continue to emphasize that whatever is taken from the preceding revelations must be judged against the sure standard of the revelation granted Muḥammad and considered to have spiritual merit in so far as it conforms to the Qur'ān and the consensus of the Muslim community as to its interpretation. The lessons drawn by Muslims from the story of Adam and Eve, thus, can best be appreciated when placed within the context of that tradition's own definition of its relationship to Judaism and Christianity. For although the names of the first couple are the same and they, too, dwell within the garden, the events are interpreted through the lens of Islam rather than the spiritual legacy of the preceding revelations.

The Islamic Understanding of Prophecy and Scripture

Islamic doctrine distinguishes between two types of prophets that are sent to humankind, the "messenger" who brings a new religion or a major revelation (*rasūl*) and the "prophet" (*nabī*) whose mission is based within an existing religion. Both those who are sent to warn and summon humanity to God and the messengers who receive scriptures are understood to share a common message, that men and women must "serve God and shun false gods" (Qur'ān 16:36). Some participants in this ongoing process of revelation are mentioned by name in the Qur'ān:

Ādam, Nūḥ (Noah), Ibrāhīm (Abraham), Ismā'īl (Ishmael), Isḥāq (Isaac), Lūṭ (Lot), Ya'qūb (Jacob), Yūsuf (Joseph), Mūsā (Moses), Hārūn (Aaron), Dāwūd (David), Sulaymān (Solomon), Ilyās (Elijah), al-Yasa' (Elisha), Yūnus (Jonah), Ayyūb (Job), Zakarīyā (Zachariah), 'Īsā (Jesus), Yaḥyā Idrīs (Enoch), Hūd, Dhu'l-Kifl (Ezekiel), Shu'ayb (Jethro), Ṣāliḥ, Luqmān, Dhū'l-Qarnayn, Uzayr (Ezra), and Muḥammad. The names and histories of others are not recorded. However, Qur'ān 10:37 confirms that every community has, in fact, received a prophet. The mission of Muḥammad and the revelation of the Qur'ān are, however, unique because they mark the culmination of the process that began with the promise made to Adam. Allah is not a different deity worshiped by Muslims and peculiar to Islam. Allah is God, the same God who has summoned humankind to his service throughout history. The same God who spoke through Torah and the Psalms and the Gospel.

The Qur'ān is understood by Muslims to be the dictated word of God, sent down to the last Prophet Muḥammad through the angel Gabriel. The Qur'ān is uncreated (*ghayr makhlūq*) according to the Sunni majority and, as the word of God, is inimitable. It is further held that its precise meaning and wording have been transmitted by numerous persons (*tawātur*), both verbally and in writing. The Qur'ān is described as unique and protected by God from corruption. Muslims believe that the Qur'ān contains no textual errors (*taḥrīf al-naṣṣ*), nor have there been errors in its interpretation (*taḥrīf al-ma'ānī*) when the analysis of the scripture has been extracted from sound reports from the Prophet Muḥammad. It is therefore a book preserved from error explained by a prophet who is himself protected from sin and error (*ma'ṣūm*).[7]

According to Islamic tradition, the revelation was complete by the time of Muḥammad's death in June 632. Although the text of the Qur'ān had not yet been copied into a single volume, its verses had been written down on various materials such as palm leaf stalks and scraps of parchment, and the text had been memorized by some members of the community. Even though the arrangement of the chapters and verses had been fixed by the Prophet before his death, and the text existed in written form and in the memories of his Companions, concerns soon arose over the preservation of the scripture. Many had perished in the wars of apostasy following Muḥammad's death, and old age would eventually claim all who had learned the scripture directly from the Prophet himself. In 633 C.E. the caliph Abū Bakr ordered Zayd ibn Thābit (d. 665 or 666), who had served as one of the Prophet's scribes, to collect the written portions of the Qur'ān and to consult those Companions who had memorized it in order to prepare a written copy of the scripture. The text was kept in the form of loose pages (*ṣuḥuf*), rather than being bound into a single volume. Following Abū Bakr's death, it was given over to his successor, 'Umar, who served as caliph from 634–44. When

'Umar was assassinated in 644 C.E., that Qur'ān was sent to his daughter Ḥafṣa for safekeeping.

In addition to this copy of the scripture, Muslim historians record the existence of other written copies that had been prepared privately by Companions of Muhammad. Among those said to have a written copy of the Qur'ān were Ubayy ibn Ka'b (d. 649), 'Abd Allāh ibn Mas'ūd (d. 652–3), 'Alī ibn Abī Ṭalīb (d. 661), and Abū Mūsā 'Abd Allāh al-Ash'arī (d. 662). It is to the variations in pronunciation found within these personal editions that Muslim historians attribute the diverse forms of recitation that began to emerge. By the time of the fourth caliph, 'Uthmān, who led from 644–56 C.E., differences had appeared in the manner in which the Qur'ān was recited to the extent that 'Uthmān sent for the copy kept by Ḥafṣa in 653. He ordered a number of copies to be prepared from that text and distributed throughout the Muslim territories. One copy remained with 'Uthmān. The so-called *muṣḥaf 'uthmānī*, 'Uthmānī text, represented the consensus of the Companions on the proper form of the text as it had been received from the Prophet.[8]

Yet the Qur'ān as it existed in its earliest written form was a sort of skeletal outline to be used as a memory aid by readers who already knew the text well from memory. Chapter headings and verse endings were indicated, and little more was given. The script consisted of consonants that had no points to distinguish letters with similar shapes from one another; vowels were not indicated. Perhaps for this reason, several regional styles of recitation developed. These were stabilized by Abū Bakr ibn Mujāhid (d. 936), based upon a statement of the Prophet to the effect that the Qur'ān had been sent down according to seven letters (*aḥruf*), or modes. Today these are known as the seven approved methods of recitation.[9]

It is this definition of the Qur'ān and its role as the final revelation that shapes the Muslim's understanding of his own religion's relationship to Judaism and Christianity and their respective scriptures. For in addition to being the dictated word of God that has been protected from corruption of content or meaning, the Qur'ān is understood to complete the process of revelation. Its invitation is universal rather than a particularized message directed at a single community. A modern text describes the relationship as follows:

> The pre-Qur'ānic scriptures, besides carrying the same basic message about Allah, master of the worlds, and man, His creation, also brought specific instructions addressed directly to particular communities of people at given points in time in history and in particular circumstances, such as the Jewish or Christian communities. Revelation before the Qur'ān, and hence scriptures before it, were in many of their details

situation oriented in nature and therefore confined to their particular frameworks. This also explains the continuity of revelation. With changing circumstances and in different situations new guidance from Allah was required. As long as the revelation and scripture were not completely universal in nature, revelation would not reach its finality.

Muḥammad was the last messenger from Allah to mankind, and he brought the final revelation from God to man. Therefore the scripture containing this revelation is the last of the Holy Scriptures.[10]

Muslim Qur'ānic Exegesis

If then the Qur'ān is believed to be the final, universal revelation that has been preserved from error, Muslim scholars engaged in interpretation of the scripture have defined very limited parameters within which to perform textual analysis. Historical-critical methods neither developed independently within Islam nor have they been widely adopted from Western scholarship. Any analysis that assumes human determination of the content or wording of the text has traditionally been regarded as suspect because it is potentially an attack upon the status of the Qur'ān itself. As Jane McAuliffe has noted:

> What the classical and modern exegetes...will not do is to consider a word or passage as incomplete or corrupt, a victim of scribal transmission. They will not entertain theories about cultural borrowing or extra-Islamic influence. Qurānic passages that appear to echo versions of Biblical narratives are not examined in order to discover their possible lines of transmission and the various shapings undergone along the way. In fact, most of the questions that fuel the historical-critical method of the Biblical scholar are, for his or her Qurānic counterpart, non-questions or even blasphemies.[11]

Because questions of authorship and evolution of content and form are outside the proper domain of *tafsīr* (exegesis), only particular types of textual analysis are performed. They are classified as being based upon "transmission" (*tafsīr bi'l-riwāyah* or *tafsīr bi'l-ma'thūr*, as it is more commonly called), "sound opinion" (*tafsīr bi'l-ra'y* or *tafsīr bi'l-dirāyah* by "sound knowledge") and "indication" (*tafsīr bi'l-ishārah*).[12]

Tafsīr bi'l-Ma'thūr

Traditionally the most highly regarded form of exegesis, *tafsīr bi'l-ma'thūr*, consists of three types of analysis. The meaning of a particular verse in the Qur'ān may be explained by referring directly to another verse in the text, an explanation may be derived from the transmitted statements of Muḥammad, or it may be based upon information transmitted from Companions of the Prophet (*al-sahābah*) or their Followers (*al-ṭābi'ūn*).

The highest form of *tafsīr bi'l-ma'thūr* is exemplified by those examples in which one verse from the Qur'ān is used to explain another. Qur'ān 2:27, for example, describes Adam's repentance following his act of disobedience in the garden:

> Then Adam learned words of inspiration from his Lord and his Lord turned towards him, for He is the Oft-Returning, Most Merciful.

The reader who seeks to understand the meaning of the phrase "words of inspiration" can find an explanation in Qur'ān 7:23:

> They said, "Our Lord! We have wronged our own souls. If You do not forgive us and bestow Your mercy upon us, we shall certainly be lost."

Thus, Qur'ān 2:37 is said to be explained by Qur'ān 7:23.[13]

A second variety of exegesis by transmission (*tafsīr bi'l-ma'thūr*) includes those verses that may be understood by reference to statements of the Prophet. When, for example, Muḥammad was asked about the meaning of "And when your Lord said to the angels, 'I am about to place a vicegerent (*khalīfah*) on earth'" (Qur'ān 2:30), he explained the physical location to which the verse referred:

> The earth was spread out from Mecca, and the angels used to circumambulate the House (the Ka'ba). They were the first to circumambulate it, and that was the "earth" which God mentioned: "I am about to place a vicegerent on earth."[14]

The third type of exegesis by transmission, which ranks below explanations drawn from the Qur'ān and the Prophet, is that provided by the Companions of the Prophet. Those who associated closely with Muḥammad during his lifetime had the opportunity to learn the meanings of the text directly from the Prophet himself. Among the best known of the Companions providing interpretations is Ibn 'Abbās (d. 687). When asked about the meaning of Qur'ān 2:30, he offered additional background information to supplement the explanation of the Prophet:

> The first to inhabit the earth were the jinn. They spread corruption thereon and shed blood, and killed each other. So God sent Iblīs against them with an army of angels, and Iblīs and those with him killed them, pursuing them as far as the islands of the oceans and the summits of the mountains. Then

he created Adam and settled him thereon. That is why He has said: "I am about to place a *khalīfah* on earth."[15]

In addition to the explanations provided by the companions of the Prophet, reports by Followers (*al-tābi'ūn*) who transmitted from the Companions are also to be given consideration. These individuals are often described as belonging to the Meccan, Medinan, or Iraqi groups because of the geographical area in which they lived and the individual Companions from whom they transmitted material. The Meccan group, which included Mujāhid (d. 722), 'Ikrima (d. 723), and 'Atā' (d. 732) among its best-known members, formed around Ibn 'Abbās. The Medina circle included among its prominent companions 'Ubay b. Ka'b, while the Iraqi cities of Kufa and Basra were home to the pupils of Ibn Mas'ūd (d. 652–53).[16]

Āl-Rābi' ibn Anas (d. 711), one of the Medinan Followers, offered the following exegesis of Qur'ān 2:30 to support the conclusion that the proper understanding of the term *khalīfah* is that of "successor" or "replacement of the jinn":

> God created the angels on Wednesday, and he created the jinn on Thursday, and He created Adam on Friday. And a group of the jinn disbelieved, so the angels came down to them on earth and fought with them. There was blood, and there was corruption on earth.[17]

The most famous of the classical *tafsīr bi'l-ma'thūr* works is that of Ibn Jarīr al-Ṭabarī (d. 923), *Jāmi' al-Bayān fī Tafsīr al-Qur'ān,* from which the above examples were taken. al-Ṭabarī's massive work (thirty volumes in the 1903 and 1911 Egyptian editions) provides analysis of the language and meaning of each verse of the Qur'ān along with commentary drawn from the Prophet, Companions, and Followers. al-Ṭabarī also records many accounts from the Jewish and Christian communities detailing events before the coming of Islam. Second to al-Ṭabarī is the work of Ibn Kathīr (d. 1372) titled *Tafsīr al-Qur'ān al-'Aẓīm* that emphasizes explanations of the Qur'ān derived from other verses within the same text. Other well known Sunni commentaries include Abu al-Layth al-Samarqandī's (d. 983) *Baḥr al'Ulūm*; the *Kashf wa'-l-Bayān 'an Tafsīr al-Qur'ān* of Ahmad ibn Ibrāhīm al-Tha'labī (d. 993) and its abridged version, *Ma'ālim al-Tanzīl* prepared by Ḥasan ibn Mas'ūd al-Baghawi (d. 1116); and *al-Durr al-Manthūr fī'-l-Tafsīr bi'l-Ma'thūr* of Jalāl al-Dīn al-Suyūtī (d. 1505).

The nineteenth and twentieth centuries have produced three important Sunni works. The first of these is the *Tafsīr al-Qur'ān al-Ḥakīm,* better known as *Tafsīr al-Manār* because portions of the work were serialized in the Egyptian periodical *al-Manār*. Its authors, Muḥammad

'Abduh (d. 1905) and Rashīd Riḍā (d. 1935), attempted to harmonize the discoveries of the modern era and the spiritual legacy of Islam. A second work that was published in Egypt has also appealed to many Muslims struggling to define the relationship between faith and modernity. Sayyid Qutb (d. 1966), the author of *Fī Zilalāl-Qur'ān*, argued for the reintegration of Islam and society to create a community in which true social justice, prosperity, and political strength are derived from submission to God's revelation. Abū'l A'lā Mawdūdī of Pakistan (d. 1979) authored the third commentary *Tafhīm al-Qur'ān*, which has been translated into English as *Understanding the Qur'ān*. Mawdūdī's work has been influential among Muslims in the Indian subcontinent and internationally among readers of the English translation.[18]

Tafsīr bi'l-Ra'y

The second type of exegesis, *tafsīr bi'l-ra'y*, interpretation based upon sound knowledge, is rather controversial. The most conservative religious scholars have historically condemned the production of any exegesis that departs from the opinions of the Companions and Followers. Such is the opinion expressed by the well-known fourteenth-century scholar Ibn Taymiya: "He who turns away from the opinions of the Companions and Successors and their *tafsīr* in adopting what is opposed to that, he is in error; indeed he is an innovator (*mubtadi'an*), for they were more knowledgeable as to the *tafsīr* of the Qur'ān and its meaning."[19]

Ibn Taymiya's observation reflects the concern of many religious scholars that the text could easily be interpreted to reflect the particular perspective of the commentator. The philosopher al-Rāzī (d. 1209), for example, brings a decidedly rational method of analysis to the text as he seeks to integrate orthodox exegesis and the philosophical and theological positions of the scholarly community of his day. In his commentary on the question asked by the angels in Qur'ān 2:30 as to why God would "place therein one who will spread corruption" while the angels proclaim God's praise, al-Rāzī explains that the verse confirms the notion that God cannot be the source of evil. "This proves that the angels did not allow that evil should come from God. They attributed corruption and the shedding of blood to the creature not the Creator."[20]

A modern text on Qur'ānic exegesis takes a more moderate approach, emphasizing that *tafsīr* of this type is acceptable when based upon reason and interpretation (*ijtihād*) of sound sources. It should never be based upon conjecture or personal opinion. As the author reminds his reader, neither the Companions nor the Followers allowed themselves to indulge in conjectural interpretation. Ibn 'Abbās reported a statement of the Prophet that "He who says (something) concerning the Qur'ān without out knowledge, he has taken a seat of fire."[21]

The best known of the classical texts is that of al-Zamakhsharī (d. 1144) entitled *al-Kashshāf*. Despite the fact that it reflects the philosophical perspective of the rationalist Mu'tazilī school of philosophy, the author's sophisticated use of grammar and lexicography as tools of interpretation have made it a standard reference work. The *Kashshāf* is often paired with *Anwār al-Tanzīl* by Abdallah bin 'Umar al-Baydawī (d. 1286) because the latter work summarizes its contents and attempts to de-emphasize the Mu'tazilī elements. Other prominent works include *Mafātih al-Ghayb* by the above mentioned philosopher al-Rāzī (d. 1209); *Rūh al-Mā'anī* by Shihab al-Dīn Muḥammad al-Alūsī al-Baghdādī (d. 1850); and *Tafsīr al-Jalālayn* by Jalāl al-Dīn al-Maḥallī (d. 1459) and Jalāl al-Dīn al-Suyūṭī (d. 1505).[22]

Tafsīr bi'l-Ishārah

Exegesis by signs or indications is particularly associated with Sufism, the mystical tradition of Islam, since its purpose is to uncover the subtle allusions of the text. However, religious scholars have reminded practitioners that there should be no radical disagreement between one's own inspired analysis and the plain meaning of the verse, nor should the exegesis contradict other verses in the Qur'ān or documented exegesis provided by the Prophet.

Yet the scholars' insistence that *tafsīr bi'l-ishārah* conform to rigorous standards, and preferably bear some relationship to recognized interpretations of the text, has not prevented flights of esoteric analysis. Ibn 'Arabī (d. 1240), for example, explains the protests of the angels in Qur'ān 2:30 as the consequence of their ignorance of the true status of humanity:

> The angels are veiled from the manifestation of the meaning of divinity (*ilahīyah*) and the divine characteristics which are in man. These belong to the societal form of the human community and the structure combining the two worlds and possessing all that is in the two realms [that is, the spiritual and temporal realms]. They knew the crude and beastly actions which denote the spreading of corruption in the earth and, shedding of blood, actions which belong to the potentiality of lust and anger. They also knew that these actions are necessary for the attachment of the spirit to the body. They knew further their own freedom from such actions because of the sanctity of their souls. This is because every class of angels can see that which is below...but cannot see that which is above it. The angels knew that it was inevitable in the process of the attachment of the luminous spirit of the higher realm to the mundane body that a kind of harmony with the body on the one hand and the human spirit on the other must exist.

This is the carnal soul which is the abode of every evil and
source of every corruption. The angels did not know,
however, that humanity attracts the divine light, for this is a
mystery.[23]

Two of the most widely read Sufi commentaries are al-Nīsābūrī's (d.
1327) *Gaharā'ib al-Qur'ān wa Ragā'ib al-Furqān*, which draws upon the
works of both al-Rāzī and Zamakhsharī, and Muḥyī al-Dīn Ibn 'Arabī's
(d. 1240) *Tafsīr al-Qur'ān al-Karīm*.[24]

Shi'i Tafsīr

Until this point, our survey of Qur'ānic exegesis has focused upon
the requirements of textual analysis as understood by Sunni Muslims,
who constitute approximately 85 percent of the world's 1.2 billion Muslims. However, our discussion would not be complete without a brief
reference to the differences between the Sunni tradition and that of the
Ithnā'Asharī Shi'is who constitute the majority within that community.

Both Sunni and Shi'i Muslims believe that Muḥammad received the
Qur'ān and its exegesis from the angel Gabriel; however, each community reaches a different conclusion as to whether additional individuals
were granted portions of this same privileged information. Sunni tradition affirms that the Prophet Muḥammad is the only trustworthy interpreter of the Qur'ān; therefore, all reliable exegesis must be possessed of
a pedigree of transmission that may be traced back to him. In contrast,
Twelver Shi'i doctrine teaches that the Qur'ān possesses two levels of
meaning. The first level of meaning is *tanzīl*, the Qur'ānic text as sent
down to the Prophet. On this universal level, the scripture may be understood by every intelligent person with a sufficient knowledge of the
Arabic language. The second level of meaning is *maknun*, safeguarded
by God, and is granted only to those whom he selects. This interpretive
knowledge (*ta'wīl*) is given to the Imams; they are the true heirs of
Muḥammad and the previous prophets. Their knowledge includes the
principles of continued relevance (*jarī*) and application (*intibāq*).[25]

Thus, in his commentary on Qur'ān 2:30 the Shi'i exegete al-Qummī
(d. 939) repeats the explanation provided by 'Alī ibn Abī Ṭālib, the First
Imam, (d. 661) as authoritative. 'Ali repeats the actual conversation that
took place between God and the angels and explains that they were filled
with sadness when they learned that God was about to create Adam. In
response to their inquiry God replied:

I know what you do not know; I wish to create a creature with
my own hand and make of his progeny prophets, messengers,
faithful servants, and rightly guided *Imams*. These I shall set
up as my vicegerents over my creatures in my earth. They
shall dissuade them from acts of rebellion, warn them against

my punishment, guide them to obedience to me, and lead them to my way...[26]

As is the case in Sunni exegesis, Shi'i commentary has passed through several historical phases. The first authoritative interpreters of the Qur'ān after the Prophet were the Twelve Imams. Their exegetical analysis, which was recorded by their disciples, is given equal weight to that of the Prophet because it is assumed that their knowledge of the revelation comes as an inerrant spiritual legacy from him. The first stage of Shi'i exegesis extended over a period of three centuries and concluded with the death of the last of the four deputies who had served the Twelfth Imam during the period of the Lesser Occultation (874–941 C.E.) that preceded his departure from this physical plane of existence.

The second stage saw the beginnings of written *ḥadīth* and *tafsīr* traditions. These early authors recorded material without providing extensive commentaries on it. Among the best known figures were al-Furat ibn Ibrāhīm al-Kūfi, who died in the late ninth or early tenth century, 'Alī ibn Ibrāhīm al-Qummī (d. 939), and Muḥammad ibn 'Ayyāsh al-Samarqandī (al-'Ayyāshī).

The third stage is typified by *al-Ṭibyān fi Tafsīr al-Qur'ān*, composed by Abu Ja'far al-Ṭusī (d. 1076), and the commentary of his student al-Ṭabarsī (d. 1153) titled *Majma' al-Bayān fi Tafsīr al-Qur'ān*. Whereas the commentaries of the second period reflected the formative, isolationist perspective of the Shi'i community of the time, al-Ṭusī and al-Ṭabarsī composed comprehensive commentaries drawing upon the rich, intellectual legacy available to them.

The fourth stage was a period of consolidation, coinciding with the rise of the Safavid dynasty in Iran in the early sixteenth century. Important works of the period include Mullā Muḥsin Fayḍ Kāshanī's *al-Ṣafī fi Tafsīr Kalām Allāh al-Wafī* and Mullā Muḥammad Bāqir Majlisī's *Biḥar al-Anwār,* both of which reflect upon every branch of Shi'i religious tradition.

Sayyid Muḥammad Ḥusayn al-Ṭabātāba'ī (d. 1981), author of *al-Mizan fi Tafsīr al-Qur'ān*, represents the final stage of Shi'i exegetical activity. His commentary offers not only traditional Shi'i exegesis of the text, but philosophical and sociological perspectives as well. Like his counterparts in the Sunni community, the author attempts to reach the educated young Muslim audience and provides exegesis that draws upon the legacy of Shi'ism and shows its relevance to modern life.[27]

The Influence of Judaism and Christianity on the Qur'ān and Its Exegesis

The goal of Qur'ānic exegesis according to Muslims is to clarify the meaning of the text employing information found within the Qur'ān itself and interpretations that can be documented as reflecting the Prophet's own explanations to the greatest extent possible. *Tafsīr* produced by Muslims is, as we have seen, based on a system that ranks the material used to interpret the Qur'ān. The most authoritative source of information is, of course, that which is taken directly from the Qur'ān itself to analyze a particular use of language or elaborate upon the meaning of the text. The Prophet, who is protected from sin and error (*ma'ṣūm*), is the second source of sure guidance. The Companions who were instructed by him and, finally, their own students, who could be trusted to convey knowledge with a pedigree extending from their masters back to Muḥammad, are the third source of authoritative interpretation.

Very early on, however, Muslims became aware that additional and sometimes contradictory information was available from the Jewish and Christian communities. Islam's self-definition as the final and complete revelation that supersedes that of the two preceding monotheistic faiths precluded the elevation of biblical materials to a status equal to that of the Qur'ān.

Yet the familiar biblical characters of Adam and Eve, Noah, Abraham, Ishmael, Isaac, Lot, Jacob, Joseph, Moses, Aaron, David, Solomon, Elijah, Jonah, Job, John, Jesus, and Jethro also appear in the Qur'ān as does Mary, the mother of Jesus. In what sense, then, could Muslims legitimately make use of the texts and exegesis of their fellow monotheists to supplement the knowledge contained in Qur'ānic accounts?

It appears that the question of whether a Muslim could make use of the legacy of Judaism and Christianity to supplement the Qur'ān had already arisen in the lifetime of Muḥammad. Abu Hurayra, one of the Prophet's Companions, reported the following tradition:

> The people of the scripture (Jews) used to recite the Torah in
> Hebrew and they used to explain it in Arabic to the Muslims.
> On that Allah's apostle said: "Do not believe the people of the
> scripture or disbelieve them, but say: 'We believe in Allah and
> what is revealed to us.'"   (Qur'ān 2:36)[28]

On another occasion Muḥammad is reported to have told his followers: "If the people of the Book tell you something, do not either accept it as true or reject it as false, for they may tell you something true and you may reject it as false or tell you something which is false but you may accept it as true."[29]

To Muḥammad's admonition that Muslims should neither accept nor reject information provided by Jews and Christians may be added the sterner warning of another of the Prophet's Companions, Ibn Mas'ūd. He is reported to have answered, "Do not ask the *ahl al-kitāb* (the People of the Book) about anything (in *tafsīr*) for they cannot guide you and are themselves in error..."[30]

Ibn Mas'ūd's remark points out a second objection that would be raised against using information provided by Jews and Christians, that of *taḥrīf*, error. Muslim religious scholars have agreed that their fellow monotheists are in error. They have debated only whether their misunderstandings are the result of errors in their scriptural material or errors in interpretation of the text by the Jewish and Christian communities. Consequently, when Muslims have read the scriptures of Judaism and Christianity, they have consciously attempted to do so through the lens of the Qur'ān, constantly aware that any contradictions that appear must necessarily be weighed against the sure standard of the Qur'ān, the final dictated word of God. Exegetes, then, typically reject contradictory material and report details extracted from Jewish and Christian texts. Since the Qur'ān does not specifically identify the food consumed by Adam and Eve in disobedience to God's command, al-Ṭabarī, for example, provides the opinions of Jewish commentators on Genesis along with the speculations of his fellow Muslims. Ultimately, however, he refuses to accept the account of the older religion. He concludes that the name of the plant cannot be precisely determined; and since the Qur'ān does not specify its identity, the information must not be necessary for Muslims to have.[31] In other cases, the stories of preceding prophets are employed to construct a universal history. From the Muslim perspective, the stories of the prophets are awful examples (*'ibar*) of how preceding prophets were ignored, and their disobedient communities were punished.[32]

The insistence that biblical materials be evaluated on the basis of conformity to the Qur'ān and explanations of the Prophet has continued among Muslim scholars. Recent works on the sciences of the Qur'ān (*'ulum al-qur'ān*) that seek to instruct the average educated Muslim as to how the Qur'ān is to be read and interpreted, repeat the formula already established by the classical authors of commentary: Those accounts provided by Jews and Christians that are known to be true because the revelation to Muḥammad confirms them may be accepted. Other materials are to be absolutely rejected because they are proven false by the revelation granted Muḥammad. A third category is neither to be accepted nor rejected as false.[33] In no instance is information to be acknowledged as true merely because it is accepted as such within the Jewish or Christian communities. When modern Muslims encounter the scriptures of Judaism and Christianity, they continue to judge them to be a source of supplemental detail to the Qur'ān, and that only in so far as information may be verified by reference to the Qur'ān or confirmed through the statements of the Prophet.

If then Muslims reject any notion of human influence upon the style or content of the Qur'ān and describe the contributions of Judaism and Christianity as being of limited importance in the production of Qur'ānic exegesis, Western scholarship presents a very different picture. Modern Western scholarship documents an environment in which the population of the Arabian peninsula had access to a rich array of religious teachings by the time of Muḥammad's birth in 570 C.E. Jews had settled in the Hijaz and Yemen no later than the second century C.E., and both Nestorian and Monophysite Christianity were represented. In addition, new followers were won through missionary efforts. The two faiths proselytized among their pagan neighbors, as did travelling merchants. Customers could acquire scriptural information, *aggadoth* about the patriarchs and rabbis or narratives about the apostles, depending upon the spiritual affiliation of the merchant.

Although the main body of Christian literature in this region was in Syriac, portions of the Bible may already have been translated into Arabic for liturgical use or for purposes of missionary activity. In the case of the Arabian Jews, it appears that the scriptures continued to be read in Hebrew and then translated for the benefit of potential converts and members of the congregation who were not able to understand the original. Accounts from the early Muslim community record that Muḥammad and his followers on occasion had listened to the Torah being read in Hebrew and then explained to the audience in Arabic.[34]

As might be anticipated, one of the questions that has long intrigued Western scholars has been that of the influence of the two older traditions upon Muḥammad and the Qur'ān. Given the parallels found in scriptural content and the availability of information on Judaism and Christianity in Arabic, to what extent was the Qur'ān's content shaped by their influence? Muslim scholars obviously reject any human influence upon the book that is regarded as the dictated word of God. Among Western academics attempting to trace local influences have been scholars such as J. Bouman, who argues for a dominant Jewish influence, and others such as J. S. Trimingham, who claims to detect a stronger Christian element.[35]

Among the most important contributions of Western scholarship, however, have been works documenting the history of the Qur'ān's compilation and variant readings of the text. Theodore Noldeke's *Geschichte des Qorans*, which was originally published in 1860, was the pioneer work in this area of scholarship. The first volume examined the origin of the Qur'ān. The second, which was enlarged by Friedrich Schwally, discussed the history of its collection. The third volume, which was edited by Gotthelf Bergstrasser and Otto Pretzl, was dedicated to the history of the text. The three-volume series appeared 1909–38.[36] In the meantime, I. Goldzieher published *Die Richtungen der islamischen Koranauslegung* in 1920, a second foundational work.[37] Two of the best-known scholars publishing in English were Richard Bell, whose *Introduction to the Qur'ān* focused on the sequence of the revelation, and Arthur Jeffrey. Jeffrey's *Material for the History of the Text of the Qur'ān* argued that many texts with variant readings were present in the early community.[38]

A second, related area of interest to Western-trained scholars has been that of the influence of Judaism and Christianity upon the exegesis of the Qur'ān. New converts to Islam from Judaism and Christianity brought with them knowledge of their former religions. 'Abd Allah ibn Salam (d. ca. 663) was a rabbi before his conversion, and Ka'b al-Ahbar (d. 652) is said to have read and explained the Torah in the Medina mosque. In addition, several Companions of the Prophet, including 'Abd Allāh ibn 'Abbās who later transmitted exegesis of the Qur'ān, were known to be interested in biblical stories and exegesis.

As members of the early community sought to explain the Qur'ān, information provided by Jews and Christians quickly found its way into exegesis in the decades following Muḥammad's death. From Jews came legends about the creation, stories about the prophets *(qisas al-anbiya')*, and accounts of the Israelites from the time of Moses' death and their arrival in the promised land. From Christians came miracle stories of Jesus and stories of the apostles and saints. By the first half of the second Islamic century, the statement of the Prophet to the effect that it was permissible to transmit accounts from the Jews *(haddithū 'an banī Isrā'īla wa-lā haraja)* was widely repeated and was used to justify narrating Jewish lore and traditions that had been recorded by Muslim scholars. In contrast to the hesitation apparently expressed by an earlier generation, biblical materials were now sought out and found their way into popular literature relating stories of the ancient prophets, Qur'ānic exegesis, *hadīth*, and historiography.[39]

However, Muslim acquaintance with biblical material seems to have remained limited to *qisas al-anbiyā'* type stories for the first two centuries. Ibn Qutayba (b. 828) appears to be the first author who supplemented a legendary version of creation with genuine passages from the Bible.[40] And when biblical passages have been quoted from the original source, they have been used for particular purposes. Muslim authors who have since used biblical passages have frequently done so in the service of Islams rather than presenting them to readers as alternative sources of authoritative spiritual guidance equal to the Qur'ān. They have been quoted to explain the history of Israelite prophets and patriarchs who were seen to be Muḥammad's predecessors. Such was the purpose of Ibn Qutayba (b. 828) in *Kitāb al-Ma'arif* and al-Ya'qūbī in his *Ta'rīkh*. Other authors, including al-Maqdisī (d. 966) and al-Biruni (b. 973), have quoted Jewish and Christian scripture to explain their beliefs and practices to curious Muslim readers. Still others, notably Ibn Rabbān (b. 810), have used the Bible for apologetic purposes or to argue that the Jewish scripture has been abrogated with the coming of Islam, as did Ibn Ḥazm (b. 994 CE).[41]

Modern writers continue to use quotations from the Bible to explain Judaism and Christianity to Muslim readers. More commonly, however, direct quotations from the scriptures are used in apologetic or polemical writings. Rather typical of the genre is Maurice Bucaille's *The Bible, The Qur'ān and Science* that has been widely translated for international distribution and even made into a video.[42] The author writes for an audience that is familiar enough with the teachings of the older religions to ask about contradictions that exist between them. To counter the claims of Judaism and Christianity, Bucaille examines examples taken from the scriptures of all three traditions in light of the discoveries of modern science to show that the Qur'ān best reflects the facts presented by science.

Sources of Disagreement

The conflict between Muslim views of the history of the text (*Textgeschichte*) and exegesis and some of the theories developed by modern scholars ultimately centers around methods of textual analysis applied to the Qur'ān and the authenticity of the *ḥadīth*, traditions relaying Muḥammad's speech and actions as reported by his Companions. While the Muslim community rejects any possibility of human influence on the form or content of the Qur'ān and teaches that the Qur'ān was already preserved in its final form by the time of the Prophet's death in 632 C.E., based upon the documented accounts of Muḥammad's Companions, modern Western scholarship has challenged these assumptions. John Burton, for example, argues that traditional Muslim accounts of the Qur'ān's textual history are a fabrication, although the text itself is "probably in the form in which it was organized and approved by the Prophet."[43] John Wansbrough concludes that the Qur'ānic canon was not fixed until the early ninth century.[44] Therefore, those traditions reporting its textual history are obviously forgeries.[45]

In addition, the traditional Muslim reliance upon transmitted reports from Muḥammad as authentic accounts of his exegesis of the Qur'ān has been challenged. If the traditions that purport to contain the Prophet's analysis of the Qur'ān are likely to be forgeries, then *tafsīr* based upon them is likewise questionable. As Jane McAuliffe has observed:

> The whole history of the text and its canonization, as understood by Muslim scholarship, depends upon the historical authenticity of accepted *ḥadīths*. Such, too, is the case with the Muslim understanding of the history of exegetical activity. The interpretations of such early commentators as Ibn 'Abbas and Ibn Mas'ud are all in the form of carefully documented *ḥadīths*. In fact, the formative period of Qur'ānic *tafsīr* amounts to little more than a compilation and classification of the relevant explanatory *ḥadīths*. By attacking the orthodox Islamic understanding of *ḥadīth*, Western scholars…have thrown the issues of the Qur'ān's canonization and its early exegesis open to question. Furthermore, since exegesis based

on *ḥadīth* (*al-tafsīr bi'l-ma'thūr*) remains the backbone of all subsequent Qur'ānic interpretation, this latter is equally jeopardized. In fact, the basic Muslim belief…that the Prophet is the principal (non-Qur'ānic) interpreter of the Qur'ān is, for such scholars, a piece of historical nonsense.[46]

However, the issue of the authenticity of the *ḥadīth* is far from resolved within the Western academic community itself. Scholars are divided between those who regard most, if not all, of the *ḥadīth* literature to be of later origin and those who argue that at least some of the traditions are genuine or date to the very early years of the Muslim community. Ignaz Goldzieher in his seminal study concluded that only a few traditions can be attributed to Muḥammad; most "reflect the historical and social development of Islam during the first two centuries."[47] Joseph Schacht reached a similar conclusion, arguing that "every legal tradition from the Prophet, until the contrary is proved, must be taken not as an authentic or essentially authentic, even if slightly obscured, statement valid for his time or the time of the Companions, but as the fictitious expression of a legal doctrine formulated at a later date."[48] Other scholars have challenged the theory that all written traditions are necessarily later fabrications. Nabia Abbott seeks to present evidence for early and continuous transmission of written *ḥadīth*, including those giving Qur'ānic exegesis. As evidence she provides a collection of papyri from the mid-eighth to mid-ninth centuries.[49] Likewise, Fuad Sezgin's supplement to Carl Brockelmann's *Geschichte der arabischen Literatur* also argues for earlier dates for written tradition of *ḥadīth*.[50]

The distance that separates proper analysis of the Qur'ān as defined by traditionally trained Muslim exegetes and the methodologies employed by modern Western-trained scholars is vast indeed. It could, perhaps, best be compared to the similar divide that separates conservative Jews and Christians from academics who employ the tools of modern scholarship in their efforts to detect subtle traces of the theological perspectives of biblical authors or define the historical Jesus. And, just as their counterparts in Judaism and Christianity must address the challenges raised, so too will Muslim intellectuals be required to respond. As once their predecessors stood to define Islam's place in relation to the preceding religions and declared the Qur'ān to be the final revelation, so now must this generation define Islam's place in relation to the new intellectual tradition.

Suggestions for Further Readings

Translations of the Qur'ān

Each of the authors approaches the translation of the Qur'ān from a somewhat different perspective. Arberry captures something of the beauty of the Arabic original. Pickthall emphasizes sound translation that reflects mainstream Sunni readings of the text. The 'Ali edition includes both the Arabic original along with the translation of the text. This author also includes brief translations of commentary. 'Ali has been widely distributed among English speaking Muslims.

'Ali, Abdullah Yusuf. *The Holy Qur'ān, Text, Translation and Commentary.* Brentwood, Md.: Amana Corporation, 1989.

Arberry, A. J. *The Koran Interpreted.* New York: The Macmillan Company, 1955.

Pickthall, Muhammad M. *The Meaning of the Glorious Qur'ān: An Explanatory Translation.* New York: Mentor Books, 1963.

General Articles on the Qur'ān

Adams and Welch provide a good introduction to the Qur'ān and its history.

Adams, Charles J. "Qur'an: The Text and Its History." In *The Encyclopaedia of Religion.* London: Macmillan, 1987, 156–76.

Welch, Alford. "al-Ḳur'ān." In *The Encyclopaedia of Islam.* New Edition. Leiden: E. J. Brill, 1954, 5:400–429.

Exegesis of the Qur'ān

Ayoub provides an excellent introduction to Sunni and Shi'i exegessis. Al-Ṭabarī offers an example of the style and materials used by Sunni exegetes; Von Denffer's book is a summary of the Sunni understanding of the nature of the Qur'ān and its interpretation.

Ayoub, Mahmoud. *The Qur'ān and Its Interpreters.* Albany: State University of New York Press, 1984.

al-Ṭabarī, Abu Ja'far Muhammad ibn Jarir. *The Commentary on the Qur'ān.* Abridged, translated, and annotated by J. Cooper. Oxford: Oxford University Press, 1987.

Von Denffer, Ahmad. *'Ulum al-Qur'ān: An Introduction to the Sciences of the Qur'ān.* London: The Islamic Foundation, 1983.

Muslim Writers on Judaism and Christianity

Both authors give a good introduction to Muslim uses of materials from the two older traditions.

Adang, Camilla. *Muslim Writers on Judaism and the Hebrew Bible.* Leiden: E. J. Brill, 1996.

McAuliffe, J. D. *Qur'ānic Christians: An Analysis of Classical and Modern Exegesis.* Cambridge: Cambridge University Press, 1991.

[1]Islam is the youngest of the three great monotheistic traditions, its founder, Muḥammad, having died in 632 C.E. And it is perhaps the simplest of the three traditions to summarize. Most Muslims would agree that their faith can be described as standing upon five practices and six points of doctrine. The practices required of the Muslim are the means by which the mind and body are trained in the service of God. The six principle doctrines of Islam in parallel fashion affirm the relationship of God and humanity.

These five practices and six points of doctrine are shared by all of the world's 1.2 billion followers of Islam. The two significant divisions within Islam are between the Sunni who constitute approximately 85 percent of the world's Muslims and the Shi'i. These divisions within Islam are the result of differences over how the revelation is to be interpreted and political authority is to be exercised within the community. Shi'ism has often been described as a charismatic tradition because one of its most basic tenets is that God has sent a series of perfect interpreters of the revelation so that humankind can be rightly guided. These sinless individuals descended from the Prophet Muḥammad are the imams. The functions of both spiritual and political guidance are thus vested in the imam of the age. Divisions within Shi'ism have historically occurred over disagreements regarding the number and identities of the imams. However, the majority of Shi'i Muslims are Ithna' Ashirī or so-called "Imami" Shi'is or "Twelvers" because of their belief that God has sent twelve imams, the last of whom went into occultation (*ghaybah*) in the ninth century C.E. Since his withdrawal from this physical plane of existence, the task of spiritual guardianship has been undertaken by religious scholars. Modern activists believe that the political authority of the twelfth imam may also be assumed by religious scholars in order to create an Islamic government during the period preceding his return. Such was the opinion of the late Ayatollah Khomeini and the ideological origin of the Islamic Republic of Iran.

Sunni Muslims believe that the ability to correctly interpret the revelation has been vested within the community of the faithful itself rather than an elite minority. Based upon the statement of the Prophet that affirmed that the community of Muslims would not agree upon an error in interpreting their religion, Sunnis believe that when a consensus is reached on interpretation of the revelation, it will be correct. The ability to derive laws directing the social and economic life of society is thus vested within the community as a whole. With regard to the exercise of political authority, Sunnis hold that while the ideal form of government within Islam would be a united system under a virtuous Muslim ruler, so long as the community lives under Islamic law (*sharī'ah*) it is rightly guided. Thus, for Sunni Muslims submission to the Revealed Law, rather than a particular form of government, is the hallmark of the true Islamic society.

[2]Abū Ja'far Muḥammad ibn Jarīr al-Ṭabarī, *The Commentary on the Qur'an*, abridged, translated, and annotated by J. Cooper (Oxford: Oxford University Press, 1987), 206–27. A French translation of al-Ṭabarī is also available. See *Commentaire du Coran*, abridged, translated, and annotated by Pierre Gode, 3 vols. (Paris: Editions d'Art Les Heures Calires, 1983). Two Arabic editions of al-Ṭabarī's *Jāmi'al-Bayān 'an Ta'wīl Ay al-Qur'ān* have been republished in recent years: *Jāmi' al-Bayān*, ed. Maḥmud Muḥammad Shakir and Aḥmad Muḥammad Shakīr, 16 volumes, (Cairo: Dar al-Ma'arif, 1955–69); and *Jāmi' al-Bayān*, 30 vols. in 15 (Beirut: Dar al-Fikr, 1405/1984). See also: J. McAuliffe, "Qur'ānic Hermeneutics: The Views of al-Ṭabarī and Ibn Kathīr," in *Approaches to the History of the Interpretation of the Qur'ān*, ed. A. Rippin (Oxford: Clarendon Press, 1988), 46–62.

[3]See Annemarie Schimmel, *Mystical Dimensions of Islam* (Chapel Hill: University of North Carolina, 1975). Professor Schimmel provides a fine introduction to the symbolism of the creation account as understood within the mystical tradition of Islam.

[4]al-Ṭabarī, *Commentary*, 238–44. Cooper's translation of *Jāmi' al- Bayān* uses the Cairo edition edited by M. M. and A. M. Shakir. Readers who wish to consult the Arabic text will find the page references to the Shakir edition in *Commentary*.

[5]al-Ṭabarī, *Commentary*, 250–57.

[6]Ibid. See also M. J. Kister, "Legends in *tafsīr* and *ḥadīth* Literature: The Creation of Adam and Related Stories," in *Approaches*, 86–114.

[7]For a discussion of the nature of the Qur'ān see Alford Welch's "al-Ḳur'ān" in *The Encyclopaedia of Islam*, 5:400–429. New Edition, E. J. Brill, 1954–. See also Issa Boullata, "The Rhetorical Interpretation of the Qur'ān: *i'āz* and Related Topics," in *Approaches*, 139–57.

Properly speaking, every translation of the Qur'ān is an interpretation of the text since it reflects the translator's editorial choices as to the intended meaning of each word. Because the Qur'ān is God's speech, the power and depth of meaning of the original can never be properly conveyed into another language. Therefore, Muslims believe that only the original Arabic language text should properly be called the Qur'ān. All other translations, regardless of the language, are interpretations of the scripture.

There are several interpretive translations currently available in English. The best known of these is A. J. Arberry's *The Qur'ān Interpreted,* which first appeared in 1955. Arberry continues to be popular because he attempts to capture both the meaning and something of the beauty of the Arabic original. Muhammad M. Pickthall's *The Meaning of the Glorious Koran: An Explanatory Translation* was first published in 1930 and has since been reissued many times. Pickthall is widely used because the author translates each verse so as to reflect the meaning assigned it by the most authoritative Sunni commentators. A third author whose translation has been widely distributed among English speaking Muslims is Yusuf Ali, whose translation is entitled *The Holy Qur'ān.*

[8]Ahmad von Denffer, *'Ulūm al-Qur'ān: An Introduction to the Sciences of the Qur'ān.* (London: The Islamic Foundation, 1985), 31–56. The author provides the standard Sunni history of the transmission and compilation of the Qur'ān.

[9]Ibid.

[10]Ibid.

[11]Jane D. McAuliffe, *Qur'ānic Christians* (Cambridge: Cambridge University Press, 1991), 30.

[12]See especially al-Ṭabarī, *Commentary,* ix–xxxvi, and Von Denffer, *'Ulūm,* 134–41. On the history of *tafsīr* see: Fred Leemhuis, "Origins and Early Development of the *tafsīr* Tradition," in *Approaches,* 13–30.

Von Denffer provides the following explanation of the difference between *tafsīr,* exegesis proper, and *ta'wīl,* interpretation of the esoteric meanings of the text:

"*Tafsīr* in the language of the scholars means explanation and clarification. It aims at knowledge and understanding concerning the book of Allah, to explain its meanings, extract its legal rulings and grasp its underlying reasons. *Tafsīr* explains the "outer" (*zahīr*) meanings of the Qur'ān. *Ta'wīl* is considered by some to mean the explanation of the inner and concealed meanings of the Qur'ān, as far as a knowledgeable person can have access to them. Others are of the opinion that there is no difference between *tafsīr* and *ta'wīl*." Von Denffer, *'Ulūm,* 121–22.

[13]al-Ṭabarī, *Commentary,* 264–65.

[14]Ibid., 208.

[15]Ibid., 209.

[16]Von Denffer, *'Ulūm,* 126–128.

[17]al-Ṭabarī, *Commentary,* 209.

[18]Von Denffer, *'Ulūm,* 140. See also: Charles Adams, "Abu'l-'Ala Mawdudi's *Tafhim al-Qur'ān,*" in *Approaches,* 307–23. Few of the important commentaries have been translated even in part; only the Arabic originals are available.

[19]Norman Calder, "Tafsīr from Tabarī to Ibn Kathir: Problems in the Description of a Genre, Illustrated with Reference to the Story of Abraham," in *Approaches to the Qur'ān,* ed. G. R. Hawting and Abdul-Kader A. Shareef (London: Routledge,1993), 132.

[20]Mahmoud Ayoub, *The Qur'ān and Its Interpreters* (Albany: State University of New York Press, 1984), 39.

[21]Von Dennfer, *'Ulūm,* 130.

[22]Ibid., 136–37.

[23]Ayoub, *The Qur'ān,* 79.

[24]Ibid., 33–34.

[25]B. Todd Lawson, "Akhbari Shi'i Approaches to *tafsīr,*" in *Approaches to the Qur'ān,* 173–210. See also M. Ayoub, "The Speaking Qur'ān and the Silent Qur'ān: A Study of the Principles and Development of Imami Shi'i *tafsīr,*" in *Approaches,* 177–98. See also Ayoub, *The Qur'ān,* 85.

[26]Ayoub, *The Qur'ān,* 86.

[27]Ibid.

[28]Von Denffer, *'Ulūm,* 133–34.

[29]Ayoub, *The Qur'ān*, 32.

[30]Von Denffer, *'Ulūm*, 134.

[31]al-Ṭabarī, *Commentary*, 248.

[32]Alford Welch, "al-Ḳur'an," *Encyclopedia of Islam*, New Edition, 5:180.

[33]Von Denffer, *'Ulūm*, 134.

[34]Camilla Adang, *Muslim Writers on Judaism and the Hebrew Bible* (Leiden: E. J. Brill, 1966), 2.

[35]Ibid., 4. See J. Bouman, *Das Wort vom Kreuz und das Bekenntnis zu Allah: Die Grundlehren des Korans als nachbiblische Religion* (Frankfurt-am-Main: Otto Lembeck, 1980); and J. S. Trimingham, *Christianity Among the Arabs in Pre-Islamic Times* (London: Longman, 1979).

[36]Theodor Noldeke, et al., *Geschichte des Qorans*, 2nd rev. ed.; vols. 1 and 2, rev. Friedrich Schwally; vol. 3, rev. G. Bergstrasser and O. Pretzl (Leipzig: Dieterich'sche Verlagsbuchhandlung, 1909–38).

[37]Ignaz Goldzieher, *Die Richtungen der islamischen Koranauslegung* (Leiden: E. J. Brill, 1920).

[38]Richard Bell, *Introduction to the Qur'ān* (Edinburgh: The University Press, 1953); and Arthur Jeffrey, *Materials for the History of the Text of the Qur'ān* (Leiden: E. J. Brill, 1937).

[39]Adang, *Muslim Writers on Judaism*, 6–22. See also Gordon Newby, *The Making of the Last Prophet* (Columbia, S.C.: University of South Carolina Press, 1989), 1–32.

[40]Ibid., 112–17.

[41]Ibid., 133–38.

[42]Maurice Bucaille, *The Bible, the Qur'ān and Science,* trans. A. D. Pannell and the author (al-Ain: Zayed Welfare Center for New Muslims, n.d.).

[43]John Burton, *The Collection of the Qur'ān* (Cambridge: Cambridge University Press, 1977), 239.

[44]John Wansbrough, *Qur'ānic Studies: Sources and Methods of Scriptural Interpretation* (Oxford: Oxford University Press, 1977), 46–47.

[45]Ibid.

[46]McAuliffe, *Qur'ānic Christians*, 25–26. For a discussion on the *ḥadīth* as a source of Qur'ānic commentary see R. M. Speight, "The Function of *ḥadīth* as Commentary on the Qur'an, as Seen in the Six Authoritative Collections," in *Approaches*, 63–81.

[47]Ibid., 22.

[48]Ibid., 23.

[49]Nabia Abbott, *Studies in Arabic Literary Papyri, Vol. 2: Qur'ānic Commentary and Tradition* (Chicago: University of Chicago Press, 1967).

[50]Fu'ad Sezgin, *Geschichte des arabischen Schrifttums, Band I: Qur'anwissenschaften, hadith, Geschichte, Fiqh, Dogmatik, Mystik bis ca. 430 H* (Leiden: E. J. Brill, 1967).

6

The Bible in the Orthodox Church

Demetrios J. Constantelos

An Introduction to the Orthodox Church

I was once asked in Lexington, Massachusetts, if we Greeks still believe in Zeus. I said, "Yes we do, but we have baptized him; we call him Jesus!" On another occasion in Los Angeles, California, I was approached by a group of tourists about to leave for Athens, who, in all seriousness, asked me, "Are there any Christians in Athens today? After all, Saint Paul was there so many years ago." These episodes speak volumes, revealing that Christians do not know each other. We do not know each other and so we must ask ourselves, "Are we willing and open to learn of other traditions?"

When speaking of Christianity in today's world, as historians we speak of Western Christianity and of Eastern Christianity. During the Middle Ages they would simply refer to Greek Christianity in the East, and Latin Christianity in the West. Of course, things have changed, but even in the present day when we speak of Western Christianity we mean the Roman Catholics and the various churches of the Reformation, such as Presbyterians, Lutherans, Episcopalians or Anglicans, and so on. When we speak of the Eastern Orthodox today, certainly we include churches that go by the name of Greek Orthodox, Russian Orthodox, Romanian Orthodox, but we also speak of the Oriental Orthodox, such as the Coptic Orthodox, the Abyssinian Orthodox, the Armenian Orthodox, and so on. In this age of the ecumenical movement we have a task, we have a responsibility as Christians to know each other before we get to know the rest of the world.

The Eastern Orthodox Church was known, until very recent years, as simply the Greek Orthodox; Greek, not as a nationalistic name but as a cultural name, was used in the Roman Empire where Greek culture dominated the Eastern Christianity as did Latin in the West. The Eastern Orthodox Church (estimated to include 220–250 million people) is one church, one church in fifteen independent jurisdictions or administrative units. Each unit is *autocephalous* and autonomous. *Autocephalous* means self-governing, having their own head. Each unit is in full sacramental communion and comprises the one fully catholic and orthodox church of Christ. When I say sacramental communion, it means simply that a person of the Russian jurisdiction can go to a Greek jurisdiction, or one of the American jurisdiction can go to a British jurisdiction for the sacraments of the church, baptism, eucharist, and the others. The ecumenical patriarchate of Constantinople has jurisdiction over Orthodox Christians living in Turkey, parts of Greece, northern and western Europe, North and South America, Australia, and New Zealand. The ecumenical patriarch is considered the first among equals. The second patriarchate of Alexandria in Egypt is the patriarchate for all Africa. The third patriarchate is the patriarchate of Antioch in Syria with Christians in Syria, Lebanon, Iraq, and Iran, and other parts of the world. The patriarchate of Jerusalem has authority over the Christians in Palestine, Israel, Jordan, Arabia, and Mount Sinai. The patriarchate of Russia, which includes the greatest number of Orthodox Christians in Russia, also includes other states outside of Russia. There are patriarchates of Serbia, Romania, Bulgaria, Georgia (southern Russia), and other places. In addition to the patriarchates, there are nine churches with rank of *autocephalous*, autonomous churches, such as the Church of Cyprus, the Church of Greece, the Church of Poland, the Church of Albania, the Church of Czechoslovakia, and the Church of Finland. The Orthodox Church in America is not yet fully recognized as autonomous, but is in the process of receiving full accreditation by the rest of the churches. Thus, we speak of one church made up of fifteen or so *autocephalous* units much as we speak of three persons in one God in the Trinity and one God in three persons.

It is important to emphasize that all the Eastern Orthodox constitute one church. This is the case because the Orthodox conception of unity is sacramental and spiritual, and not administrative. As the Pan-Orthodox Council, which met on the island of Rhodes in 1961, put it, "Our church is not made of walls and roofs, but of faith and life. We believe that the sister Orthodox churches, in maintaining the saving faith of our fathers, are preserved in this unity with divine archetype, the mystical and supernatural unity of the Holy Trinity. And in this unity which cannot fundamentally be troubled."

Orthodox theologians today tend to emphasize a biblical theology in the light of patristic exegesis and the experience of the community in history. The church is more than an organization; the church is an organism, a living organism, even though it also has organizational dimensions. Orthodoxy believes in a continuum, that is, in an uninterrupted continuity throughout history that takes us back to the person of Christ. The Orthodox have the sense that indeed the church has an unbroken continuity of history, of doctrine, of practice, for two thousand years. Orthodox theology today is perceived as a matter of the mind, but also of the heart and the servant of the community at large. Theology is studied not for its own sake, but for the edification of the faithful. It is understood not only as the champion of religious knowledge, but as a steward of the tradition in which that knowledge is applied for the good of the community, indeed for the world. Orthodox theology is less concerned with intellectual exercises, with academic exercise of the mind. It is much more concerned with the broader tradition of the needs of the faithful.

The Cultural Context of Christianity

Recent discussion within Orthodox theology has stressed the need for a rediscovery and respect of the theology of the early and undivided church. It is thus crucial to understand the religious and cultural environments, the political and social circumstances in which the church grew. Judaism, Hellenism, and Roman imperialism were the three important forces that influenced the genesis, the growth, and the universality of Christianity. Jewish monotheism and messianic expectations, Greek cultural unity through language and thought, and Roman political unity constitute a three-legged organism upon which the Christian edifice was built. The founder of Christianity, Jesus of Nazareth, was seen as the Messiah, the *Christos*; Christos being the Greek name for Messiah. As the New Testament shows, it is not Jesus of Galilee that saves; but it is Jesus as the Christ that saves. It is the theology of Christ that made Christianity universal, but also reveals its Jewish background. Christianity knows that "in diverse ways and in various manners God spoke to us in years past" (Heb. 1:1). Christianity inherited its cosmology and anthropology, much of its ethics and prophecy from Judaism and sees Christ as the fulfillment, culmination, and completion of a covenant between humanity and the Creator God of Genesis, the God of Abraham.

However, the Christ-event was perceived as something more than the arrival of a Jewish messiah. Christ was perceived as the preexistent *logos* of the Greeks, the very incarnation of the *logos*. "In the beginning was the *logos*, and the *logos* was with God, and the *logos* was God," as we read in John 1:1. Long before the establishment of political unity under Roman rule and the Roman authority, the Greeks had achieved a cultural and linguistic unity in the Mediterranean world—east and west, as far as present-day India. Christianity was born in a Hellenized Judaism, and it achieved its propagation in the Greek world. The Eastern Orthodox possess a strong historical conscience and a sense of continuity, which is explained in terms of both history and theology. Jesus was born in Bethlehem of Judea, but the principle theater of his life and teachings was the region of Galilee. Eleven of his twelve disciples were also natives of the same province, which, at the time of Jesus, was heavily Hellenized. Its inhabitants were viewed with disdain by some in Jerusalem, and the district was called the land of the Gentiles (Mt. 4:15). For more than three hundred years Galilee had been subject to influences of Greek ideas, customs, and culture. This mixed and heavily Hellenized population of Galilee received Jesus as the anointed one, as the Christ. And Jesus the Christ, the founder of Christianity, was accepted as the fulfillment of Hebrew messianism and as the Greek *logos*. In his person we have the convergence of Hebrew expectations and the Greek quest for the unknown god. The Gospel of Matthew is the clearest source of the Hebraic understanding of Jesus, whereas the Gospel of John reveals Christ as the Greek *logos*, the preexistent God who in time and space assumed flesh and walked among human beings as God-human, that is, as the *theanthropic* one. As one of the early Church Fathers, Irenaeus, said, "God became what we are that we may become what God is." The Gospel of John, more than any other New Testament book, is in the heart of Orthodox theological thinking. Jesus the Hebrew becomes the Christ whom the Greeks, the representatives of all the Gentiles, also seek (Jn. 12:20). The long search of the Greeks culminated in the discovery of Jesus the Christ.

Theologically, the coming of the Greeks to see Jesus is most significant. The Greeks represented the world outside Judaism, and their conversion to Christ secured Christianity's universality. When Jesus exclaimed that "the hour has come for the Son of Man to be glorified" (Jn. 12:23), he understood the ecumenical implications of the first Gentiles meeting with him. But this was more than a meeting between Jesus of Nazareth and the Greeks. Symbolically, it was a meeting between Christianity and the Greek inquisitive mind, between ethical Judaism and philosophical Hellenism. In the person of Jesus the Christ the Orthodox see the fulfillment of God's promise to all humankind. The Orthodox are conscious of the fact that Christianity was born and raised in the Greek-speaking and Hellenized eastern part of the Roman Empire.

In his excellent volume, *The Spirituality of the Christian East*, Roman Catholic theologian Thomas Spidlik, a professor at the Oriental Institute in Rome and also a member of The Society of Jesus, has summarized what the Orthodox consider a principle of great significance. He writes, "We must stress one principle, and stress it hard, that the Latin church originated from the Greek church as a branch grows from a tree trunk. The church was implanted by the Greeks and expressed itself in the Greek language."

The Bible in the Faith and Life of the Orthodox Church

Having seen the origin and context of the Christian faith from the standpoint of the Orthodox Church, discussion can now turn to the important aspects of the Bible's place in the faith and the life of the Orthodox church. These are, (1) the nature of the Bible, (2) its canon and authority, (3) its relationship to the authority of the church, that is, the community of believers, and (4) its place in the worship of the community and the private life of the individual believer.

The Nature of the Bible

The question of the nature of the Bible might be answered this way: The Bible is certainly an encyclopedia. An encyclopedia of seventy-six books written in the course of some one thousand years by more than sixty authors, and it is indeed a *theanthropic* document. It is a divine and human record that reveals God's creative and providential invasion and involvement in history and the response of the human being to God's plans and presence in history. The Bible takes God's existence for granted and relates how the world came into being, what went wrong with it, and God's plans for its reconstruction and ultimate salvation. Though it speaks about the totality of creation, the focus is on God's supreme creature, the human being. The Bible is *theanthropic* because God is the source of inspiration and the protagonist among the numerous persons and events described in the Bible. But it is also a human document. Human beings are the concern of the Bible and its main objects, but also the instruments of its writing and its codification. Primarily it is a book of religion, but it includes much material of historical, literary, geographical, and cultural value. The Eastern Orthodox consider the Bible as the written memory of God's activity in history and God's relationship to humankind. It does not reveal everything that God is and what God is not. In many respects it is a mystery. The main purpose for which it was written is that human beings may believe and by believing they may have life. The written word is only part of God's revelation. There is much diversity in its accounts, style, chronologies, descriptions, and poetry, but there is also a unity, a centrality in its message and its purpose. It introduces a linear approach to history. It looks forward to fulfillment and the *eschaton*, the end of time.

As a partial memory recorded in history by human beings, the Bible cannot be understood in separation from the historical experience and the consciousness of the community of believers, whether of the old or the new covenant, that is, among Israelites and the Christian people today. It is for this reason that the Bible is considered the book of the community, depending on the community's authority and approval of its authenticity, its inspiration, and its interpretation. It was written for practical and circumstantial needs and in different historical circumstances. This means that the Bible is not the totality of God's word of revelation. God's word has been revealed in various ways and diverse manners, including the order and beauty of the cosmos, human conscience, and natural law. What is common to human consciousness and morals, the mind and mouth of philosophers, poets, and prophets of many people, culminating in the *Logos* of the God-made-man, the incarnate *Logos* of God, Christ.

Thus, the word of God can be discerned within, but also outside the Bible. Natural revelation, however, is propaedeutic, preparatory to the supernatural, more direct revelation, first through God's elect prophets and finally through God's preexistent *logos* who became human. Revelation means truths disclosed by God through special persons and methods. There are truths about God that can be learned through man's natural endowments. Original sin, identified with man's disobedience, did not destroy the image of God in the human, and it did not eliminate the human's capacity to seek the fulfillment of the likeness. Thus, revelation reaches us through God's activity in history, whether through human beings or other means. We have truths of revelation and truths of reason or nature. There are truths understandable by reason and truths accepted by faith. Early Christian theologians viewed all the prophets of the Old Testament and all the New Testament writers as charismatic individuals, gifted personalities. The writers of the Bible were perceived as persons who possessed a state of mind that made them certain that they stood in a personal relationship with eternal God. They thought that they were possessed by God. Church Fathers and many ecclesiastical writers or theologians did not consider prophetic inspiration as a mechanical communication dictated by God's Spirit in Hebrew, Aramaic, or Greek, but as an inner voice, an awareness, known during the ecstatic state of being in which the prophet, the apostle, or the evangelist experienced and witnessed God's presence. In speaking of all scripture as divinely inspired we mean that God's Spirit is the inspirer and giver, and the human being is the receiver. The two are cooperators. They are, as Saint Paul would call them, *synergoi*.

The Eastern Orthodox does not see God's word coming to an end with the work and teachings of Jesus Christ. God's word is being constantly revealed through the Holy Spirit, the Paraclete. Through the church, through the community of believers, there perpetuates the redeeming and sanctified work of God the Father through Jesus Christ. Thus, the word of God is in a written form and also as a tradition that has penetrated the life of the community throughout the centuries. Much of this memory has been codified in decisions of church ecumenical councils. Much of this memory has been experienced by the believers throughout history. It is for this reason that the Orthodox retain a strong historical consciousness and insist on the value of apostolic traditions, the patristic ethos, and the experience of the Church Fathers and of the saints of the church. God's truth revealed in the history, whether preserved in written form or oral traditions, incorporated in the experience of the church, serves to emphasize the rule of God, who is active in creation, judgment, mercy, and salvation.

The first part of the Bible, known as the Old Testament, reveals that God exists, creates, and intervenes through signs and symbols. Individuals, prophets and priests, kings and shepherds, in particular, have been used as examples of God's providence and concern for humankind. Its role was to prepare the way for the New Testament, which is viewed as the high point of God's revelation in Jesus Christ, who is the end of an era and the beginning of a new one. It is for this reason that we read in the New Testament that the time was fulfilled. It is for this reason that to the present day the Old Testament is viewed by the Orthodox as really preparatory, propaedeutic, which means that indeed it is not exactly of equal value with the New Testament. The New Testament is the fulfillment. Indeed Jesus said, "I have come not to abolish but to fulfill" (Mt. 5:17). It is for this reason that the Old Testament is not read during the divine liturgy, but it is always read during vesper services. Vespers prepare the way for the main service, the eucharist. And indeed we read the Old Testament but selectively because many of the books are simply preparing the way for the fulfillment that is achieved in the New Testament. The New Testament is the beginning of a new era. The Old Testament is an ending.

Whether in the Old or the New Testament, divine revelation was recorded under the inspiration of God's Holy Spirit. But inspiration is understood in a dynamic way. The writer of a book was not a passive receiver of messages, but an energetic and conscious instrument recording the message in his own style under his own intellectual and grammatical presuppositions. For the Orthodox, inspiration is known as *theopneustia*, that is, how God inspires. It is an elevated state of being that makes the grasp and recording of revelation possible. The Holy Spirit inspires the writer, but it is this writer who writes and speaks, not as a mechanical, passive instrument, but in full control of his senses.

Thus, the biblical author may display his human shortcomings, his broad or limited education, and indeed his intellectual and social background. Thus, for the Eastern Orthodox, the Bible is the inspired word of God in terms of content rather than style, grammar, history, or frame. Very few, if any, Orthodox theologians accept the word by word inspiration of the scriptures. It is for this reason that the Orthodox church has never had any serious disputes concerning the application of the historical-critical method in its approach to exegesis and hermeneutics. Orthodoxy's concept of historical thinking determines the biblical theology. In fact, Theodore of Mopsuestia (c. 350–428), an Antiochene theologian, was one of the first serious biblical scholars to approach the Bible critically.

The Canon and Authority of the Bible

The Bible includes the Old Testament, made up of the Hebrew canon of thirty-nine books and also a second list of books known as the Deuterocanonicals or *Anaginoskomena*. These terms simply mean second list. The thirty-nine books of the Hebrew canon are the first list. There is a second list of ten books and, of course, a third list, of twenty-seven books, known as the New Testament. All of them, the three parts, make up the Bible of Orthodox Christians. The Greek translation of the Old Testament, including the Deuterocanonicals, was the original Bible used by the early Christian community, and it remains to the present day the official text of the Orthodox Church. The early church as a whole did not take a definite position in favor of or against the Deuterocanonicals. Churchmen and ecclesiastical writers of both the Greek East and the Latin West were not in full agreement. Some preferred the shorter Hebrew canon, others preferred the longer canon, which included the Deuterocanonicals. This translation of the books of the Hebrew Bible, known as the Septuagint, was begun in the third century B.C. and was used by the Jews of the Diaspora because Greek was the language of the people throughout the Mediterranean world.

The disagreements over the canon by churchmen and ecclesiastical writers from both the Greek East and the Latin West remain to the present day. Some prefer the Hebrew canon and others the longer canon. The ambivalence of ecumenical and local synods—the first ecumenical council in Nicaea in 325, the local synod of Rome in 382, the local synod of Laodicea in 365, and the council of Hippo in 393—was resolved by the synod in Trullo in the year 691, which adopted the longer list, that is, the forty-nine books all together. Indeed, ultimately the Deuterocanonicals were adopted as inspired books. However, they were considered good for reading, good for spiritual edification, on occasions even as sources of doctrine, but as a whole not for doctrine. The most serious justification for the adoption of the Deuterocanonicals was their frequent use in the worship of the life of the early church. Books such as Tobit, Judith,

Wisdom of Solomon, Wisdom of Sirach (Ecclesiasticus) are frequently used in liturgical prayers and hymns of the ancient and medieval church and frequently in vesper services, which means that the experience of the early church is really what determines the canonicity of these books. Christians in the Greek Middle Ages used them for many, many centuries. One will find churchmen and theologians down to the twelfth century using these books interchangeably with other books. So, once again, the experience of the church has taken the lead. The official text of the Old Testament used by the Orthodox includes the following deuterocanonical books: 1 Esdras, Tobit, Judith, Wisdom of Solomon, Wisdom of Sirach, Baruch, 1–3 Maccabees, and the Letter of Jeremiah. Parts of the Deuterocanonicals, such as Susanna, Song of the Three Children, and Bel and the Dragon, appear as parts of Daniel. The canonicity of the deuterocanonical books is still disputed in some Orthodox theological circles, but as a whole they have been accepted in the Bible.

The Relationship of the Bible to the Community of Faith

The question of whether or not the authority of the Bible stands opposed to the authority of the church is a serious theological issue. The prevailing opinion is that once the canon of the Bible has been established, its authority becomes absolute. But the church remains its continuous and watchful guardian. The Bible's inspiration, canonicity, and authenticity depend on the church's consent. The Bible is the book of the church, of the community. Revealed truth preexisted the written word, and the community, both in the sense of old and new Israel, that is, the synagogue and the church, preceded the writing of the scriptures. It took the Jewish community nearly 500 years to determine the canonicity of the books. The establishment of the Hebrew canon was a long process. The decision as to which books, the laws and the prophets and the writings, is traditionally assigned to a council that took place around the year A.D. 90 or 100. Likewise, the canonicity of the New Testament was a long process that lasted into the fifth century. In the beginning we did not know which books were valid. The authority of the gospels was established, then the authority of some of Paul's letters, and finally the others. But it was Saint Athanasius of Alexandria who decided or determined the outcome. Right in the middle of the fourth century he was the one who said, "These twenty-seven books constitute the New Testament." Now the community, the church, came together and by the year 451 the New Testament canon was established.

Now the Bible is a record of truth, but not the truth itself or the totality of the record of revelation. Truth itself is God himself, and the totality of revelation would mean a disclosure of God's personal being, who is incomprehensible and a perpetual mystery. Last, there are limitations of the written word, whose purpose is to nourish faith, to provide

hope, to broaden the human being's vision, to lead to a personal experience of God in the present life, and to bring one to communion with
God in the hereafter. The distinction between revealed truth as written
words and tradition explains the reason why Eastern Orthodoxy emphasizes the importance of the church authority, the authority of the
believing communion. The church is the pillar and ground of the truth,
we are told in 1 Timothy 3:15. And Christ promised that the *Paraclete*,
the Holy Spirit, would guide the apostles and through them the church
to all the truth (Jn. 16:13). The disciples of the apostles were admonished
to guard the fruit that had been entrusted to them by the Holy Spirit
who dwells with the faithful. The church proclaims and guards those
divine truths, written and unwritten.

Scripture and tradition coexist in complete harmony with each other.
Ecclesia (church), as a people called out by God to be God's instruments
and witnesses, existed long before the Bible's writing and the Bible's
codification. Whether as a people of God in ancient Israel or as a new
people of God in the Christian community, it was God's people who
first witnessed God's mighty deeds in history through his prophets and
finally his own *Logos*, that is, Christ, who became human in order to
save humanity. The Bible itself was produced within the *Ecclesia*, within
the church, for specific reasons, and for the needs of its own people.
What was not incorporated in the book remained a fluid, living testimony, and a living experience that found its way in the writings and
commentaries of Church Fathers, into prayers and liturgical texts, and
certainly into decisions of ecumenical councils. The totality of God's revelation that is necessary for salvation infuses the life of the church. That
is why all the services in the Orthodox Church are replete with biblical
quotations, the mind of the Bible within the experience of the community in prayer.

The Bible in Worship and Personal Life

Notwithstanding this holistic understanding of revelation, the Bible
still occupies the central position in the Orthodox Church's faith and
life. Doctrinal truths, ethical teachings, liturgies, and prayer life all have
biblical foundations. The Bible's authority is not minimized by ecclesial
authority. The church, however, remains the lawful custodian and the
authentic interpreter of divine revelation, whether it presents itself as
Holy Scripture or as Sacred Tradition. The indwelling Holy Spirit guides
and directs the church, especially when it is assembled in an ecumenical
council. An ecumenical council, in particular, is the supreme authority
on matters of doctrinal truths. Divine revelation through God's word
and prophecy, mighty deeds, and especially God's infinite *logos*, his teachings, death, and resurrection, was believed by the early church assembled
in worship. The human being is not only a rational animal, but also a

religious being. Religion means an instinctive worship of the divine. Worship is of primary importance to Eastern Orthodoxy, for worship consists of the liturgy of the Word and the liturgy of the mystery of the eucharist, the Lord's supper. For this reason, the first part of an Orthodox church service is instructional, catechetical teaching. The second part is the mystery, the mystery of the death and resurrection of Christ. The example was set by the early church. The believers devoted themselves to the teachings of the apostles, to prayer, and to breaking of the bread. Teachings, prayers, the mystery. It is not only symbolic that the book of the gospels occupies the central place on the altar table of the Orthodox. There is no service in the Orthodox Church that does not include readings from the Bible—psalms, prophets, and especially the New Testament books. Liturgical texts, hymns, and prayers are filled with biblical passages or inspired and encircled with the spirit, images, and symbols of the Bible.

Icons are symbols of the presence of the metaphysical in a physical form. Icons make the invisible visible, and the visible is elevated to the invisible. The community is made up of invisible and visible entities, that is, the believers in heaven and the believers on earth. This is the ecclesiological concept of what the church is. But on the same altar we find the chalice, that is, the tabernacle with the host. The liturgy of the Word and the liturgy of the eucharist are the basis of sermons and catechetical instruction. Listening to the exposition of the written word and participating in the mystery of the eucharist within the community constitute the supreme religious experience for the Eastern Orthodox believers. The interpretation of scripture and the celebration of the eucharist are the two principal unifying poles between the ancient and the ongoing life and thought of Eastern Orthodoxy.

With very few exceptional cases, Eastern Orthodoxy has always encouraged individual Bible reading for inspiration, edification, and the strengthening of the individual's spiritual life. "May the sun arise and find you with a Bible in your hand," are the words of Evagrios Pontikos, and they summarize the patristic and traditional stand of Eastern Orthodoxy toward individual reading of the Bible. The reading of the Bible assumes a state of praying and presupposes a sense of humility. The word of God is easy to understand, but also a mysterious word to comprehend. The Bible is everyone's book, but is not for everyone's interpretation. Subjective interpretation that may lead to misunderstanding and extreme individualism should be subject to the objective interpretation of the church. Subjective interpretation, usually the task of the pastor or preacher, is expected to rely on the objective exegesis of the church's theology. And there is no authentic theology outside the historic experience of the community of the church and its teachings. It is not possible for the modern believer and the church collectively to turn their backs on past centuries of accumulated wisdom and historical investigation. Thus, the emphasis and the value of the patristic mind and the biblical ethos of the church. In the light of the church's role in preparation, preservation, transmission, and interpretation of the gospel tradition, biblical studies in Eastern Orthodox theology today is permitted to use the methods of biblical criticism. This leads to neither biblical literalism nor biblicism, both of which tend to create a bibliolatry. Just as one might become an idolator by worshiping the icon, so also it is very possible for someone to worship the Bible, to become a bibliolator. Both extremes must be avoided. The authority of the Holy Spirit provides the criteria of authenticity that separate and reject what does not belong to the Bible, preserving its fullness and its harmony with the living witness of the church in history.

Suggestions for Further Reading

Agouridis, Savas. *The Bible in the Greek Orthodox Church*. Athens: University of Athens, 1976.

Barrois, Georges. *Scripture Readings in Orthodox Worship*. Crestwood, N.Y.: St. Vladimir's Seminary Press, 1977.

Bratsiotis, Panagiotis. "The Authority of the Bible: An Orthodox Contribution," in *Biblical Authority for Today*. Ed. A. Richardson and W. Schweitzer. Philadelphia: Westminster Press, 17–29.

Breck, John. *The Power of the Word in the Worshipping Church*. Crestwood, N. Y.: St. Vladimir's Seminary Press, 1986.

Constantelos, Demetrios J. *Understanding the Greek Orthodox Church*, 3d. ed. Brookline, Mass.: Hellenic College Press, 1998.

Florovsky, Georges. *Bible, Church, Tradition: An Eastern Orthodox View*. Belmont, Mass.: Norland Press, 1972.

Hopko, Thomas. "The Bible in the Orthodox Church." *St. Vladimir's Theological Quarterly* 14 (1970): 66–99.

Stylianopoulos, Theodore. *The New Testament: An Orthodox Perspective*. Brookline, Mass.: Holy Cross Orthodox Press, 1997.

7

Scripture in the Catholic Tradition

Joseph A. Fitzmyer

My introductory remarks have to do with what may be called the ups and downs of the Bible in the Roman Catholic tradition. There were times when the Bible was widely read in the course of the history of the Roman Catholic Church. There were times too when the Bible was read in Latin and only in Latin, and there were no vernacular translations. There were also times when there were vernacular translations, but they were all translations of the Latin Vulgate. The Bible in the Roman Catholic tradition suffered very much from what took place in the sixteenth century, for the Reformation had a major impact on the way the Bible was used in the Roman Catholic Church. The stress of the sixteenth-century Reformers on the Bible, especially in vernacular translations, caused a negative reaction among Catholics of that time. After that episode, Catholics went through another period that may be called Catholic fundamentalism. It was not a fundamentalism like that in some Protestant churches of the last century and a half, but it was a form of fundamentalism that most Catholics themselves were not aware of. Beginning in the mid-twentieth century, however, since 1943 roughly, a new direction was taken, and since then interest in the Bible in the Roman Catholic Church has grown in astounding proportions. This rapid survey of the ups and downs of the Bible in Roman Catholicism serves to introduce my further remarks, which will be made under four headings: (1) The Catholic Bible; (2) The Role of the Bible in Catholic Tradition; (3) The Historical Interpretation of the Bible; and (4) The Modern Catholic Interpretation of the Bible.

The Catholic Bible

It is necessary, first of all, to clarify what the Bible is for Roman Catholics. What is the Catholic Bible?

(1) For Roman Catholics, the Bible is, in general, what it is for Protestants and Orthodox Christians. In other words, we recognize the Old Testament and the New Testament, the Hebrew Scriptures (as the Old Testament is often called, especially among the Jewish people), plus the Christian Scriptures, the New Testament. Today, some people prefer to call them the First Testament and the Second Testament. Whatever one may call it, it is basically the same collection of sacred writings.

(2) The New Testament is the same for the Roman Catholics as it is for Protestant and Orthodox Christians. All twenty-seven books are identical. Catholics, however, do not admit a canon within the canon. In other words, Catholics do not downgrade certain parts of the New Testament canon. The Epistle of James is not an epistle of straw, as Martin Luther once characterized it in the sixteenth century, calling it "*eine rechte strohern Epistel,*" a real strawy epistle.[1] Catholics do not put the New Testament books on three different levels, as he did.

(3) As far as the Old Testament is concerned, Catholics usually distinguish between protocanonical books and deuterocanonical books. There are twenty-four books in the Hebrew Scriptures, or the Jewish Bible. (As Christians count them, there are thirty-nine.) For Catholics, they are the protocanonical books, canonical books of the first class. Deuterocanonical is the name used for the seven extra books of the Old Testament that Protestants usually call the Apocrypha (Judith, Tobit, Wisdom, Ecclesiasticus [or Sirach], Baruch, and 1 and 2 Maccabees).[2] In addition to the seven books, there are also the extra chapters of the book of Daniel and the book of Esther. *Deuterocanonical* is a term that has been used among Catholics ever since it was coined by Sixtus of Siena, who lived 1520–1569. It denotes what Jerome himself called canonical books and passages of "the second order."

The trouble with the term *Apocrypha* is that it means far more than the seven deuterocanonical books and the additional passages of Daniel and Esther. The deuterocanonical books, as Catholics understand them, are not simply equated with the Apocrypha. In the Protestant way of thinking, the Apocrypha include certain books that Catholics would not consider deuterocanonical. They would not be canonical in any sense, but are simply apocryphal for Catholics too: 3 and 4 Esdras, 3 and 4 Maccabees, Psalm 151,[3] Psalms 152–155,[4] The Prayer of Manasseh.[5]

(4) Why is there this difference in the Old Testament canon? The canon of the Old Testament used by Catholics is derived from the Alexandrian collection of Jewish sacred writings. It goes back to the canon used by Greek-speaking early Christians who adopted the Old Testament from the Greek-speaking Jews of Alexandria in Egypt. It is the Bible that was used by the New Testament writers, because in the vast majority of the instances where the Old Testament is quoted by a New Testament writer the quotation has been derived from the Greek form of the Old Testament used in Alexandria, which is often called the Septuagint. The difference between the Catholic and the Protestant Old Testament exists today because, at the time of the Reformation, Martin Luther and other Reformers reverted to the collection of biblical books used by the Jews of Palestine, and that distinction has been with us ever since.[6] In other words, the Protestant tradition, which has limited the canon of the Old Testament to the Jewish collection of the Hebrew Scriptures that was current in Palestine, broke with the tradition in the early church of using the Alexandrian collection of biblical writings translated from Hebrew.

Another distinction must also be made, namely between the so-called Alexandrian canon and the Septuagint. The Alexandrian canon did not include everything that is found in the Septuagint. A modern edition of the Septuagint has all the protocanonical and deuterocanonical books of the Hebrew Scriptures or the Old Testament, but in addition it has other writings that are apocryphal. Thus, in a modern edition of the Septuagint one will find such writings as Esdras A, 3 and 4 Maccabees, Psalm 151, the diverse Odes, and the Psalms of Solomon. Moreover, this problem is compounded, because some of the Greek books that are found in the Septuagint have turned up in modern discoveries in forms that are different from the traditional way in which the book was read in Greek for centuries. A good example of that is the book of Tobit. For centuries it was read in a Greek form found in two great manuscripts, Alexandrinus (A) and Vaticanus (B). Then in 1844 a German scholar, Constantin von Tischendorf (1815–74), went to Mount Sinai and at the Monastery of Saint Catherine discovered the famous manuscript of the Greek Old Testament called today Sinaiticus (S). In Sinaiticus he found a form of the book of Tobit that is longer than that of Alexandrinus and Vaticanus. The book of Tobit in a modern printed edition of the Septuagint is given in both the shorter (A, B) and the longer (S) form.[7] Thus, the *modern* Septuagint has been growing over the years, and one must be careful about what is meant by that term.

The end result is that the Catholic Old Testament is closer to the Old Testament used by Christians of the Orthodox churches than it is to the Old Testament used by the Protestants.

(5) Moreover, the Catholic Bible for centuries was a Latin Bible. Here I am talking about the whole Western church tradition. The church of

western Europe for a long time read the Bible only in Latin. There were two different forms of the Latin Bible: *Vetus Latina*, which means the Old Latin (version).[8] That was the Latin translation of the Bible that existed before Jerome (345–420) and in several different forms. There was the *Vetus Latina Itala*, which was used in Italy, and the *Vetus Latina Afra*, used in Africa. Because of this difference of form, especially of the Latin Old Testament, Pope Damasus in the fourth century wanted Jerome to produce a new translation to supplant these different Latin translations. Jerome began working on his translation from the original languages (Hebrew and Greek) in A.D. 385. What he produced in Latin is known today as *Vulgata Latina*, or the Vulgate.[9] The nature of Jerome's work was different in different parts of the Old Testament. Sometimes he just spruced up the Latin translation in the *Vetus Latina*; at other times he completely translated the biblical text anew. Jerome was mainly interested in what he called the *hebraica veritas*, "the Hebrew truth," by which he meant the meaning of the Hebrew text of the Old Testament. This above all he wanted to render in contemporary Latin. He did not care for the Septuagint, the Greek translation of the Old Testament, which some theologians of his day, such as Augustine, considered to be inspired. Jerome preferred to translate the Old Testament from Hebrew into Latin, and that is what one has in the Vulgate today.

Jerome could translate Hebrew and Greek but, surprisingly enough, could not translate Aramaic. We know that from a letter that he wrote when he was asked by two bishops to translate the book of Tobit into Latin. He finally agreed to accede to their request, even though he really did not want to do it, because he considered the book of Tobit to be part of the canon of second order, what Catholics today call a deuterocanonical book. His letter to bishops Chromatius and Heliodorus is often used as a preface to the Vulgate form of Tobit. In it he tells that he dashed off the translation of Tobit in one day's work. He could not translate it himself, so he found a Jew who could speak both Aramaic and Hebrew, who translated the Aramaic text of Tobit into Hebrew for him, which he then translated into Latin and dictated to a secretary. That explains the form of the book of Tobit in the Latin Vulgate. For centuries this was the form of the book that was read in the Catholic Church of western Europe. Today we have texts of Tobit in Aramaic and Hebrew from among the Dead Sea Scrolls,[10] and many phrases and clauses in them are quite different from Jerome's translation.[11]

The Latin Bible continued to be used until the time when scholars in the Renaissance period began to translate the Bible into vernaculars, into the different contemporary languages. A good example would be Luther's Bible in German.[12] There were various antecedents of the English Bible prior to the so-called *King James Version*, the Authorized Version of 1611. The Latin Bible, too, continued to be used, and initially English Bibles for Catholics were all translated from the Latin Vulgate. This was partly a reaction to Protestants, who were using vernacular Bibles translated from the original languages. The Catholic Church reacted against that and initially would have nothing to do with vernacular Bibles, even if they were translated from the original languages, because it esteemed the historic Latin Vulgate.[13] Eventually it was translated into English. The *Douai-Rheims* is the famous English Bible that was used for centuries in the English-speaking Roman Catholic Church. In 1582 the New Testament was translated, and then in 1609 the Old Testament.[14] It was eventually revised in 1749–52 by Bishop Richard Challoner (1691–1781).[15]

The Council of Trent in 1546 defined for Roman Catholics the canon, its deuterocanonical and protocanonical books, so that the canon is closed.[16] Nothing more can ever be added to the Catholic Bible. If tomorrow we were to discover a heretofore unknown but genuine letter of Paul of Tarsus, it would never become part of the Catholic Bible. Other churches might think it proper to include it, but Catholics would not. The Council of Trent defined the canon on two principles: first, long use of the books, with all their parts, in the church, and second, their use in the Latin Vulgate.

There have been other Catholic English translations of the Bible beyond the *Douai-Rheims*. For example, in this century Ronald Knox produced an individual translation of both the Old and New Testament,[17] but it too was a translation of the Latin Vulgate, though Knox himself said that he always kept his eye on the original Greek or Hebrew text. It remained, however, a translation of the Latin Vulgate. The same would have to be said about the original *Confraternity of Christian Doctrine* version,[18] which, after considerable revision based on the original languages, became the *New American Bible*. For in 1943 Pope Pius XII issued an encyclical letter, *Divino afflante Spiritu*, on the promotion of biblical studies in the Catholic Church, and that encyclical changed the whole process and attitude toward the Bible.[19] Pius XII insisted on the Bible being used in the Catholic Church according to the original languages. Henceforth, Catholics were to translate the Bible into modern English, modern German, modern French, and so on, basing their version no longer on the Latin Vulgate but on the Aramaic, Greek, and Hebrew texts of the canonical writings. A good example of such a translation is now the *New American Bible*, a Catholic Bible rendered from the original languages.[20]

The Role of the Bible in Catholic Tradition

(1) The first thing that must be said is that Catholics regard the Bible as the Word of God. In employing this term, however, one must make several distinctions. For Catholics, Jesus Christ is the incarnate Word of God, taking that notion from John's Gospel: "In the beginning was the Word, and the Word was with God, and the Word was God...And the Word became flesh" (Jn. 1:1, 14). So "Word of God" can refer to Christ,

the Word of God Incarnate. The Bible may tell us about the Word of God Incarnate, but it is not the Word of God in that sense. A second way in which one can understand "Word of God" is as God's message to humanity. When one speaks of God revealing things to Moses or to the prophets, one uses "Word of God" in a prebiblical sense, the message about divine things revealed that existed before it was written down. Through Jesus Christ, too, the "Word of God" came as a message, and before it was reduced to writing in the New Testament books, it already existed. That message is not yet identical with the Bible. The third way one can understand the "Word of God" is the *written Word of God*. The Bible is for Catholics the written Word of God. This term and these distinctions Catholics hold in common with most other Christians, even if they do not habitually use such terminology.

(2) Catholics also talk about the Bible containing the revelation of God, or what God has revealed to humanity. Sometimes there is difficulty in understanding the term "revelation." An easy way to begin talking about it is to use the frequent biblical expression, "And God said…" It is a mode of God's self-revelation to humanity. That self-revelation would include not only what God has said, but also what God has done for his people, Israel of old and Christians, and who has manifested himself in the person and message of Jesus. The God who speaks and the God who acts is thus the revealed God. So revelation is the self-manifestation of God in word and deed to human beings.

Now someone might ask, "But isn't that what is in the Bible?" Yes, that is what is in the Bible, but there is also more, because not everything in the Bible is revealed. To think that the Bible is God's revelation from beginning to end is an oversimplification. The Bible also presents to us, for example, forms of prayer that human beings address to God. These are not necessarily revelations of God. Another example would be the collection of human wisdom sayings found in the book of Proverbs or Qoheleth (Ecclesiastes). One such saying reads, "It is better to live in a corner of the housetop than in a house shared with a contentious wife" (Prov. 21:9 and 25:24). Is such a proverb a revelation of God or about God? Is God revealing something about himself in such a saying? No. There are many such things, many human things, in the Bible that are not a revelation of God. So one must make a distinction. Is the Bible the Word of God? Yes. Is the Bible a revelation of God? Not entirely. It contains a revelation of God in both the Old and New Testaments, but it also contains what is only human wisdom.

(3) For Roman Catholics the Bible, the written Word of God, is inspired. This notion is derived from 2 Timothy 3:16, "All scripture is inspired by God…," and 2 Peter 1:21, "men and women moved by the Holy Spirit spoke from God." Those are the two main passages that Protestants, Catholics, and Orthodox appeal to for the notion of biblical inspiration.

One must remember, however, that both of those passages were referring to writings of the Old Testament. The church in its tradition has extended that idea of inspiration to the New Testament and considers it just as much inspired as the Old Testament. That is a theological extension of the notion set forth in Scripture itself (2 Tim. 3:16; 2 Pet. 1:21). In other words, biblical inspiration refers to all the Old Testament from the first word to the last, and to all the New Testament from its first word to its last. If this is sometimes maintained as a form of verbal inspiration, it does not mean for Catholics that God has actually dictated the words to some human scribe. What is meant is that God has moved an ancient human being to record in writing a message to guide his people, Israel of old or Christians. Now that message might simply be a catalog of human wisdom like the book of Proverbs, but it could also be divine wisdom being communicated by God to humanity for their guidance and salvation. For all the different proverbs, human wisdom though they be, God also wanted codified and written down to guide his people. Though they are not necessarily a revelation of things divine, they are all inspired; and because they are inspired, they manifest God's concern for his people. That is the notion behind biblical inspiration for Catholics.

(4) Catholics also maintain the inerrancy of Scripture, but realize that this is a somewhat problematic idea. The Bible itself does not speak about its own inerrancy. "Inerrancy" in English is a word derived from Latin *inerrantia* and from the Latin theological tradition of the church that tells about the Bible not containing error. There are, indeed, places in the Old and New Testament to which theologians often appeal to support the notion of inerrancy, for example, Numbers 23:19, Deuteronomy 18:20–22, or John 10:34–35. Such texts indicate that the Word of God will not come to an end or will not fail. This is not the same thing as inerrancy. For Catholics inerrancy is a deduction from the inspired character of Scripture. Because God's Spirit has been involved in the writing of Scripture, he does not inspire error. But if all Scripture is inspired from one end to the other, it is not all inerrant. Biblical inspiration and inerrancy are not necessarily coextensive. For instance, there are many psalms where people praise God or beg God's assistance. Such human expressions in praise of God or in prayer to him are not involved in the issue of inerrancy. No one would say that they contain error, but they are not usually considered when the quality of inerrancy is discussed. Similarly, some historical statements made in the indicative, often in the past tense, might seem at first sight to involve inerrancy, but not necessarily so. In the Catholic tradition inerrancy is not understood quantitatively, but is rather understood formally of the whole. It tells us that the Bible "teaches firmly, faithfully, and without error that truth which God wanted put into the sacred writings for the sake of our salvation."[21] In other words, all the salutary truths and the statements concerning human salvation in the Bible are inerrant. The question,

however, whether God created the world in six days (Gen. 1:1—2:3) would not be a matter guaranteed by inerrancy; so Catholics do not have to squirm in explaining what is meant by "day" in such a passage. Nevertheless, the larger issue of the religious truth, that God is responsible for the existence of the world, is indeed taught with inerrancy and is without error. The purpose of the doctrine of inspiration and inerrancy is to indicate that the Bible does pass on without error the truths that are necessary for human beings and their salvation.

(5) The purpose of the Bible itself is to pass on the Word of God in order to build up Christians and lead them to proper conduct and eventually to their graced salvation. Why did God see to it that ancient human beings would record his message in writing for humanity? Because it is a distillation of many of the utterances made by Moses and the prophets, and later by Jesus of Nazareth during his earthly life, utterances that are important for the instruction and guidance of humanity.

The Bible is, then, for Catholics the supreme grace of God after Jesus Christ. Jesus is the first and foremost grace, and the second is the Bible. The earliest books of the New Testament do not pass on to us *verbatim* what Jesus did and said, but rather an interpretation of the Christ-event. Paul's letters, especially the uncontested seven,[22] were all composed before any of the gospels, so that they pass on to us an interpretation of what Jesus Christ meant for humanity even before the story about him was compiled and written down. Such an interpretation of Christ is part of the purpose of the Bible.

The Historical Interpretation of the Bible

The question we come to now is one of hermeneutics: the rules that tell us how to read and understand the Bible. What governs our understanding of the written Word? What governs the meaning of the written Word of God? Because of the ups and downs that the Bible has had in the Catholic Church, it is necessary to say something about how the Bible was once interpreted and understood; in the next section I shall deal with how it is understood and interpreted today. For the way the Bible was once interpreted in the church affects the way that it is interpreted today.

(1) From the earliest patristic times one finds two sorts of interpretation of the Bible in the church. The first is called its *literal sense*: what the inspired human author directly expressed and intended to convey by what he wrote. It involves the meaning of the words employed, the meaning of phrases, the meaning of paragraphs, and the meaning of the whole book. It is what is sometimes called the textual meaning, contextual meaning, and relational meaning. For example, what does the expression *soma Christou*, "body of Christ," mean for Paul? Anyone who

studies that expression will find that Paul uses it in three different ways. Sometimes it means the historical, crucified body of Jesus (Rom. 7:4); sometimes, the church (1 Cor. 12:27–28); and sometimes the Eucharist or the Lord's supper (1 Cor. 10:16; 11:24). How does one know which one to use in a given place? It depends on the context, the contextual meaning, what is behind the expression. The relational meaning also helps to explain how "body of Christ" functions in Pauline theology as a whole. That meaning thus forms part of the larger context in which any given phrase in Paul's letters would have to be understood. Questions of this sort aid in determining what is the literal sense of a given expression in Paul's writings, what he meant when he wrote about the "body of Christ."

(2) The second mode of interpreting the Bible in early patristic literature, and one also found frequently in the Middle Ages, is called its *spiritual sense*. It was usually an allegorical interpretation that sought to bring out the christological meaning of the Hebrew Scriptures for Christians. A famous example comes from the *Epistle of Barnabas* (early second century A.D.), chapter 9, paragraph 7.[23] In order to show that the circumcision to which Abraham submitted "the slaves born in his house or bought with his money" (Gen. 17:23) was done looking forward to Jesus, the author of the epistle uses the number 318, the number of the men of Abraham's household according to Genesis 14:14, and interprets it allegorically. The number "eighteen" is considered first, because in Greek it is written *iota eta* (IH), which are also the first two letters of the name Jesus in Greek (*IHSOUS*). The letter *tau* (T) is used as the way of writing "three hundred" in Greek, and because it has the shape of a cross, it became for the author of the epistle a clear reference to Christ and his passion. The author of the epistle fails to tell us what the meaning of the circumcision of Abraham and his household was (its literal sense); instead, he seeks to find only a hidden meaning in the Genesis story that would refer to Christ (its spiritual sense). Thus, almost from the beginning of the Christian church there was this mode of interpreting the Old Testament christologically and allegorically. Early Christians wanted to interpret the Old Testament and find Jesus in some way or other in all that they read. That became the allegorical interpretation of the Bible, and it is found in many different forms in patristic writers.[24]

(3) In time, these two modes of interpretation, the literal and the allegorical, developed into two different schools of patristic interpretation: the Antiochene school, which stressed the literal interpretation of the Bible; and the Alexandrian school, which practiced the allegorical or spiritual mode of interpretation.

Origen, who used at times a critical method of interpreting the Bible to ascertain its literal sense, became famous for his use of the spiritual sense. For him the spiritual sense was far more important than the literal sense, and he employed it in interpreting the Old Testament as pointing to Christ, especially when he was in controversy with various opponents, whether pagan or Jewish.

(4) Eventually these patristic modes of interpretation led to what has been called the medieval four senses of Scripture. In the Middle Ages, it was the method of the Alexandrian school that continued among the theologians, who often acknowledged four senses for every verse in Scripture. In the dictum of the thirteenth-century Dominican theologian, Augustine of Dacia:

> *Littera gesta docet, quid credas allegoria, moralis quid agas, quid speres anagogia.* (The letter teaches facts; allegory, what you are to believe; the moral sense, what you are to do; the anagogical sense, what you are to hope for.)

Every verse of the Old and New Testament could have these four senses. Note, however, how in this mode of interpretation faith has nothing to do with the literal sense. Strangely enough, in this medieval view, the literal sense would not tell Christians what they must believe, but the allegorical sense would be what is to be believed.

Although Thomas Aquinas (1225–1274) admitted the four senses of Scripture, he nevertheless wrote:

> All the senses are based on one, namely, the literal from which alone an argument can be drawn, and not from those which are said by way of allegory…Yet nothing is lost to sacred Scripture because of this, because nothing necessary for faith is contained in the spiritual sense which Scripture does not clearly pass on elsewhere by the literal sense.[25]

In effect, Thomas wrote off the three nonliteral senses, the allegorical, moral, and anagogical. While still admitting that there were three other senses, he saw clearly that he was breaking with the tradition that elevated them.

There is a sort of irony in this development, because the allegorical interpretation of Scripture continued by and large until the time of the Renaissance and the Reformation. Then came the Renaissance with its *recursus ad fontes*, "return to the sources," and a renewed interest in the meaning of original texts and sources. Scholars began to read Hebrew and Greek, which had been largely neglected during the Dark Ages. This resulted in a break from the allegorical or spiritual way of interpreting Scripture. That interest pushed back to the literal sense again.

The same interest in the literal sense is seen in the Reformers, Luther and Calvin. Luther, especially in his translation of the Bible into German from the original languages, and Calvin, with his commentaries and other theological works, usually went back to the literal sense of scripture. And yet, that allegorical interpretation continued in the Roman Catholic Church, often in opposition to the efforts of the Reformers, precisely because it had been the vogue for so many centuries and thus historical in a sense. There was opposition to vernacular Bibles and to the Lutheran emphasis of *sola scriptura,* by scripture alone. The Bible was seen, consequently, by some as the Protestant Book, and this led to an exaggerated emphasis on tradition.[26]

(5) The movement toward the literal sense continued, however, and was aided by the Enlightenment at the end of the eighteenth century, and then in the nineteenth century by the so-called rationalist philosophies. It was also furthered by the light that the significant archaeological and historical discoveries were shedding on the Bible from the end of the eighteenth century and throughout the nineteenth. Most people today do not realize what an impact those discoveries made on the interpretation of the Bible. For example, the Rosetta Stone was discovered in 1796 by some of the soldiers in Napoleon's army in Egypt, but it was not until 1822 that Jean François Champollion, a Frenchman, deciphered it. It took another fifty years before Richard Lepsius perfected the understanding of Egyptian hieroglyphics. Then for the first time (in the modern world) the hieroglyphs, in which ancient Egyptian literature had been written, were read, and the literature of the Egyptians, Israel's neighbors to the west, was finally opened up. Then people began to realize, for example, that Egyptian historical, poetic, and wisdom texts were similar to the writings in the Bible.

Similarly, in 1839 the Assyrian and Babylonian counterpart of the Rosetta Stone, the Behistun Inscription, was deciphered. Then, for the first time the literature of Israel's neighbors to the east was opened up, and scholars discovered that the Mosaic law had counterparts in the Assyrian and Babylonian law codes, such as the code of Hammurabi (1792–50 B.C.). Thousands of historical documents were discovered, such as the chronicles of the Assyrian king Sennacherib (705–681) and the Babylonian king Nebuchadnezzar (605–562). These documents, contemporary with parts of the Old Testament, in thus coming to light, provided a rich historical context against which one had to interpret the Bible. That meant that one could never go back to the allegorical way of interpreting the Bible or to the spiritual senses that were in vogue for so many centuries.

(6) All of this eventually impinged on the Catholic interpretation of the Bible, and in 1893 Pope Leo XIII issued an encyclical letter, *Providentissimus Deus,* to guide Catholic biblical studies.[27] Leo XIII encouraged Catholic biblical scholars to utilize the many new resources, but he also uttered various cautions against the rationalist interpretation of the Bible that had come out of the Enlightenment. Fifty years later Pope Pius XII brought Catholic biblical interpretation into the

modern age when he issued his own encyclical *Divino afflante Spiritu*,[28] which was revolutionary, as far as Catholics and the Bible were concerned. He insisted, first of all, on the translation of the Bible from the original languages. That changed the emphasis on the Latin Vulgate that had been used for centuries. Secondly, he insisted on the interpretation of the Bible in its literal sense: It was the duty of the Catholic exegete to uncover the sense of the words that were composed by the ancient human author. Thirdly, he directed that one must do this according to the literary form or genre in which the various writings of the Bible had been composed. The discoveries of the nineteenth century had brought about the realization that parts of the Bible were written according to the contemporary conventions of certain genres. In other words, one began to realize that a poem is not the same thing as an epistle; that the wisdom literature is not the same thing as the Mosaic law. Thus the ancient counterparts in neighboring literatures that had come to light impinged on the interpretation of the Bible, and so one could never go back to that old pre-critical way of reading the Bible. Fourthly, he admitted that one could not really interpret the Bible according to "the unanimous consent of the Fathers," because it was practically nonexistent. Pius XII said all of this while still asserting the inspired character of the Bible. He noted that its text was inspired because it was written by human beings moved by God to record God's message in the form of language and literature that they knew, with all the excellence, elegance, and foibles of their mode of writing. Certain parts of the Bible are miserably written; for example, the book of Revelation is composed in very poor Greek. If one were to ask, "Did God inspire such Greek?" the answer would be, "Yes, he inspired it in just that way." Friedrich Nietzsche, in *Beyond Good and Evil*, says, "It is curious that God learned Greek when he wished to turn author—and that he did not learn it better."[29] In other words, God's Word comes to us with all the marks of humanity.

The Modern Catholic Interpretation of the Bible

(1) The literal sense of Scripture is ascertained by using what is often called the historical-critical method of interpretation. This is a mode of interpretation that is conducted according to critical literary and historical principles. Sometimes people say that this method came into being at the time of the Renaissance, and sometimes at the time of the Enlightenment, but neither opinion is correct. The method, even though it was not then called historical-critical, has been traced back to pre-Christian times in Alexandria. In the second and first centuries B.C. that Egyptian city was a great center of learning with a famous library and museum. The scholars who worked in the Alexandrian library dealt with the text of Homer's *Iliad* and *Odyssey* and other Greek classics. They tried to get the best manuscripts and establish the best readings; they

sought to interpret the different writings and epics. Their method may have been a little more primitive than it is today, but it was the beginning of the literary criticism used for literature, and also for the Bible.

It is also the method that Origen (185–254) and Jerome (345–420) employed among the Church Fathers. For example, Origen's famous book, the *Hexapla*, put the Old Testament in six columns: the Hebrew text, a Greek transliteration of the Hebrew text (for pronunciation purposes), then the Septuagint translation, followed by three other Greek translations. Origen did this because he wanted to establish the best reading of the text, the best way of understanding it, and the best way of interpreting it. When Jerome was working on the translation of the Hebrew Bible into Latin, he too was employing the critical methods he had inherited from earlier Greek scholars.

Sometimes people are annoyed when they hear the word "critical" or "historical-critical" because they think that scholars are criticizing the Bible. That is not the point of it at all. The method is called "critical" because it is using the technical, literary, and scientific way of reading an ancient text, what philologians do in studying the classical literature of ancient Greece and Rome. The proper use of criticism for interpretation is necessary because the Bible did not drop from heaven, written in King James English. It was written in ancient languages, which are not ours, and consequently one has to make an effort to understand that ancient inspired text.

(2) Because of the encyclical of Pope Pius XII of 1943, *Divino afflante Spiritu*, Catholics today use the historical-critical method along with other interpreters, Jewish and Protestant. They adopt the same interpretative principles that Protestant and Jewish commentators had been using for long decades, perhaps even centuries. Though Pius XII never used the expression "historical-critical method," it is obvious that that is what he was talking about.

As an example of such interpretation, one can consider the instruction of the Biblical Commission, a group of Catholic scholars that meets once a year in Rome to study various questions in order to help the Pope and Vatican officials in biblical matters that may affect church teaching. In 1964 the Commission issued a document, *Instructio de historica evangeliorum veritate*, "Instruction on the Historical Truth of the Gospels."[30] The most important word of the Latin title was *de*, "about," because the Commission did not insist on the historical truth of the gospels. It discussed rather their historical truth and made an important distinction of the three stages of gospel tradition: Stage 1, representing what Jesus of Nazareth did and said (roughly A.D. 1–33); Stage 2, representing what the apostles and disciples preached about what Jesus did and said (roughly A.D. 33–65), that is, the period of apostolic preaching prior to the writing of the gospels; Stage 3, representing what the evangelists wrote down, having culled, synthesized, and explicated the preaching of the prior stages (roughly A.D. 65–95). That means that what we have in the canonical gospels is the record of Stage 3 and only a reflection of Stages 2 and 1. Thus, Catholics are spared from a fundamentalistic interpretation of the gospels, as if Stage 3 represented a verbatim account of Stage 1. This approach to the gospel tradition reckons clearly with the form-critical study of the gospels and has made good use of the historical-critical method.

(3) Finally in 1993, the centenary of Pope Leo XIII's encyclical, the Biblical Commission put out another document on *The Interpretation of the Bible in the Church*.[31] That document more or less suggests the way the Bible should be interpreted in the Roman Catholic Church today. It comes out strongly in support of the historical-critical method, speaking of it as "indispensable" and "required," because the Bible is a product of ancient human writing. The Commission also acknowledges all sorts of other approaches to the Bible, such as literary, narrative, rhetorical, semiotic, or canonical approaches, as well as sociological, psychological, liberationist, and feminist approaches. These different approaches may have to be taken into consideration in the interpretation of a given book or passage, but the Commission makes it clear that none of these approaches can stand by itself and none of them is a substitute for the historical-critical method. They serve, however, as refinements or correctives of that basic method. In other words, they enable certain aspects of the Bible to come to the fore that perhaps have been neglected earlier.

The Commission looks upon the historical-critical method as neutral. This aspect must be stressed, because ever since the time of the Enlightenment it has been used with presuppositions that have created problems for many people. For example, at the time of the *Leben-Jesu Forschung* in nineteenth-century Germany the historical-critical method was employed with a rationalistic, deist, and antidogmatic philosophy that used the gospels merely as historical sources and ignored their religious teaching. That was the beginning of the so-called quest for the historical Jesus, which has its contemporary counterpart in the Jesus Seminar in the U.S.A. That quest started toward the end of the eighteenth century, and Albert Schweitzer in his book *The Quest of the Historical Jesus*[32] exposed what was afoot. He showed that the nineteenth-century lives of Jesus were written "with hate, not so much hate of the Person of Jesus as of the supernatural nimbus with which it was so easy to surround Him" (in church tradition). The Commission, however, recognizes that the historical-critical method, being neutral in itself, can be used with such presuppositions, but it can also be used with the presupposition of faith. In other words, a right-minded Christian can make use of that method to interpret the gospels without trying to undermine the spiritual or religious meaning that they are trying to convey.

(4) Finally, this approach to Scripture emphasizes that the Bible, as far as Catholics are concerned, is part of a living-faith tradition. The Christian community is guided by its faith commitments and tradition, and consequently the Bible will always have to be interpreted in the context of that faith and tradition, because that living-faith tradition has grown out of the Bible itself. In other words, such tradition has not grown up independently of the Bible; it is a tradition that has developed out of the Bible. Thus it has become also a guide for the interpretation of the Bible.

As *Dei Verbum* of Vatican Council II has put it for Catholics, "Sacred Tradition and sacred Scripture form one sacred deposit of the Word of God, which is committed to the Church." "There exist a close connection and communication between sacred Tradition and sacred Scripture. For both of them, flowing from the same divine wellspring, in a certain way merge into a unity and tend toward the same end."[33] In other words, in the Catholic tradition the Bible does not stand alone; one always has the Bible and Tradition. Tradition is simply a way of interpreting the Bible in the light of what has grown out of the Bible itself.

The famous Lutheran distinction between Scripture as the *norma normans non normata* and tradition as the *norma normata* is used by some Catholic theologians too. Accordingly, Scripture is the norm that norms but is not normed, whereas Tradition is the norm that is normed (i.e. by Scripture). In other words, Scripture is thus the guide *par excellence* for Catholic doctrine and life. This distinction has been used by Karl Rahner[34] and is useful in relating Scripture to Tradition. Another way used by Catholic theologians is to speak of the two merging together, as did the Vatican Council II in the above quotation.

These, then, are the ways in which Roman Catholics in the twentieth century use the Bible and learn from it what God has revealed for them. Scripture and Tradition are both guides for Catholic life and teaching, because they feed the faith of the community, of which Scripture is the prime inspiration.

Suggestions for Further Reading

Fitzmyer, Joseph A.*The Biblical Commission's Document "The Interpretation of the Bible in the Church: Text and Commentary."* Subsidia biblica 18. Rome: Biblical Institute Press, 1995. Available from Loyola University Press, Chicago.

———. *Scripture, The Soul of Theology.* Mahwah, N. J.: Paulist Press, 1994.

The Pontifical Biblical Commission. *The Interpretation of the Bible in the Church.* Vatican City: Libreria Editrice Vaticana, 1993. Reprinted by United States Catholic Conference, Washington, D.C. 1994.

---

[1]See "Preface to the New Testament (1522/1546)," *Werke: Weimar Ausgabe, Deutsche Bibel*, 6. 10; *Luther's Works*, 35. 362.

[2]A mnemonic for remembering the named books is "J. T. Web and the two McCabes."
[3]This psalm is canonical for Orthodox Christians.
[4]Psalms 152—155 were part of the psalter in a Syriac Bible. Psalms 151, 154, 155 have turned up in Hebrew form in one of the Dead Sea Scrolls, 11QPs[a] (see J. A. Sanders, *The Psalms Scroll of Qumrân Cave 11*, Discoveries in the Judaean Desert 4 [Oxford: Clarendon, 1965], 53–76).
[5]An appendix to many editions of the Latin Vulgate includes the Prayer of Manasseh, 3 and 4 Esdras, Psalm 151, and the Epistle to the Laodiceans, but they are not considered canonical in any sense by Catholics. That is why these apocryphal writings have been relegated to the appendix. The appendix is not found in the so-called *Neovulgata* (*Nova Vulgata Bibliorum Sacrorum Editio* [Vatican City: Libreria Editrice Vaticana, 1979]).
[6]See F. F. Bruce, *The Canon of Scripture* (Downers Grove, Ill: InterVarsity, 1988), 98–104.
[7]See the manual edition of A. Rahlfs, *Septuaginta*, 2 vols., 8th ed (Stuttgart: Württembergische Bibelanstalt, 1935), 1. 1002–39. Compare R. Hanhart, *Tobit* (Septuaginta: Vetus Testamentum graecum auctoritate Academiae Scientiarum Gottingensis editum 8/5 (Göttingen: Vandenhoeck & Ruprecht, 1985).
[8]See the critical text of much of the *Vetus Latina* in the series *Vetus Latina: Die Reste der Altlateinischen Bibel*, ed. Monks of Erzabtei Beuron (Freiburg im Breisgau: Herder, 1951–). There is no English translation of the *Vetus Latina*.
[9]See R. Weber, *Biblia Sacra iuxta Vulgatam versionem*, 2 vols. (Stuttgart: Württembergische Bibelanstalt, 1969). It contains the appendix with the Apocrypha mentioned above in n. 5.
[10]I published the Aramaic and Hebrew texts of Tobit in 1995; see "196–200. 4QpapTobit[a] ar, 4QTobit[bd] ar, and 4QTobit[e]," *Qumran Cave 4: XIV. Parabiblical Texts, Part 2*, Discoveries in the Judaean Desert 19, ed. M. Broshi et al. (Oxford: Clarendon, 1995), 1–76 (+ pls. I–X).
[11]One of my graduate students (Vincent Skemp) at the Catholic University of America, Washington, D.C., is currently writing a dissertation on the book of Tobit. He is comparing the Vulgate text of Tobit with the Qumran Aramaic and Hebrew fragments of Tobit and the other Latin and Greek versions of the book.
[12]See *Das Neue Testament deutsch von D. Martin Luther: Ausgabe letzter Hand 1545/46: Unveränderter Text in modernisierter Orthographie* (Stuttgart: Deutsche Bibelgesellschaft, n.d.).
[13]See H. Cotton, *Rhemes and Doway: An Attempt to Shew What Has Been Done by Roman Catholics for the Diffusion of the Holy Scriptures in English* (Oxford: University Press, 1855).
[14]*The New Testament of Jesus Christ, Translated Faithfully into English out of the Authentical Latin...in the English College of Rhemes* (Rhemes: John Fogny, 1582 [repr. English Recusant Literature 1558–1640 series, vol. 267; London: Scolar Press, 1975]); *The Holie Bible Faithfully Translated into English out of the Authentical Latin...by the English College of Doway*, 2 vols. (Doway: L. Kellam, 1609–10 [repr. English Recusant Literature 1558–1640 series, vols. 265–266; London: Scolar Press, 1975]).
[15]*The Holy Bible Translated from the Latin Vulgate... Revised... by Bishop Richard Challoner, A.D. 1749-1752* (Baltimore, Md.: John Murphy Co., 1899; repr. Rockford, Ill.: Tan Books and Publishers, 1971).
[16]J. Neuner et al.; *The Teaching of the Catholic Church as Contained in Her Documents* (Staten Island, N. Y.: Alba House/Mercier Press, 1967), 59–60.
[17]R. Knox, *The New Testament of Our Lord and Saviour Jesus Christ: A New Translation* (New York: Sheed & Ward, 1944); *The Old Testament Newly Translated from the Vulgate Latin...*, 2 vols. (New York: Sheed & Ward, 1950). Cf. R. Knox, *The Holy Bible: A Translation from the Latin Vulgate in the Light of the Hebrew and Greek Originals* (New York: Sheed & Ward, 1944, 1948, 1950).
[18]*The New Testament of Our Lord and Savior Jesus Christ Translated from the Latin Vulgate* (Paterson, N. J.: St. Anthony Guild Press, 1941).
[19]See J. J. Megivern, *Bible Interpretation*, Official Catholic Teachings (Wilmington, N. C.: McGrath Publishing, 1978), 316–42, esp. 326.
[20]See *The New American Bible Translated from the Original Languages with Critical Use of All the Ancient Sources by Members of the Catholic Biblical Association of America* (Patterson, N. J.: St. Anthony's Guild Press, 1970). Cf. *The Catholic Study Bible: The New American Bible Including the Revised New Testament*, ed. D. Senior (New York: Oxford University Press, 1990); *The Revised Psalms of the New American Bible* (New York: Catholic Book Publishing Co., 1991).

[21]Vatican Council II, *Dei Verbum*, 11 (*The Documents of Vatican II*, ed. W. M. Abbott, [New York: Herder and Herder/Association Press, 1966], 119).

[22]I.e., those that are generally admitted to be of genuine Pauline authorship: 1 Thessalonians, Galatians, Philippians, 1 Corinthians, 2 Corinthians, Philemon, and Romans.

[23]See K. Lake, *The Apostolic Fathers with an English Translation*, Loeb Classical Library, 2 vols. (Cambridge, Mass.: Harvard University, 1965), 1. 372–73.

[24]See further my articles "Problems of the Literal and Spiritual Senses of Scripture," *Louvain Studies* 20 (1995): 134–46; and "The Senses of Scripture Today," *Irish Theological Quarterly* 62 (1996–97): 101–17.

[25]*Summa Theologica* I, q. 1, a. 10 ad 1.

[26]Involved here was an exaggerated emphasis on the interpretation of scripture according to "the unanimous consensus of the Fathers" (Council of Trent, 8 April 1546, "Decretum de libris sacris et traditionibus recipiendis"; cf. *Teaching* [n. 16 above], 61).

[27]See J. J. Megivern, *Bible Interpretation* (n. 19 above), 193–220.

[28]See n. 19 above.

[29]Apophthegm 121 in *Beyond Good and Evil*, Modern Library (New York: Boni and Liveright, n.d.)

[30]"Sancta Mater Ecclesia," *Acta Apostolicae Sedis* 56 (1964): 712–18; an English translation of the instruction can be found in the *Catholic Biblical Quarterly* 26 (1964): 305–12; or the *Tablet* (London) 218 (30 May 1964): 617–19. My translation, along with a commentary on the text of the instruction, can be found in the appendix of *A Christological Catechism: New Testament Answers: New Revised and Expanded Edition* (New York/Mahwah, N. J.: Paulist, 1991), 119–62.

[31]See J. A. Fitzmyer, *The Biblical Commission's Document "The Interpretation of the Bible in the Church: Text and Commentary"*, Subsidia Biblica 18 (Rome: Biblical Institute Press, 1995); available in the U.S.A. from Loyola University Press, 3441 North Ashland Avenue, Chicago, IL 60657 (tel.: 773-281-1818 or 800-621-1008; fax: 773-281-0555).

[32]See A. Schweitzer, *The Quest of the Historical Jesus: A Critical Study of Its Progress from Reimarus to Wrede*, 3d ed. (London: A. & C. Black, 1954), 4.

[33]*Dei Verbum* §10 and §9 (see *Documents* [n. 21 above]), 117.

[34]"Scripture and Theology,"in *Theological Investigations* 6 (Baltimore, Md.: Helicon, 1969), 89–97, esp. 93; "Bible, B. Theology," in *Sacramentum mundi,* 6 vols. (New York: Herder and Herder, 1968–70), 1. 171–78, esp. 176–77.

8

Luther, the Reformers, and the Bible

David C. Steinmetz

It would be an exaggeration to say that the Reformation grew out of a desire on the part of laity for good preaching, but it would not be entirely false.[1] While it was not the case in the late Middle Ages that there was absolutely no preaching at Sunday mass, it was not an activity very much done by local parish priests. Preaching was done, of course, by members of mendicant orders—orders like the Dominicans, Franciscans, Augustinians, and Carmelites—either in the local chapel of the order or in some village church. But preaching was not the central act of Christian worship. The central act of Christian worship was the celebration of the Lord's supper in a special, highly ritualized, and very dramatic way. To become a priest was not primarily a matter of learning how to talk to a large group of laity about the Bible, but learning how to celebrate the sacraments of baptism, penance, eucharist (or Lord's supper), matrimony, and extreme unction. The priest was not primarily an explainer of texts, but a celebrator of mysteries.

There is now considerable historical evidence that laypeople in England and in the free imperial cities of the Holy Roman Empire developed a hunger for good preaching. In order to satisfy this hunger, which was not altogether satisfied by hearing a few sermons by an occasional mendicant friar, the laity in the free imperial cities endowed preaching positions at important churches, using funds from the public treasury. They called such preachers *Leutpriester,* or people's priests, and expected them to preach every Sunday and on all feast days. Laypeople in important cities, including the city councilmen, decided that they were tired of going to church and listening to no sermons or bad sermons by priests who were pathetically ineffective preachers. They were willing to support their spiritual aspirations with public funds, not with the church offerings, and to engage as *Leutpriester* secular priests like John Geiler of Kaisersberg and Huldrych Zwingli, who had made enviable reputations already as riveting preachers. The *Leutpriester* was a person whose only responsibility was to preach and preach well on every Sunday and every feast day (there are lots of feast days in the liturgical calendar so the *Leutpriester* preached with some frequency). Of course, he did not have to say mass or hear confession or baptize babies or participate in any of the myriad liturgical acts, though he was free to do so and undoubtedly did. But he was not hired to be a celebrator of mysteries; he was hired to preach.

The most famous preacher in late medieval Germany was in fact a preacher in the Strasbourg cathedral by the name of John Geiler von Kaisersberg (1445–1510). Every Sunday and every feast day, Geiler ascended the pulpit in his church at Strasbourg to preach in German. There were as yet no pews, so the people just gathered around the pulpit, which was located in the nave. The nave was the part of the church where the people assembled to pray and observe the consecration of the host. The area in the front of church was dedicated to the celebration of the mystery of the eucharist and set off from the nave by a rood screen. Geiler preached for two hours every Sunday and in fact preached two sermons back to back. He took an hourglass with him into the pulpit. The first hour he preached an exegetical sermon on one of the lessons of the day taken from the Bible. After turning the hourglass over, he preached a second sermon on a larger theme or a problem. For example, he once preached a series of sermons on Sebastian Brant's book *The Ship of Fools.* His normal pattern was thus to preach both exegetically and thematically every time he entered the pulpit.

Because Geiler was dedicated to the task of preaching, he wanted to justify its importance. But it must be understood that in medieval theology preaching was a good deal less important than the sacraments. It was not as important as the sacraments because preaching, unlike the sacraments, was not thought to communicate saving grace. Preaching was doctrinal instruction. It taught what one ought to believe. Preaching was instruction in morals, what one ought to do. Preaching was often catechetical; teaching the creed, the Lord's Prayer, the Ave Maria, and the Ten Commandments. But preaching was not regarded as an instrument by which God gives grace to sinners. In medieval theology God gives grace to sinners through sacraments. Sacraments are a set of liturgical actions through which God always and infallibly gives grace. According to medieval Catholic theology, when a baby is baptized, its original sin is washed away and the child is inserted into the church. When an adult Christian participates in the sacrament of penance, his or her sins committed since the last confession are pardoned and eternal punishments are reduced to temporal works of satisfaction. In the celebration of the eucharist, Christ the Lord is living and present in the bread and wine in order to feed the recipients and to give them the provisions they need to find their way through life, until finally at the end they reach the heavenly Jerusalem. Saving grace is given through sacraments. That notion is absolutely fundamental to medieval Catholic theology.

However, grace is not given through preaching (or, to speak very precisely, only a kind of preparatory grace that disposes one to receive the fuller grace given through the sacraments). Preaching is an invitation to come and participate in the sacraments. It may be instruction about what sacraments are. But it is not a means of grace as the sacraments are. The priest, who preaches, persuades his parishioners to avail themselves of the sacraments, especially penance and the Lord's supper. He would not invite them to baptism, since everyone in his parish had been baptized already as an infant. The preacher might talk about confessing one's sin, about being reinstated in the grace from which one has fallen. He might urge his parishioners to receive communion as well as watch the consecration of the host. But he would not leave them with the notion that hearing sermons is the center of Christian worship. The medieval parish was a eucharistic fellowship, and the priest had been ordained above all to celebrate the mass.

Both he and his parishioners shared the conviction that grace comes through the sacraments. There in bread and wine and water Christ is present to renew one for the Christian pilgrimage though life. All a sermon does or can do is move men and women to the sacraments and to encourage them to embrace the moral life appropriate to the grace they have received.

Which brings us back to Geiler the *Leutpriester*. His sole responsibility was to preach. But if grace was given through the administration of sacraments and not through preaching, it seems that Geiler has in fact been given a much less important job than the priests who do not preach but who say mass. Why should Geiler stand in his pulpit and preach for two hours, if, in the end, preaching plays such a subordinate role in medieval parish life? So Geiler tried to write a cogent explanation why preaching was important for the church and offered his own theory. To do so he had to argue against some assumptions of medieval theology. In medieval theology the most important event of all Christian worship was the celebration of the eucharist. Indeed, priests were primarily ordained so that they could stand at the altar, share in Christ's priesthood, and thereby participate in the miracle by which bread and wine were transformed into the body and blood of Christ. The eucharist was not merely a sacrament; it was highest of all the sacraments. In all the other sacraments only Christ's power was present, but in the eucharist, Christ the living Lord was bodily present under the species of bread and wine as both the high priest who offers sacrifices and the victim offered. It therefore seemed to Geiler's contemporaries beyond dispute that the most important thing for a priest to do was preside at the eucharist.

Geiler gave a very sophisticated and important justification for preaching that still assumed the central importance of sacraments. He argued that preaching is an activity that participates in the dignity of the sacrament to which it is attached. If someone asked what is the sacrament to which preaching is attached, Geiler responded that it was primarily attached to the sacrament of penance because sermons characteristically prompted sinners to seek forgiveness. Penance is in some ways a stronger sacrament than the eucharist. The eucharist can only take away venial or lesser sins, whereas the sacrament of penance can remove mortal or serious sins.

On one level there really is no difference in medieval Catholic theology between sins. All sins are evidence of disobedience to God and therefore, considered in themselves, are worthy of eternal punishment. But God in his grace has decided not to regard all sins as equal, but to regard some sins as venial, sins that do not break one's friendship with God, and other sins as mortal, sins that destroy one's friendship with God. Even Christians can commit mortal sins, which, if unforgiven, can merit eternal punishment by God. The eucharist has the power to remove venial sins. But mortal sins, such as breaking any of the Ten Commandments, require the offender to undergo the discipline of penance. Geiler thought the logic was clear: If preaching is associated with penance and if penance alone can remove the mortal sins of the baptized, then preaching is more important than saying mass, since the eucharist can only remove the lesser faults that do not break friendship with God. The stronger the sin, the stronger the sacrament. Thus, in this respect, if not in every other respect, penance is more important to sinners than hearing mass and preaching, which calls to penance, more important than presiding. Geiler's argument, however, did not persuade many people that preaching was more important than consecrating the elements. However much the laity hungered for good preaching, they did not conclude that it was more important than the eucharist.

What we have in the late Middle Ages is a hunger for good preaching and the need for an adequate justification for its importance. It would be misleading to say that the Reformation was a movement whose only importance was to justify the importance of preaching. But it could be said that the Reformation offered a stronger justification than Geiler could find. The Protestant relationship to the Bible elevated preaching as a kind of sacramental act that bestowed grace and therefore regarded it not as something that was less important in the life of the church, but, in theory at least, something that was equal in importance to the sacraments.

From the standpoint of medieval Christians, Protestant worship seems to be dominated by a good deal of talking. Protestant ministers for the most part (there are exceptions) do not kiss icons, or incense altars, or venerate relics, or understand themselves primarily as priests leading a sacramental community. Protestant ministers of almost any denomination regard themselves more as preachers of the Word than as the celebrators of mysteries. Preaching (except when the Lord's supper or baptism are administered) is not only an element in Protestant worship; it is clearly the central element. It is not uncommon to describe the Protestant pastor as "the preacher," even though the minister's role is by no means restricted to the office of preaching. Even Lutherans who keep the crucifix and eucharistic vestments do not adore the eucharist or collect relics of Martin Luther. How did this change come about? The reasons can be found in the changes that were introduced during the Reformation.

The Transformation of Protestant Worship

Luther began his career as a professor of biblical studies, primarily Old Testament, in the University of Wittenberg, the same university in which his younger colleague, Philip Melanchthon, served as professor of classics and New Testament. Through his study of the Old Testament, Luther became very impressed by the biblical notion of the Word of God. The Word of God is a very complex idea for Luther, and elements in that complex meaning eventually play an important role in the transformation of a group of dissident Catholics into what is known today as Protestantism. Luther distinguished in the somewhat antiquated German of his day between two different kinds of words. Luther called one kind of word a *Heissel-Wort* and he called the other kind of word a *Thettel-Wort*. A *Heissel-Wort* is a word used to affix a name to something that already exists—a wall, a book, a window. All of these things existed before they were called by their respective *Heissel-Wörter*. Calling is a way of fastening a label to something already there.

But a *Thettel-Wort* is an altogether different kind of word. When a *Thettel-Wort* is spoken, it brings into existence something that did not exist before. A *Heissel-Wort* is incapable of bringing nonexistent things into existence; it can only label a thing once it exists. Luther finds examples of *Thettel-Wörter* in the opening chapters of the Bible. According to Genesis 1 God created heaven and earth by speaking. God said "Let there be light" and suddenly there was light. A *Thettel-Wort* is a deed-word, a word which, once uttered, brings into existence a thing that did not exist before and could never have existed apart from that spoken word. For Luther the instrument by which God creates and redeems the world is his *Thettel-Wort*.

What exactly is the Word of God for Luther, granted that it is first and foremost a *Thettel-Wort*? The answer to that question is fairly complicated. When the Bible talks about "the Word" as Luther reads it, it is talking simply about God's speech, God's speaking. The primal or most basic way of understanding "the Word" is to realize that it is the original speech of God, before heaven and earth came into existence, spoken again in the creation and redemption of the world. This is the most fundamental form of the Word of God. Luther's second way of talking about the Word of God can be found in the opening chapter of the Gospel of John where it says, "In the beginning was the Word, and the Word was with God, and the Word was God. He was in the beginning with God." It is obvious that this text is not talking simply about the speech of God. The Gospel of John has in mind an incarnate Word, the Word that is made manifest in Jesus of Nazareth. And so Jesus Christ is the second way in which Luther will talk about the Word of God. As the incarnate Word. Jesus Christ is the perfect Word that God speaks, the perfect expression of the will and intention of God, the perfect reflection of the mind and being of God.

A third way to talk about the Word of God is to talk about the Bible. The Bible is the Word of God in a variety of ways for Luther, but, as it will soon be clear, the Bible is important because it witnesses to Jesus Christ. And there is a sense in which—this is not quite so true for Calvin as for Luther—the Bible as a *written* Word is a little less a Word from God than as a *spoken* Word. That is why for Luther it is the old oracle respoken, which becomes the vehicle for God to speak again. From the spoken Word through the written Word to the spoken Word again. The words from the Wesley hymn capture what Luther has in mind: "He speaks and listening to his voice new life the dead receive."

A fourth way to talk about the Word of God is to talk about preaching. In the words of Heinrich Bullinger in the Second Helvetic Confession (1562–1566): *Praedicatio verbi dei est verbum dei*; "The preaching of the Word of God *is* the Word of God." It does not say that the preaching of the Word of God signifies the Word of God or that the preaching of the Word of God is a witness to the Word. Preaching is more than a witness to God's Word; insofar as it is an event in which the voice of

God is heard again, it *is* the Word of God. What this means in its sixteenth century context is that *just as* Catholics believe that when mass is said, Christ is really present in the creaturely elements of bread and wine, so Protestants now claim that when a sermon is preached, the life-giving Word of God *is* really present in the creaturely elements of human speech. The Word of God *is* present because through culturally determined human language God again speaks a culturally transcendent Word. God speaks not *Heissel-Wörter*, words with which he simply names things that already exist; God speaks a *Thettel-Wort*, a Word that transforms the current state of affairs so that things cannot remain the way they were before. Preaching is not just a report of something happening elsewhere or of something that happened two thousand years ago. As Luther understands the concept of the Word of God in preaching, it is not just an act in which Ezekiel's oracles, which were *once* a living Word, are recollected. Rather, at the hands of the preacher, Ezekiel's oracles become again the Word of God, powerful and lifegiving in our own time and place.

Bernard Lord Manning once defined a sermon, properly done, as "a manifestation of the incarnate Word from the written Word by the spoken Word." That is more or less what Luther also has in mind. The incarnate Word is offered in the text of scripture. When the preacher bears witness to Christ, the incarnate Word, he or she is not bearing witness to something else, something alien, something other, but to the Word as flesh in the word as written, by the word as spoken. Preaching *is* the Word of God in no less a sense than the word spoken in creation. Through human preaching God is once again doing his unremitting work of grace and judgment, of creating and destroying. We must therefore be very careful how we use the Bible. When dealing with the Word of God, written and spoken, we are dealing with something extremely powerful. It comes with all the force that created the world out of nothing.

Finally, the fifth sense of Word of God for Luther is found in the way the church lives from the once-again spoken Word of God. Pastoral conversation can be the Word of God. Luther understands that public preaching is a function that has been delegated to the pastor. But when the pastor was given the function of this public preaching, that assignment of responsibility did not release any parishioner as a baptized Christian from the obligation to witness to Jesus Christ by word and deed. Thus every baptized Christian becomes a bearer of this very dangerous Word of God that can make alive, create, and renew, but can also destroy.

It is now clear that we are moving in a different direction from Geiler von Kaisersberg, who tried to justify preaching by attaching it to the sacrament of penance. Luther provides a wholly new foundation. There is, for Luther, one means of grace. And that one means of grace is the Word of God in all its complexity and power.

This means that the sacraments themselves are now looked upon as vehicles of the same Word as preaching. For Luther these were the three sacraments: baptism, the eucharist, and what he calls the keys (which refers primarily, though not exclusively, to preaching). The Word of God is the means of grace active in baptism, preaching, and the eucharist. The Bible, of course, plays a crucial role in all of this, but it is not just the Bible that is the Word of God. Christianity is not, as Luther likes to point out, a scribal religion. One can swallow twelve Bibles whole and it may not necessarily do one any good. One can master Hebrew philology— Luther thinks that is useful—but philology and grammar cannot tell you in the end what the Bible is about. What it is about we will see below.

The Word and the Sacraments

How does the Word relate to the sacraments? If the Word of God is *the* sacrament, then what is baptism, for example? Is baptism mere water? Luther answers by going back to an old saying of Augustine (354– 430): *Verbum accedat ad elementum et fit sacramentum;* "The Word is joined to the element and a sacrament occurs." What Augustine was talking about in this context was primarily the formula of consecration: "I baptize you in the name of the Father, and of the Son, and of the Holy Spirit." The formula is joined to the element, in this case water, and the sacrament takes place. But Luther now has in mind something more than just the words of the formula. What occurs in baptism is that *the* Word of God—this *Thettel-Wort* that created heaven and earth, and is the Word that will destroy it—this powerful Word is joined to water. It is this Word, not the water itself, that inserts the baptized into Christ. Luther thought that infant baptism was a much more perfect form of baptism than adult baptism. Adults think they are bringing something to baptism to make it effective; that is, they are bringing their rationality, their capability for understanding the gospel. But Luther believed that anyone who comes to God is like a baby. Like babies, adults bring nothing to God. What makes both alive is the Word of God that has joined the water to make it the water of baptism. Baptism is a visible Word of God. It is addressed to the eyes and not to the ears. But it is no less a word for all that. Baptism is the Word that made heaven and earth joined to water.

The eucharist is also the Word. It is a visible proclamation of the Lord's death until he comes. The sermon may have been wretched. The sermon may have been Pelagian or Manichaean or Donatist. But however miserably the sermon may have failed to preach Christ, the eucharist will correct it. Whenever the eucharist is celebrated, Christ is proclaimed. Therefore, the proclamation of Christ in the Lord's supper is again a manifestation of the incarnate Word, joined not to human speech but to bread and wine and water. But the power of the Word remains the same.

When discussing the eucharist as a Word of God, Luther was not talking about *Heissel-Wörter*, words that are in the end not very important, but about a *Thettel-Wort* in visible form.

What are keys? Keys deal with the power to bind and loose from sin, especially among the already baptized. In traditional Catholic theology the keys are tied to the sacrament of penance. For Luther, the power of the keys is exercised from the pulpit. When the Word is proclaimed, faith is awakened and sinners are redeemed. They are released from bondage, not by the preacher, not even by the old written oracles. They are released by the power of the speech of the living God who, when he speaks, creates and redeems. Therefore the power of the keys is exercised in the local church first by preaching.

Secondly, the power of the keys is also exercised in ordinary conversation, Christian to Christian. Every Christian has, because of baptism, the right to hear confession and to absolve from sin. It is not priestly ordination that confers this power, nor does the power reside in the person who absolves, but in the Word of judgment and forgiveness that even the laity can speak. It is no longer ordination by a bishop that gives such power. Luther has reconceived what it is to be a minister. Authorization for ministry does not reside in persons who have been ordained, but in the Word that they carry. Therefore, those ministers who carry the Word of God are authorized by the Word of God they carry, and if they fail to carry that Word (as Luther felt had happened in the old church), they lose their authorization. When laypeople speak the Word of God to each other, it is as effective as if it were spoken by the pope. Laity can bind and loose from sin because the binding and loosing does not reside in them. It resides in the Word they are carrying. It is the Word that is being carried that authorizes the act.

With Luther's new understanding of what the Word of God is, there is an enormous shift in his understanding of ordination. It is no longer the office as an ontological state that matters at all. Those who have been ordained to proclaim the Word, to celebrate the sacraments, and to preside at worship, have simply taken on a new job. They are not new people. Protestants, to speak crudely, get a new job; Catholics through ordination become different persons. For Luther, pastoral ministry is a job like any other job. And, in fact, Luther wants to argue that it is not a job more important than other jobs. Luther is opposed to the halo effect. He is deaf to the notion that to go into church work is to assume a holy job. Why should one think that what the pastor does is more holy than what the farmer does? Why is it more holy than what the housewife does? All vocations, properly done and offered to God, are sacred work. If a person can learn Hebrew and Greek, can understand and explain the creed, can talk plainly to ordinary people, has a sympathetic ear, can understand the Bible, can live a disciplined life of prayer, and has passed qualifying examinations, then the church should ordain him. Pastoral ministry is a job like all others, because the authorization to do it resides in the Word that is proclaimed and not in the person who does it. Therefore, the poorest minister who proclaims the Word publicly is more important than the most gifted person who stands in the pulpit and talks about other things. It also means that laypeople have not been absolved from responsibility for the ministry of the Word, simply because they are not called to preach themselves publicly from the pulpit. The ministry of the Word belongs to all the baptized.

Luther and the Bible

Having considered the larger concept of the Word of God for Luther and the Reformers, we now turn more specifically to the Bible. If we inquire about the way Protestants read the Bible, we discover that in the end it was not all that different from the way it was read in the medieval Catholic Church, in spite of the fact that Protestants kept suggesting it was very different. It would be very misleading if, in thinking of Luther and the Bible, we think of the Bible as a very simple, uncomplicated book. It is quite simplistic to think that for the Reformers the Bible is just a kind of straightforward narrative and that the Protestant Reformation is about lectures to people about the content of the Bible, the content of which is unproblematic and straightforward. The Bible, for Luther, is a very complicated book. When you open the Bible, you open a book that is full of antinomies and tensions.

But today such tensions are frequently avoided. Television evangelists love to tell us that if we will only become a Christian in the way they prescribe, all our problems will be resolved. And there are even subspecies of these popular evangelists who say that faith (and a donation to the televangelist) will get the naive believer the new BMW for which he had long been praying. When the fact of the matter is that if one becomes a Christian, one will have a whole set of new problems one never had before, problems that could easily have been avoided by leaving Christianity alone. Telling martyrs, as they are filing in to the Colosseum to be eaten by lions, that their faith has solved all their problems is not exactly true. Having a Bible is also not an enterprise without some difficulties, problems, and tensions of which Luther was painfully aware.

Luther was not terribly interested in critical questions about the Bible, questions such as who wrote what, when it was written and under what circumstances, who was king at the time, and whether these oracles are in the proper order, or whether the order of oracles ought to be rearranged or changed. Luther was not as interested in what we call historical-critical questions as we are, although he and his contemporaries had historical questions of a sort. Luther was more interested in a whole set of other problems and questions. For him the Bible was not primarily information about the migration and activities of ancient Semites. It was *the* book through which God claimed individuals and nations. If in fact the Bible was not the vehicle for the living Word of God that claims and marks the people of God, then it was not more interesting to read and study than the *Iliad* or the *Odyssey*.

In Luther's case he was even less interested in critical questions than many of his contemporaries. For example, when Luther translated the Bible into German, he took the Pentateuch and renamed it. He called the book of Genesis First Moses, Exodus he called Second Moses, and so forth, to the book of Deuteronomy, which he called Fifth Moses. When somebody objected, "But Dr. Luther, Moses dies in Fifth Moses (Deuteronomy) and the book still goes on," Luther answered, "Ach, it does not really matter. It is still Moses' book." In short, Luther was not terribly interested in critical questions. What was important to Luther was that scripture contains a great treasure. The importance of scripture did not so much lie for him in the scripture itself as in the Christ who is contained in scripture and who is accessible to us only by means of scripture. Let me cite a passage from Luther's *Table Talk*, written down by students at his table, which illustrates this point:

> I beg and admonish faithfully all devout Christians that they be not offended or stumble over the simple stories related in the Bible nor doubt them. However poor they may appear, they are certainly the words, history, and judgments of the high divine Majesty, Power and Wisdom. For this is the book which makes all wise and clever people fools and can only be understood by simple people as Christ says. Therefore let go your own thoughts and feelings and esteem this book as the best and purest treasure as a mine of great wealth which can never be exhausted or sufficiently excavated. Thus you will find the divine wisdom which God presents in the Bible in a manner so simple that it tamps down the pride of clever people and brings it to naught.[2]

That is, he said it is very easy to read the stories of the Bible and offer critical judgments about them. Take Jonah and his fish, for example. Jonah was thrown overboard from a ship on a storm-tossed sea, and was swallowed by a large fish, in whose stomach Jonah found oxygen but no digestive juices. Jonah remained in the belly of this fish and was transported for quite a long time until he was then deposited conveniently on the shore. This tale seems on the face of it a poor, simple story. God has given us poor and simple stories because we are proud people who would rather have abstract metaphysical arguments or narratives in which the heroes are never ridiculous. Not only does Jesus say that one must come to him as a child, the Bible gives one the opportunity to become childlike. For those who want to think great and powerful thoughts the Bible tells these simple stories. But that is good, says Luther, because the door to the kingdom of heaven is a door too low for a proud person to enter.

Luther describes the Bible in the following way: "In this book one finds the swaddling clothes and the manger in which Christ lies and to which the angel directs the shepherds. Those swaddling clothes are shabby and poor, yet precious is the treasure wrapped in them for it is Christ."[3] But the poor and shabby stories are important because they are the manger in which Christ is born. You can look for Christ elsewhere, but you will not find him, except in this manger. You are going to find Christ wrapped in poor, simple off-putting stories of the Bible. Moreover, you cannot have the Christ child without the swaddling clothes. No Bible, no poor and shabby stories, no Christ.

While the Bible often tells simple stories, the stories point to a God who is not simple at all. One of the stories that Luther uses to illustrate the complexity and problematic character of God is the story about a Syro-Phoenician woman (Mt. 15:21–28). The woman has a sick daughter and she has heard of Jesus' healings, so she comes to Jesus and asks Jesus to heal her daughter. Jesus gives her a very brusque rejoinder to push her away. He says to her, "Is it fair that I give the bread that belongs to the children to a dog?" He calls her a dog, which displays a fairly typical attitude toward people of her ethnic background. So she says to him the following: "Truth, Lord, yet the dogs eat at the crumbs which fall from their master's table." Luther loved her answer. Jesus called her a dog, and she replied that dogs always get the crumbs from the table. Then Jesus answered her, "Oh woman, great is your faith. Let it be unto you even as you will." This is one of Luther's favorite stories. It comes up several times in the course of Luther's life and always to make the same point. Luther says, "Is not this masterly? She catches Christ by means of his own words." What Luther admires is how bold she is and that she uses the very words he has spoken to catch him. Jesus compares her to a dog, which she admits, and then she asks no more than to be treated like a dog.

> Whither could he turn? He was caught. No dog is denied the bread crumbs under the table. They are a dog's rightful share. Therefore Christ takes heed of her and submits to her will so that she is no longer a dog but has become a child of Israel. And this was written in order that we might be comforted and that it might be made manifest to us all how deeply God hides his grace from us. And that we should not judge him according to our feeling and thinking about him, but in accordance with his Word. For here you see that Christ, although he

showed himself hard, pronounced no final statement by
saying no to her, but all his answers, though they sound like
"No," are not yet "No" but are indefinite. Therewith is shown
how a heart should stand firm in the midst of temptations. For
as hard as we view them, so Christ feigns to be. A heart hears
and understands nothing but "No," and yet it is not "No."
Therefore sweep your heart clean of all such feelings and trust
firmly in God's Word and grasp from above or from underneath the "No" the deeply hidden "Yes" and hold onto it just
as this woman did, and keep a firm belief in God's justice.
Then you have won and caught him with his own words.[4]

One of the things that Luther discovers in the Bible is that the oppo-
nent who keeps one from God may, in fact, be God himself. Luther found
two faces of God in the Bible, though he was certain that both belonged
to one God. There is the face of God in the law, which makes demands
and judges. The God who makes these demands is a God who is serious
about them. Our conscience agrees with the law and finds it easy to
believe in a God who commands and punishes. Furthermore, law is not
restricted to the Old Testament. One can see this face of God in the New
Testament as well as the Old. It is the face of God that makes demands
and judges. There is also a second face of God, of a God who is merciful
and forgives sins. With this face of God, conscience does not agree because the conscience knows it is not really just to forgive sins. Justice
demands punishment. One therefore encounters in the Bible both "yes"
and "no." Law speaks a "no" to sinners, a "no" that conscience says is
right. However, if one believes God's "no" in the law and does not believe God's "yes" in the gospel, then it will be God who keeps one from
God. But what one must to do is this: against the "no" of God's law,
believe the "yes" of God's gospel. Like the Syro-Phoenician woman one
must grasp by faith the deeply hidden "yes" underneath the "no." In
other words, the road to God is a road to which we are drawn to God by
God, but it is a road on which we are also opposed by God. It should
now be clear that for Luther the Bible is a very complicated book.

Finally, Luther raised the question of canon. For Luther, the reopen-
ing of the question of canon was, however, on an altogether different
basis from the basis on which it was originally settled by the early church.
The question Luther raised was simply, Does this book teach well the
notion that we are justified by Christ freely by faith alone through God's
grace? If it does, then it belongs in the canon. If it does not, perhaps it
should be removed. Luther was not very happy about the book of James,
which gives the impression that believers are justified by their good
works rather than by faith. About the book of Revelation he made the
biting comment that a revelation should be revealing. He liked the Gospel

of John better than the Synoptic Gospels, because the Gospel of John gave readers the words of Christ that can teach us today, while the Synoptics spent more time on Christ's deeds, events that are long past. So for a brief period of time, Luther raised the question whether the canon ought to be reconceived. But in the end, he did not press the issue. He returned to the Hebrew canon, omitting the so-called apocryphal books. Still one of his favorite verses is taken from the Apocrypha, Sirach 2:1, "My son, if you would serve the Lord prepare yourself for temptation." But the theological critique of the canon he finally abandoned.

Suggestions for Further Reading

Battles, Ford L. "God Was Accommodating Himself to Human Capacity." *Interpretation* 31 (1977): 19–38.

Leith, John H. "John Calvin: Theologian of the Bible." *Interpretation* 25 (1971): 329–44.

———. "The Bible and Theology." *Interpretation* 30 (1976): 227–41.

Runia, Klaas. "The Hermeneutics of the Reformers." *Calvin Theological Journal* 19 (1984): 121–52.

Steinmetz, David. *Luther in Context.* Reprint ed. Grand Rapids: Baker Books, 1995.

———. *Calvin in Context.* New York: Oxford, 1995.

Wallace, Ronald S. *Calvin's Doctrine of the Word and Sacrament.* Grand Rapids: Eerdmans, 1957.

---

[1]This is a lightly edited talk that was given *ex tempore* to a large class of undergraduates in the King College Chapel.

[2]Martin Luther, *D. Martin Luthers Werke: Tischreden* (Weimar: H.Böhlau, 1912–1921), 6:16.

[3]Ibid.

[4]Martin Luther, *D. Martin Luthers Werke: Kritische Gesamtausgabe* (Weimar: H. Böhlau, 1883–1919), 17.2:203.

9

The Story That Is the Bible: A Contemporary Protestant Approach

James S. McClanahan

The Story

Nearing the end of this series of articles, "Living Traditions of the Bible," the question may still be asked: As Protestants who are aware of the Bible's complex history and our own distinct heritage, what do we do with the Bible? How do we interpret it: as a whole collection of authoritative books? its separate sections? its individual books?

In part, the preceding chapters of this book are an exercise in thinking of the Bible as a great story. In fact, as Christians, we would like to say "The Great Story." The history of the development of the canon has demonstrated that the two collections of the Christian Bible—the thirty-nine books of the (Protestant) Old Testament and the twenty-seven books of the New Testament—are the definitive and authoritative sources for the foundation of faith in the Living God. From the Christian perspective, God has entered human history to carry out his purposes for his people. The Bible is the definitive narrative and interpretation of God in history; it may be said to be God's story. This story is found in the two parts of the Bible, the two testaments. The Christian church's recognition of this goes back at least to the second century C.E. when a set of Christian and/or apostolic writings was set alongside the Jewish canon of scriptures. This second canon, or *new* testament, was believed to be the authoritative interpretation of what was believed to be the fulfillment of the former, or *old* testament, covenants and promises.

In so doing, affirmations and a denial of beliefs were made. In agreement with Judaism, the keeping of the Hebrew Scriptures in the Christian canon indicated that Christianity believed it shared with Jews a large part of the Great Story of the Bible. But it differed from Judaism and parted company with it by adding a second testament as the second part and completion of the Great Story. Christianity believed that the story and meaning of Jesus as set forth in its second or New Testament formed the continuation and fulfillment of the story of God in history. With Islam there are also significant differences. While affirming certain Old Testament events and characters, both Judaism and Christianity do not share in many of Islam's stories and interpretations derived from the Old Testament. Further still, Christianity and Islam differ significantly in their evaluation of the person and place of Jesus. Islam recognizes Jesus as a great prophet. But for Christianity, Jesus is much more than a prophet. Jesus is the final and complete revelation of the Living God, not the Qur'ān.

This brings us back to the consideration of the Bible as story. The questions may be asked: What kind of story is it? Why should we call it a story at all? Is it a true story? How so? In what way or ways do we treat story as foundational for faith in God?

First of all, the Bible may be said to be a record of the salvation of God; that is, it is the record or story of God's salvation or God's saving works in history. The Bible is not simply, or even *primarily,* a book that instructs us as human beings in how we should live; that is, telling us what is right and wrong, how we should treat one another and live in society. Certainly, it has parts that do this to some real degree (that is, the laws of the Torah; Proverbs; Jesus' Sermon on the Mount; the ethical specifics in the epistles). But in this, the Bible is not unique. Human beings in all kinds of cultures possess and formulate laws and customs that enable them to live well, peaceably, even humanely and compassionately with each other. Such instruction, important as it is, then, is not primarily what the Bible offers to its readers.

Rather, when one looks at the Bible—just taking a cue from Genesis or the Gospel of Luke, for instance—one immediately encounters a kind of history, a story about God at work in human history. This story more specifically begins with a revelation and promise to an ancient man named Abraham and culminates in that promise's fulfillment in one of his Jewish descendants named Jesus from Galilee. Thus, the Bible as a whole is distinguished or given its particular shape by its historical progression. The writer of Hebrews catches this emphasis with his opening verse: "*Long ago* God spoke to our ancestors in many and various ways by the prophets, but in *these last days* he has spoken to us by a Son..." (Heb. 1:1–2a). The apostle Paul in 2 Corinthians 1:20 says: "For in him every one of God's promises is a 'yes.' For this reason it is through him that we say the 'Amen,' to the glory of God." The biblical narrative tells of God who has acted in history, and this makes biblical faith very different from much mystical and Eastern religion in which history and historical events are not truly important. What gives biblical faith its foundation and shape is exactly that. History is crucially important because it is the theater of the progression of God's saving acts. In this way, then, we may understand the Bible to be record of God's salvation.

In line with this is a second observation. In the telling or unfolding of this progressive story, we need to be aware of what happens when we hear this story. The Bible's emphasis, or what it wants to impact us with foremost, is not instruction (laws, principles, ethics) but incarnation (God in our midst). The Bible is not so much an ever-increasing book of rules or regulations, but an ever-increasing book of revelation—the revelation of God himself, of God with us, of God for our salvation. After decades, even centuries, of hearing much of the narratives of both the Old and New Testaments as moral stories from which we should learn, it is sometimes difficult to remember that, more often than not, the real character in the story we need to be aware of is God, and the more wonderful truth of God's faithfulness in spite of human unfaithfulness. It is because God is faithful that the story goes on and on. The prologue of John's Gospel captures this dimension with the words of 1:17–18: "The law indeed was given through Moses; grace and truth came through Jesus Christ. No one has ever seen God. It is God the only Son, who is close to the Father's heart, who has made him known."

Consider this synopsis of the Story. It begins with God's address to humankind before the fall, continues afterward with a word of promise and hope (Gen. 3:16). The word is understood in Christian theology as enlarged upon and given specific action in the promise to Abraham in Genesis 12:1–3. It is repeated and expanded with each of the patriarchs—Isaac, Jacob, Joseph. It finds genuine fulfillment in part with the people of Israel whom God redeems from Egypt as promised to Abraham (Ex. 3:6ff). More fulfillment is realized when Israel conquers Canaan. Then, the promises enlarge more with the words given to both David and Solomon in terms of an eternal dynasty. These promises are picked up, repeated, and repromised throughout Israel's turbulent and disobedient history. The prophets speak again and again of what God has yet to do in fulfillment of his promises, and they even develop the growing theme of a new covenant and a new age for Israel, more glorious than anything known in its history so far. The New Testament claims that a more glorious new covenant and age has begun realization in the person and ministry—and especially the death and resurrection—of Jesus Christ.

For this reason, there is no great divide between the two testaments. Neither can they be truly understood apart from each other. The Old Testament is the first or preliminary part of the one story of the Bible; the New Testament is the second and complete part. To use a movie analogy, to drop the Old Testament from the New Testament is like trying to understand and appreciate the third part of the *Star Wars* trilogy, *Return of the Jedi*, without knowing the first two parts of the story, *Star Wars* and *The Empire Strikes Back*. But it is more profound than that. Because while the film trilogy has a progression and completion of its story from a narrative point of view, the Christian claim is that the story we read in the Bible beginning with the first or Old Testament must lead to the conclusion we read in the second testament. Or as Augustine expressed it, "The New is in the Old concealed; the Old is in the New revealed" (for example, *Reply to Faustus*,§ 76).

The Bible, then, is the record or history of redemption. Most Christians believe this record is also God's inspired revelation. And God's revelation—telling God's acts in two testaments—follows or sets forth this wonderful history in an overall story form, a story that is the unfolding of God's incarnation (God with us), the ways God has been with us, and how he finally and in fulfillment of all that went before ultimately came to us in the incarnate Son. "Grace and truth came through Jesus Christ."

The second aspect of considering the Bible as the history of redemption is the particular way that the central character of the great story is presented: the God who speaks and acts. The God of the Bible is a God who is bound to history, that is, though the God of the Bible is presented as the Lord over history and transcendent, distinct from the creation, this God has chosen in his freedom to do something in our history, and still does. From the time God "calls" Abraham to go forth from Ur to Canaan, to his "summons" to Moses to whom he reveals his own name and then leads the people of Israel out of a world ruled over by a pantheon of nature gods who can neither act nor speak, to his word given through the prophets of Israel, calling them to covenant obedience and the promise of a future deliverance, to the advent of the Son disclosed in the Word made flesh, the reader of the Bible is dealing with a God who is presented as acting and speaking in human history. Yes, the words of God are given through the words of human beings in history, but the source and authority of those words is God.

As such, we may see that the Bible presents us a "deed plus word" salvation. According to the Bible, God's redemptive acts are always accompanied by an interpretative word. The words are given in order to properly understand the acts. More often than not, the acts are preceded by a foretelling. God addresses humans, telling them what he is going to do. God then does what he says. Then, he explains what he has done in fulfillment of his original word. We may think of God's word to Moses, speaking of his coming redemption of Israel (Ex. 3), then the acts of redemption, and the interpretative word of fulfillment (Ex. 19). God reminds the prophet Amos that he shows his servants what he will do (3:7–8). Jesus, too, speaks of his coming death and resurrection; the events transpire as told in the gospels; then we see Jesus explaining what he has done (Lk. 24:44ff; the epistles are an even further and more detailed elaboration of the work of God in Christ).

There is a wonderful dynamic in the scripture. The words are connected to the acts. Without an interpretative word, the acts would be unclear as to their meaning. Without the acts of God but only words, one is left with revelation "hanging in the air." But the word-act-word pattern is seen again and again. Now, functionally, a particular word may be descriptive or it may be interpretive. And, all revelation is by necessity selective. Not everything has been said (Jn. 20:30; 21:25). Yet in fact, from the Christian viewpoint, the entire canon of Christian scripture is word-act-word in form. One may consider the entire Old Testament as the pre-word that sketches what God is going to do in redemption; then God acts decisively in the Christ event; finally, God speaks again, a post-word setting forth in inscripturated form the authoritative interpretative word that is the New Testament. In this manner, most Protestants believe that the Bible as a whole is the written Word of God, as its two-part canonical form presents us with the authoritative record and interpretation of the acts and words of God for redemption's sake. If we keep in mind this word-act-word shape, we will more accurately handle then the contours of the Bible.

A third observation we may make in looking at the Bible is to see it as "christocentric." This is to say that the whole story of the Bible, the words and acts of God, comes to its climax in the Christ-event. Everything in redemptive history converges in Christ from the New Testament perspective. The church's order of the New Testament canon bears this out. The gospels, though not chronologically written first, are at the front of the Christian part of the canon because they set forth the climactic story of redemption in the person of Christ. Four interpretative presentations—gospels—set forth the life, teaching, ministry, and most importantly, the death and resurrection of Jesus. We are presented with God incarnate, God with us, God in the act of redemption. The book of Acts continues the story of Christ now present with his church by the Spirit, and demonstrates that the gospel was meant for and made it to the whole world when it arrived in Rome. The epistles of the New

Testament then explain more fully the person and work of Christ, emphasizing more especially the meaning of his death and resurrection that the gospels actually only describe and whose deeper meaning can only be implied. For instance, while the gospels tell us of his coming death as a "ransom" and for "forgiveness," it remains for the epistles to more fully explain how and why this is the case. Finally, the canon of the New Testament closes triumphantly with an apocalypse, sounding the chord of Christ's ultimate sovereignty and the church's ultimate completion and perfection with God. In Revelation, the final chapter, or the epilogue, of God's story is foretold, but the reality remains to be accomplished in full.

Surveying the whole story of the Bible, we see that the route is not a straight or smooth one. The story takes twists and turns; there are apparent stops and starts. God's people make terrible mistakes and, humanly speaking, seem to jeopardize the whole enterprise of redemption. Yet, at other times, they make great strides and demonstrate wonderful faith and obedience and heroics. Like us, they praise God one moment, and in the next are sometimes stunned and perplexed at what God's acts and words mean. But more amazing still is the fact that the story continues. God remains faithful; God remains true; God picks up the pieces; God renews his covenant; God makes new promises; though men may fail, God does not. Certainly, it is this reality that makes the new beginning of the New Testament a story that is told with breathless wonder. When John the Baptist appears in the first century C.E., it is believed by many that God is on the move again redemptively (Lk. 3:15). We hold our breath through the awful weekend of crucifixion, only to be confronted with the bright light of resurrection. We wonder with the apostles what it is that has happened, and with them we strain at grasping the implications of Jesus' words: "Thus it is written, that the Messiah is to suffer and to rise from the dead on the third day…" (Lk. 24:46). As Luke explains, "[Jesus] said to them: "These are my words that I spoke to you while I was still with you—that everything written about me in the law of Moses, the prophets, and the psalms must be fulfilled'" (Lk. 24:44). The demands of the sinful situation we are in requires that God speak to us with a word of life and resurrection. As Paul says, "Faith comes from what is heard, and…what is heard comes through the word of Christ" (Rom. 10:17). Looking at the book of Acts, the recorded digests of the apostolic sermons demonstrate that they did the same thing, preaching the redemptive work of God in Christ from the Old Testament scriptures. The New Testament interprets the Old Testament. Remember Augustine's rubric: "The New is in the Old concealed; the Old is in the New revealed." The greater revelation of the New interprets the lesser revelation of the Old.

In speaking of the Bible as christocentric, we also want to say that it is not christo-monolithic; that Christ is not all that there is in the Bible. The great story leads to Christ, but the story involves from the beginning the people of God. God's people are part of the story, and their story in relation to God is valuable and interesting too. We should also observe that the Bible is not flat in its story or revelation. It is not all of equal importance; it is all important, but not equally so. Chronicles is important, but not as much as Isaiah. Philemon has significance, but not as much as Romans. Yet all of the Bible's parts are legitimately part of the story and important as such. We may say that the Bible has a certain terrain about it. Like life itself, there is the mundane and the spectacular; there is the common and the not-so-common; in fact, with God there is always the new and the "once-for-all"! Keeping in mind both the Great Story that is the Bible as a whole and the different terrain or parts of the Bible is a key consideration in its proper understanding and application.

Resulting Principles

1. The New Testament teaches that Old Testament revelation is a unified whole, a promise fulfilled by Christ. Jesus is "God with us," Prophet, Priest, King, Last Adam, Second Adam, Son of God, New Israel, Lamb of God, and so on. Christ fulfills all that was promised from the beginning (Gen. 12:1–3). And this fulfillment is given its particular focus by the "sufferings and glory of the Christ." In other words, the Old Testament is not broadly messianic, but specifically so in that way. There is no division of purpose, as though there were one purpose for Israel and one for the church. This is the error of dispensationalism.

2. The New Testament is the final expression of God's revelation, the completion of what was so only in part in the past. The Old Testament was always provisional; the New Testament is the climactic reality. The Old Testament is the bud; the New Testament the flower. The Old Testament is true in its part of the story; but the New Testament is the truth in full. This is why the Old Testament, while at one level it stands on its own with integrity as story, cannot, from the Christian perspective, be *ultimately understood* apart from the fuller story given by the New Testament.

3. Though the New Testament is christocentric, it is not christo-monolithic. This means that one does not press into the Old Testament texts what became realities in the New Testament. We honor the text in terms of where it is in progressive revelation and redemptive history (one doesn't make Genesis 1 teach the Trinity; one doesn't make the "angel of the LORD" into Christ; one doesn't make David speak as though he envisioned Jesus of Nazareth, but only figures that he could speak of as he could in his own time). Each part of the Old Testament is to be

understood as part of the ongoing history of revelation. But it is moving toward the event of Christ and his sufferings. We can now address the "terrain" of the Bible, or the literary forms of the Bible that give the Bible its multifaceted shape.

The Literary Forms of the Bible's Story

It is evident that, when one looks at the Bible, one is looking at a collection of different books; in fact, one may say, one finds a set of different literary genres. The great story of the Bible is given to us in a variety of literary forms. Some forms are, by their nature, more story in form than others (i.e., Exodus or Acts). Others do not take story form at all. How do they fit into a story approach to the Bible as a whole? This we must consider.

Recently, the Anglican scholar John Goldingay has produced several volumes that I believe are helpful in this task. His *Models for Interpretation of Scripture* provides an approach to the forms of the Bible that keeps the larger narrative or story form of the Bible as primary. The remainder of this article is largely dependent upon his book, and the reader is encouraged to study it to better understand the approach outlined here.

Narrative form constitutes the major part of the Bible,[1] and because this is so, it seems reasonable to understand narrative as the key form. One of my major convictions is that the Bible is a collection of living texts, living in the sense that they confront us or tell us of the living God with whom we have to do, and living in the sense that God employs the biblical texts to address us and meet us with himself and his truth. In a story, truth is presented to us in a particular way. Goldingay says,

> A story is told in such a way as to work for an audience—for example, by means of the order in which it relates events and the rate at which it releases information. It tantalizes, teases, challenges, upsets, and makes the audience think, forces it to come inside the story and involve itself with it if it is to understand.[2]

In telling the stories of the Bible or retelling them, or, say, in telling the parables of Jesus, it is the task of the interpreter to tell the stories in such a way that, as Goldingay says, "that what the story had the power to make happen to its [original] audience will happen to us."[3]

One of the most important aspects of the stories of the Bible that many a preacher/teacher forgets is drawing out how God is present and relates to people. More often than not, we have been told about the people in the Bible stories in order to be presented models of behavior. In other words, "here is how they lived before God; therefore, so should you." But often, that really is not why the story is there at all, though if context permits or implies, that may be a point. Usually, however, there is something much more important than example (bad or good) that is being communicated in the stories of the Bible. What that is—what really is the good news—is the picture of God relating to human beings. Again, Goldingay says: "[The stories] encourage and challenge us not by giving us a clearer picture of what we should or should not do, but by giving us a clearer picture of who God is."[4] The story of the Old Testament is first God's story in history, it is first the way God is to us, before it is the story of Adam, Moses, David, or Israel. This is true of the New Testament as well. The gospels confront us with the way God has come to us in Jesus. Thus, in interpreting the stories of the Bible, the stories, being told and retold, should put the hearer in the position of those for whom and despite whom God can and will achieve his gracious purposes. Generally, the stories of the Bible in narratives are meant to keep before us the person of God, and God as he was and is to us. The interpretation of story/narrative should first and foremost accomplish this.

The second category of scripture Goldingay speaks of is "instruction" or Torah.[5] Such materials are represented by the detailed instruction given to the people of God: specifically, the law in the Old Testament and the ethical teaching of both Jesus and the epistles of the New Testament. Such instruction, however, is to be understood in the larger setting of the story concerning God and Israel and then in the story of Jesus and his followers. The prophets of Israel emphasize the ethical values and principles such as holiness, justice, mercy, and love, which they see both explicit and implicit in the law. The theologians of the gospel such as Paul and John develop a whole perspective on life lived in light of the incarnation, cross, and resurrection of Jesus (i.e., Rom. 12:1–2; 1 Jn. 1:1–5).

Now the order of these two forms of scripture is important; they demonstrate something of the terrain of the Bible. The detailed instruction or ethics of religion are derivative from the ongoing story of salvation or redemptive history. Basically, the instruction in life for the people of God (Israel and then the church) are reflections of what the great acts of God inspire: in summary, love of God and neighbor. In that sense, then, this part of the biblical message is addressed to the accidental particularities of the human situation at specific moments and in specific cultures. The Bible contains much instruction in regard to society, family, relationships, sexual behavior, property, the state, and other situations. Many of these commands applied to Israel as a nation under God or to the first century Christians in desperate times. Such specific situations are not ours today. Many commands given in the instruction portions of the Bible do not specifically apply to us in our times. "You are not to boil a kid in its mother's milk" (Ex. 23:19) is an instruction famously reported three times in the law, and yet its reason or meaning is not entirely clear to modern interpreters. At the same time, the commands of the Bible are not random. They are concrete expressions of love and obedience/obligation to God and neighbor at specific times. Part of the responsibility and challenge for us as modern day interpreters of the Bible is to discern the principle underlying the concrete situations that the specific laws reflect, and then turn that principle into concrete commands applicable to our own situations.

As such, "living interpretations" or contemporary applications must be discerned from the once-given text. The practice of this is seen in the Bible itself, as the prophets make contemporary applications of earlier-given Torah. Jesus, too, reapplies the Torah to his times, often challenging the misapplication of the Torah by his contemporaries. The apostles also must translate the moral principles reflected in the Torah to Jewish and non-Jewish Christian believers in the Greco-Roman world. Jesus himself confirms the more important principles of the Torah, but often sets principles and commands in the law over against each other in a certain priority (for example, strict observance of the fourth commandment over against human need or the acts of compassion). He broadened and extended the commandments, making clear that justice begins with the words of the Torah, but goes beyond its explicit definitions in commands; God's desire and purposes can have a greater expression that former expressions allow ("love your enemies, and pray for those who persecute you," Mt. 5:44). Still further, keeping the ongoing story of redemption in view, we see in the story of Jesus that the people of God are soon to be defined by a greater gift than the Torah, by Jesus himself who is the ultimate expression of God's mercy and justice, truth and faith. Speaking of himself, he says, "Take my yoke [instead of the Law] upon you, and learn from me," (Mt. 11:29).

The apostle Paul also does not simply restate the law of Israel as the way of understanding the way of Jesus' followers. In fact, his teaching is that the church is not under the law of Moses at all. The age of the law, which formerly belonged to the people of Israel, has given way to a new age of grace in the kingdom/reign of Christ (Rom. 6:14).

The key principles of law that underline the Mosaic law—love of God and neighbor—remain in effect, but now even they take on a renewed understanding with the salvation demonstrated in Christ. Love of God and neighbor will look somewhat different for the new Christian community of the church. Here, we may see how grasping the centrality of Christ in scripture comes to the fore. There is a kind of canon within the canon, and that inner canon that interprets or makes sense of the other is Christ and the gospel. The texts of the Bible in this area, then, come alive when by the leading of God's Spirit we can discern the principles embodied in specific scriptural commands or guidelines and transfer those principles to our own times and translate them into meaningful and applicable instruction (Torah) for the people of God today. Then, the principles of love of God and neighbor are replicated in our lives and situations that are helpful and beneficial to the body of Christ and genuinely manifest his gospel.

Prophecy is the third category of scripture that may be seen in the context of the great story of scripture.[6] Generally speaking, prophecy may be understood as the inspired speech of the servants of God who speak the word into specific situations in which they live. In the case of the Old Testament prophets, they also speak of what God is going to do in the future, sometimes depending on the response of Israel, sometimes in spite of Israel's response. To interpret them correctly largely involves understanding the prophets' historical and pastoral situations they had to address. Then, it may be that one must move from the historical particularity of the prophet who speaks God's concerns in that situation to something comparable in our own time. To create for the hearer something akin to the existential moment of the prophet's hearers for one's own time takes skill and care. Yet to do so allows for the prophet's challenging words of the past to be heard again in the present. Other cases of Old Testament prophecy may mean demonstrating their fulfillment in the New Testament, the development of the story as the New Testament understands it. As Paul says, "For in him every one of God's promises is a 'yes'" (2 Cor. 1:20).

The fourth category according to Goldingay is experiential/ revelatory scripture.[7] This includes: the Psalms, written in light of the experience of God; and wisdom literature (Job, Proverbs, Ecclesiastes), which are reflections on life in light of certain convictions. Apocalyptic literature (Daniel 7—12; Revelation) is another kind of literary form that is also reflective of life lived before God, particularly in the context of hostility or persecution. Apocalyptic requires the interpreter to discern the symbolic language of the "seer" and help the hearer to "see" like the writer. Goldingay also places parts of the epistle in this category, since they also "testify to the human experience of their writers, depend on revelation they have received, and mediate their reflection on experience and revelation."[8]

Whatever the particular passage, all scriptures may be seen in the context of the great story of the Bible. As such, it is absolutely necessary in interpreting the scriptures to listen to each scripture as it tells or takes its place in the story. To listen to the story correctly means to accept it on its own literary terms. The scriptures tell the story and stories of God their own way. Thus, the literary form of each passage is key to "hearing" that part of the story well. Here, the grammatical-historical and literary-theological tools are helpful. Further, we may say that the Bible is interested in history as well, but history on its own terms, that is history with theological interpretation. Such an emphasis is not meant to disregard the historical dimension of the Bible. Indeed, the texts clue us in to this dimension. The great story of the Bible is not a nonhistorical myth. It is not a story ungrounded in history. The concern for the historical is real and legitimate. It is a story that has taken place in our world where our stories happen; it is meant to address us who are part of the same ongoing history. The great promise of the Bible and the gospel is that the God of history has entered history for our good, our redemption; and that means that the God revealed in Jesus Christ calls us to himself by his grace and takes us up into his story, our lives into his. The story of God has largely been told in the Bible; it is by that story we are to understand ourselves and our stories. But the final chapter is yet to be written. The promise of the New Testament is that the kingdom of God is yet to more completely manifest itself. In that day, history as we know it will be transformed and there will be "loud voices in heaven saying, 'The kingdom of the world has become the kingdom of our Lord and of his Messiah…'" (Rev. 11:15). "Amen. Come, Lord Jesus" (22:20).

Finally, we may say that in approaching the Bible as "story," we do so in a way reminiscent of the sixteenth-century Protestant Reformer Martin Luther. David Steinmetz's contribution in this book (chap. 8) captures Luther's understanding of the Word of God in scripture with the story emphasis along the same lines as meant here. In the Protestant tradition, the preaching of the Bible and its stories is a kind of sacrament in which God meets us with his grace. For Luther, it is through preaching that the creative-redemptive Word of God is spoken afresh and with power for our lives. The redeeming Christ is made accessible to us through preaching the "poor and simple stories" of the Bible. Steinmetz reminds us that the Reformers were not only preaching the Bible and its stories in order that they might preach events of the past. They were preaching the Bible and its stories because they believed it to be the vehicle in which Christ the Word of God is present in creaturely human speech and transforms the current state of our lives.

As an heir of this theology of the Word, it is my belief that the largely story-and-narrative form of the Bible is not merely a historical accident. Certainly, there is something profound and wondrous about the human desire to tell and listen to stories. Perhaps, it is part of the "hard wiring" of what we are as human beings created by God and who are addressed by the same God in his redeeming work in Christ. If so, then, we should pray for the grace "for ears to hear."

Suggestions for Further Reading

Campbell, Charles L. *Preaching Jesus: New Directions for Homiletics in Hans Frei's Postliberal Theology*. Grand Rapids: Eerdmans, 1997.

Childs, Brevard S. *Biblical Theology of the Old and New Testaments: Theological Reflections on the Christian Bible*. Minneapolis: Fortress Press, 1992.

Goldingay, John. *Models for Interpretation of Scripture.* Grand Rapids: Eerdmans, 1995.

Greidanus, S. *The Modern Preacher and the Ancient Text.* Grand Rapids: Eerdmans, 1988.

McConnell, Frank. ed. *The Bible and the Narrative Tradition.* New York: Oxford University Press, 1986.

Steinmetz, D. C. "The Superiority of Pre-Critical Exegesis." In *A Guide to Contemporary Hermeneutics.* Edited by Donald McKim. Grand Rapids: Eerdmans, 1986.

Thistleton, A. C. *New Horizons in Hermeneutics.* Grand Rapids: Zondervan, 1992.

---

[1]John Goldingay, *Models for Interpretation of Scripture* (Grand Rapids: Eerdmans, 1995), 13–86.

[2]Ibid., 37.

[3]Ibid., 39.

[4]Ibid., 58.

[5]Ibid., 87–138.

[6]Ibid., 139–99.

[7]Ibid., 201–87.

[8]Ibid., 203.

10

Scripture in Modern Judaism

Michael A. Meyer

Let me begin by explaining some terms that are basic for understanding what we Jews mean by scripture. The first of these is the Hebrew word Torah. It is not easy to translate or to explain because it has multiple meanings. Often it is mistranslated as "law," likening it to the Greek word *nomos*, which does mean "law." This has the effect of furthering the mistaken idea that Judaism is a religion of law whereas Christianity is a religion of love. But, in fact, love is just as important in Judaism as it is in Christianity, and Christianity likewise has a tradition of law—of church or canon law. Torah comes from a Hebrew word whose root means "to teach." The word for teacher in Hebrew is *moreh*, which comes from that same root (y-r-h) in Hebrew. Thus, Torah means teaching—teaching in a wide sense, broader than doctrine, including practice as well as theology.

Over the course of time the word Torah acquired various meanings. In the most specific sense it refers to the Pentateuch, that is to say, the five books of Moses, the first part of the Hebrew Bible: Genesis, Exodus, Leviticus, Numbers, and Deuteronomy. These books of the Torah, in the form of a scroll handwritten by a scribe, are to be found inside the "ark," a kind of cabinet located at the front of every synagogue. Portions of the

191

Torah scroll are read regularly at worship services by either the rabbi, the cantor, or a layperson. At the life cycle event when a Jewish boy or girl reaches religious maturity, called Bar Mitzvah for a boy and Bat Mitzvah for a girl, the young person is called up to the pulpit, the scroll is taken out of the ark, and that boy or girl says the blessings before and after the reading, and reads a part of the Torah portion that constitutes the scriptural reading for that week. Thus, the five books of Moses are not only an important part of our Jewish heritage, but an integral element of our liturgy.

But the meaning of Torah may extend beyond the Pentateuch. Traditionally, Torah is understood to consist of two parts—written and oral. By the Written Torah we mean once again the five books of Moses, which according to traditional Judaism were revealed in their totality to Moses at Mount Sinai. But according to Jewish tradition, as still preserved in Orthodox Judaism, Moses received from God not only the Written Torah, but also an Oral Torah, which elaborates upon the Written Torah and which was only much later written down in the form of the Talmud.

Finally, there is an even broader definition of Torah that takes the word to mean Jewish teaching in general, not alone what was revealed at Mount Sinai. This use of Torah includes all of the traditions that accumulated over the centuries: Jewish philosophy and mysticism, the ethical literature, and legal literature—all those elements make up Jewish tradition, what one might call the "canon" of Judaism.

If one begins, however, not with the Hebrew word Torah but instead translates the English word scripture into Hebrew, one gets a different Hebrew term that is of particular interest. The Hebrew equivalent of "scripture" is the word *mikra*. Now, mikra comes from a Hebrew word which, unlike the word scripture (cf. "script"), has nothing to do with writing. Mikra comes from a Hebrew root that has two meanings: "reading," and "seeking" or "calling out." What this means is that for us Torah is not a fixed, written text. To be sure, it was written down. But as "reading" rather than "writing" it allows for new interpretations that arise from new readings of the text. Moreover, mikra continually "calls out" like a voice to the individual Jew and to the Jewish people. It serves as a channel by which God's voice calls to us. Thus, it is not really scripture, but voice. Torah as mikra means listening and answering in dialogue.

A third crucial term is *tanakh*, a Hebrew acronym that takes in Torah, in the narrow sense meaning the five books of Moses; *neviim*, which is the Hebrew word for the prophetic literature (Joshua, Judges, Samuel, Kings, and the classical prophets—Isaiah, Jeremiah, Ezekiel, and the twelve minor prophets); and *ketuvim*, or "writings," which is the name for all the other books in the Hebrew Bible (Psalms, Proverbs, Job, etc.). Tanakh is the word that represents in Hebrew what in English we call the Hebrew Bible, or for Christians, the Old Testament.

Finally, we need to introduce four connected Hebrew terms that are essential to understanding the varieties of biblical interpretation in Judaism. These were developed by the Rabbis, the Jewish scholars and sages of ancient times. The first of these is the *peshat*, or simple interpretation. This kind of interpretation tries to get at what the text says without any homiletic intent, without attempting to apply it to contemporary problems or events. Peshat represents the most basic level of biblical interpretation and has held a place of honor especially in those periods of Jewish history that tended toward rational understanding. The second is called *remez*, which literally means "hint," and refers to symbolic exegesis. Is there something that the text does not say explicitly, but at which it hints when we read it carefully? Is there a symbolic message behind the simple message? The third form of exegesis is called *derash*. It refers to the homiletic meaning of the text. Just as a Christian pastor might desire to convey more than the simple meaning of a text, from the New Testament for example, using it to teach a moral or religious lesson, so, too, rabbis and Jewish preachers from their pulpits look not only for the simple meaning of a text and what it may hint at, but also for how it may shed light on the issues of daily life. And fourth there is *sod*, the mystical or esoteric meaning. Seeking a hidden message in the text, one that points to mysteries of God and the cosmos, is an enterprise that has been limited to mystical movements in Judaism such as the Kabbalah and Hasidism. Of the four types of interpretation, the first and the third, the simple meaning and the homiletic one, have been the most prominent in modern times. And, indeed, it is to modern Judaism and its background that we must now turn.

Scripture and the Modern Branches of Judaism

There is not a single modern Judaism any more than there is any one modern Protestantism. As there are Presbyterians, Methodists, and Congregationalists, so there are various denominations in modern Judaism. The three largest are each distinguished by a particular approach to scripture. Modern Orthodox Judaism is the least critical in its treatment of the biblical text. The middle-of-the-road movement called Conservative Judaism is less fundamentalist or traditionalist in its theology and its approach to the Bible. And the third of the major Jewish streams, Reform Judaism, lies on the liberal end of the spectrum, fully open to biblical criticism. Thus, when we speak of modern Judaism, we must distinguish among the different groups that share the designation. There are approximately 13 million Jews in the world today. Of the five and a half million Jews in the United States, about three million are religiously active. Of those three million, only about 10 to 15 percent are Orthodox, with the rest almost evenly divided between Conservative and Reform. In Israel, where there are more than four and one half million Jews, the percentage of Orthodox is somewhat higher, but still not over 20 percent.

Modern Judaism begins, not surprisingly, with the Enlightenment, at the end of the eighteenth century. Its origins lie there because then Jews began a process of leaving the medieval ghetto, which removed them from the non-Jewish culture around them. For the first time, Jews began to enter the larger society and become an integral part of the modern world. They began to identify themselves culturally as Europeans while politically they developed an allegiance to the states in which they lived, whether France, England, or Prussia. They came to the conclusion that Judaism under the new circumstances must follow new paths to meet the challenges of new conditions, and one of the paths of change was to give the Bible renewed prominence. During the late Middle Ages the great Talmudic academies of central and eastern Europe had placed less pedagogic emphasis on the Bible than on the rabbinic literature, specifically on the Talmud and its commentaries. The student of Judaism spent much more time studying rabbinic tradition, the Oral Torah, than studying the Written Torah. That emphasis began to change in the late eighteenth and early nineteenth centuries when Jews increasingly returned to the Bible as central in Jewish education, indeed as the fountainhead of Judaism. In part this occurred because central and western European Jews increasingly wanted to be seen as belonging to the larger European world. The Hebrew Bible could serve as a common foundation for Jews and Christians.

What role, then, has scripture played in modern Orthodoxy? Like the conservative tendencies within Protestantism and Catholicism, Orthodox Judaism rejects biblical criticism. Orthodox Jews, whether in the modern world or the medieval, hold steadfastly to a doctrine called "Torah from heaven." That phrase is taken to mean that both the Written and the Oral Torah were quite literally revealed by God to Moses at Sinai, and therefore are wholly of divine origin, though not in the same literalist fashion as for those Protestants who believe in inerrancy of the text. Thus Orthodox Jews reject all modern attempts to suggest that any portion of the Torah was not written by Moses at God's behest. Jewish Orthodoxy does not allow for the position that the Pentateuch consists of different sources that were written at various times.

While Orthodoxy rejects biblical criticism, contemporary Conservative and Reform Judaism do not. In this they were partially anticipated by one of the medieval Jewish biblical commentators, Abraham ibn Ezra, who lived in Spain during the twelfth century. Ibn Ezra wondered about certain passages in the Bible that he had difficulty in ascribing to Moses. For example, he thought that references such as "the Canaanites were then in the land" (Gen. 12:6; 13:7) reflected a post-Mosaic composition, and he questioned how Moses could write about his own death (Deut. 34:5–8). Later, in the seventeenth century, Spinoza openly suggested that Moses did not write the Pentateuch at all, but that its author was really Ezra the Scribe (fifth century B.C.E.), during the period of the Second Temple, basing his writing on oral sources that had come down to him. Then, in the following centuries, as rationalism and historical criticism penetrated Jewish thought, as it did Christian, liberal-minded rabbis began to wonder whether it was justifiable to take literally the creation and miracle stories in the Hebrew Bible.

A leading rabbi of the Jewish Reform movement in Germany, Abraham Geiger, confided his growing doubts in a letter to a friend in 1836. He wrote, "The Talmud and the Bible too, that collection of books, most of them so splendid and uplifting, perhaps the most exalting of all literature of human authorship, can no longer be viewed as of divine origin." He went on to say,

> For the love of heaven, how much longer can we continue
> this deceit to expound the stories of the Bible from the pulpit
> over and over again as actual historical happenings, to accept
> as supernatural events of world import stories which we
> ourselves have relegated to the realm of legend and to derive
> teaching from them or at least to use them as the basis for
> sermons and texts? How much longer will we continue to
> pervert the spirit of the child with these tales that distort the
> natural good sense of tender youth?[1]

Clearly, Geiger felt the need to get away from the literal meaning of the text, which an increasing number of Jews could no longer accept, and yet to recognize the Bible's ongoing centrality and religious significance.

Until relatively recently, the Conservative movement made a clear distinction with regard to historical criticism between the Written and the Oral Torah. While criticism could legitimately be applied to the Talmud, it was considered sacrilegious to apply it to the Pentateuch. In fact, even the founder of Reform Judaism's American seminary, the Hebrew Union College, Isaac Mayer Wise, would not allow biblical criticism to be taught during the years that he was the president of the institution from 1875 until 1900. But today, for both Conservative and Reform Jews the historical study of the Bible is considered legitimate. The message of the Bible, not the specific origins of its text, is what really matters to these denominations. And that God-inspired message is independent of whether the five books of Moses were entirely written by Moses or whether there were many authors writing over a longer period of time.

In the course of time it became characteristic of Reform Judaism in particular to transfer its religious emphasis away from Torah (in the narrow sense) to the prophetic literature in the Bible. Why was it that this particular branch of Judaism should find special religious inspiration in Isaiah, Jeremiah, Hosea, and Amos? First of all, because of the universalism of much of the prophetic literature. As Jews became more and more a part of the modern world, they wanted to demonstrate that Judaism was not a tribal religion, not a religion that was focused predominantly on matters specific to Judaism, but that it was and is a religion that embraces all humanity. And where could one better find that humanity-embracing view than in prophets like Isaiah and Micah? "In the days to come the Mount of the LORD's House shall stand firm above the mountains…many people shall go…They shall beat their swords into plowshares and their spears into pruning hooks…" (Isa. 2:2–4; Mic. 4:1–4, JPS). And so the Reform movement put more and more of its emphasis upon prophetic passages, such as the famous verse from Micah: "He has told you, O man, what is good, And what the LORD requires of you: Only to do justice And to love goodness, And to walk modestly with your God." (Mic. 6:8, JPS). A second reason why Reform Judaism turned to the prophets was their preaching of social justice. Repeatedly, the prophets remind their listeners to be concerned for the downtrodden in society, for the widow, the orphan, the person who has lost his lands and has to sell himself into slavery (cf. Isa. 1:17; Am. 5:10–15). Given its rationalism and its focus on morality rather than ritual, it is therefore not surprising that Reform Jews gave preference to the prophetic literature over the specific commandments, particularly those concerning ritual observance, such as the dietary laws, which are so much stressed in the Pentateuch.

We should also take note of a modern approach to Jewish Scripture that comes neither from Reform or Conservative Judaism nor from Jewish Orthodoxy. It originates in Zionism, a secular expression of Jewish identity and the movement that brought about the establishment of the state of Israel in 1948. The Hebrew Bible assumed great importance for Zionists, but for national rather than religious reasons. If within the literature of the Bible traditional Jews stressed the five books of Moses, starting the curriculum of small Jewish children with the book of Leviticus, and if Reform Jews tended to emphasize the literary prophets, Zionism looked to a different set of books within the Hebrew Bible, those that possessed a national historical character: the book of Joshua, the two books of Samuel, the books of Kings. Those works tied ancient Israel to its land. Zionist intellectuals, in their reading of the Bible, spoke about God's promise to Abraham, about Joshua's conquest of the land, about the military exploits of the Judges, and, of course, about Kings Saul, David, and Solomon. These were texts little studied either by traditional Jews, who focused upon ritual commandments, or by universalistically oriented Reform Jews. The Bible became for Zionism the book of Israel's ancient national history. Most Zionists gave the Bible a secular interpretation, but that in no way diminished its importance in their eyes. David Ben Gurion, the first prime minister of Israel, participated regularly in a Bible study group that sought to relate the modern state of Israel to its ancient predecessor, which served to legitimate its existence. Similarly, the popular practice of biblical archaeology in Israel today, which uncovers remnants of buildings constructed by ancient Israelites, establishes a visible link between ancient and modern Israel.

Reflections on Scripture in Reform Judaism

Let us focus now on Reform Judaism, the most liberal of the movements in contemporary Judaism, in order to describe a modern Jewish approach to the Torah. When the Reform movement crystallized in the United States toward the end of the nineteenth century, anthropology was just beginning to make its appearance in American colleges and universities. The new discipline suggested that religion should be studied comparatively. Increasingly, religious thinkers therefore began to distinguish between the primitive religions studied by anthropologists and their own religion, which they deemed more sophisticated. Primitive religions were judged to be such as involved a great deal of ritual behavior, such as performing symbolic acts with hands and feet, wearing ritual garments, and the like. These acts within the monotheistic religions were seen as comparable to shamanism, fetishism, and the use of talismans. The "higher religions" were thought to be those that employed an absolute minimum of symbols. They were strictly a matter of the mind and the heart. Their message was conveyed in the words of the sermon, their longings in the words of the prayers.

But Judaism is a religion rich in symbols, none of them more central that the scroll containing the five books of Moses that is read regularly in the synagogue. Most Reform congregations continued to venerate the scroll, keeping it in its designated place in the ark behind the pulpit. In the last decades of the nineteenth century, however, there were some radicals within the Reform movement who saw the Torah scroll, too, as a primitive relic even as they continued to venerate its ethical message. In 1894, the executive board of one congregation, Temple Sinai in Chicago, Illinois, went so far as to pass the following resolution: "Whereas the congregation is the owner of the Torah scroll, the use of which in the service has been dispensed with, therefore be it resolved that the Torah scroll be donated to The University of Chicago as part of its Semitic library." What they were saying was that what really counts is the message in the books and not the symbol of the scroll. As the latter, the Torah belongs in a museum. Although most congregations kept their Torah scrolls, Temple Sinai was not the only one that began to read the weekly scriptural passages from a printed Pentateuch instead of chanting it from the handwritten parchment scroll. In some cases, they also did the readings only in English rather than beginning with the Hebrew text and only then adding an English translation.

In recent years, however, the Reform movement has moved sharply in the opposite direction. Today at a Bar or Bat Mitzvah ceremony the Torah scroll is taken out of the ark by the rabbi, given first to the grandparents, who represent the oldest generation (unless there are great-grandparents present). Then the grandparents pass the scroll on to the parents, and the parents, in turn, pass it to the boy or girl who is becoming a Bar or Bat Mitzvah. This novel ceremony is indicative of how the scroll of the Torah has fully regained its symbolic value. Even though it contains only the five books of Moses, when the scroll is passed down from grandparents to parents to children, it in fact represents Torah in the broadest sense, namely, as the totality of the Jewish teaching to which the Jewish community regularly rededicates itself. It is also interesting to note that at the time of the civil rights marches in the South and those protesting the Vietnam war—the marches in which Martin Luther King participated along with other Christian clergymen—it was not unusual for a rabbi to carry a Torah scroll on his arm, in this case because that scroll represented the collective religious conscience of the Jewish people.

There is no better source for illustrating how the meaning of Torah has changed within Reform Judaism than the official statements or "platforms" of the movement that have been adopted from time to time. The first one was adopted at a meeting in Pittsburgh in 1885, the second one in Columbus, Ohio, in 1937, and another in San Francisco in 1976. One of the planks of each of these major platforms has, of course, been the place of Torah or Bible. The 1885 Torah plank in many ways reflects the attitude toward religion that was described in the story of the Torah scroll at Temple Sinai. Its text reads:

> We recognize in the Bible the record of the consecration of the Jewish people to its mission as priest of the one God, and value it as the most potent instrument of religious and moral instruction. We hold that the modern discoveries of scientific researches in the domains of nature and history are not antagonistic to the doctrines of Judaism, the Bible reflecting the primitive ideas of its own age, and at times clothing its conception of Divine Providence and justice dealing with man in miraculous narratives.

Notice that the word used is "Bible," not "Torah," the latter being a Hebrew word. In this period Reform Jews wanted to employ language that Jews and Christians had in common and so preferred to speak of the Bible. This Bible is understood to be a human product in its literary form: "the record of the consecration of the Jewish people to its mission

Scripture in Modern Judaism 199

as priest of the one God." It represents the evidence of ancient Israel consecrating itself to God and to its mission as a "kingdom of priests and a holy nation" (Ex. 19:6). It is also valued as the "most potent instrument of religious and moral instruction." Notice that the Bible is here portrayed as an educational tool, the instrument by which the Jews are able to fulfill their religious mission as messengers of God. It is not, however, defined as divine revelation. The Torah is not understood, as Orthodox Jews would have it, as a document that came down "from heaven." Reform Jews at the end of the nineteenth century were very much concerned to justify religion in the face of science. They wanted to harmonize the Bible with geology and evolutionary biology. The assertion made in the platform is that the modern discoveries of science in the fields of nature and also of historical studies are not antagonistic to the doctrines of Judaism. How is this possible? Because the Bible reflects "the primitive ideas of its own age." In other words, the Bible does not contain truth in those areas that would conflict with science. On such subjects as how the universe came into existence, for example, the Bible has only a primitive understanding. It also has primitive ideas with regard to certain religious practices such as animal sacrifices, for example, or with regard to human institutions like slavery, which, of course, exists in the Bible, albeit in a milder form than elsewhere in the ancient world. The framers of the Pittsburgh platform thus held that there were ideas in the Bible that may have been religiously significant and morally sanctioned in ancient times, but were not applicable to their own. Biblical ideas, moreover, such as those of divine providence and God's justice in dealing with human beings, were often clothed in miraculous narratives, whether it be the parting of the Reed Sea or some of the stories told about Elijah. The Reform movement of this early period determined that the Bible retained its importance as a document that shows that the Jewish people at an early point in its history dedicated itself to the one God and to the belief in a single humanity and made the dissemination of ethical monotheism its own religious mission. The Bible was not a document containing truth on matters susceptible to scientific inquiry, but it was the principal source of religious truth, both theological and moral.

Fifty years later, in 1937, Reform Judaism adopted a new religious platform. This time it was divided into the three principal categories of Jewish theology: God, our Creator and Redeemer; Torah, our teaching; and Israel, the people dedicated to God. Here the plank on Torah begins not with the Jewish people, as it did in 1885, but with God. It reads:

God reveals Himself not only in the majesty, beauty and orderliness of nature, but also in the vision and moral striving of the human spirit. Revelation is a continuous process, confined to no one group and to no one age. Yet the people of

Israel, through its prophets and sages, achieved unique
insight in the realm of religious truth. The Torah, both written
and oral, enshrines Israel's ever-growing consciousness of
God and of the moral law. It preserves the historical precedents, sanctions and norms of Jewish life, and seeks to mold it
in the patterns of goodness and of holiness. Being products of
historical processes, certain of its laws have lost their binding
force with the passing of the conditions that called them forth.
But as a depository of permanent spiritual ideals, the Torah
remains the dynamic source of the life of Israel. Each age has
the obligation to adapt the teachings of the Torah to its basic
needs in consonance with the genius of Judaism.

This statement not only begins with God but freely uses a concept
that does not occur in the 1885 plank on Torah, namely, the idea of revelation. In Judaism, God's revelation is to be found, first of all, in nature.
In the words of the psalmist: "How many are the things you have made,
O LORD; with wisdom you have made them all. The earth is full of Your
creations" (Ps. 104:24, JPS). But God's revelation also manifests itself
through scripture. God is not only the God of nature; God is also revealed "in the vision and moral striving of the human spirit," namely in
that which is revealed to human beings by God through Torah. God's
revelation is not, however, limited to Jews—or to Christians or to Muslims. It is open to all human beings who are prepared to listen for it.
Thus, the platform declares that revelation is a continuous process, not
limited to Mount Sinai, confined to no one group and to no one age. As
God is always present, today not less than in biblical times, so too is
revelation always a possibility. Nonetheless, the people of Israel through
its prophets and sages achieved unique insight. The Bible reveals a message that was hitherto absent from the history of humanity. It is not to be
found in the history of Canaan or of ancient Egypt. The Torah, here understood broadly as both the Written and the Oral, enshrines Israel's
ever-growing consciousness of God and of the moral law. This is sometimes called progressive revelation, meaning that we learn more about
God, God's ways and God's will, in the course of history. Revelation
does not stop with the Bible. Thus, the Columbus platform says that the
Torah, broadly conceived, "enshrines Israel's ever-growing consciousness of God and of the moral law." The ancient Israelites believed that
slavery was just; our biblical ancestors were certain that the way to serve
God was through animal sacrifices offered upon an altar in the temple
in Jerusalem. But Reform Jews no longer believe either in the moral legitimacy of slavery or in the religious significance of animal sacrifices.
Clearly our religious sensibilities have changed, our own moral conscience has been educated. But that education is itself to be understood
as revelation. God not only inspired the Bible, but also postbiblical understandings of God and God's will.

According to the words of the platform, the Torah "preserves the historical precedents, sanctions and norms of Jewish life, and seeks to mold it in the patterns of goodness and holiness." In other words, Torah is not only the fount of tradition, but the process by which that tradition is shaped and reshaped in the light of our changing views of what is right and what is sacred. Torah is seen as the product of historical processes—"certain of its laws have lost their binding force with the passing of the conditions that called them forth"— but it is also a "depository of permanent spiritual ideals," ideals such as those represented by the prophets or by the famous verse in Leviticus commanding: "Love your neighbor as yourself" (Lev. 19:18). These ideals remain firm in all ages and are not subject to historical evolution. Thus, as the "depository of permanent spiritual ideals," the Torah, in its sense as Bible, remains the dynamic source of the light of Israel. Each age has the obligation to adapt the teachings of Torah to its spiritual and moral needs in consonance with the genius of Judaism. That is seen to be the task of interpretation: to take a document that goes back three thousand years and more and to make it alive and meaningful for the present day.

The third platform of the Reform movement, adopted in San Francisco in 1976, likewise has a plank entitled Torah. What is of particular interest here is that the sequence of the triad—God, Torah, Israel—differs from that of the previous platforms. The 1885 platform began with the people of Israel that dedicated itself to God. The 1937 platform began with God who reveals Torah to Israel. This statement presents the sequence as follows:

> Torah results from the relationship between God and the Jewish people. The records of our earliest confrontations are uniquely important to us. Lawgivers and prophets, historians and poets gave us a heritage whose study is a religious imperative and whose practice is our chief means to holiness. Rabbis and teachers, philosophers and mystics, gifted Jews in every age amplified the Torah tradition. For millennia, the creation of Torah has not ceased and Jewish creativity in our time is adding to the chain of tradition.

In setting forth the idea that Torah results from the relationship between God and the Jewish people, this platform suggests that Torah is not a finished revelation that God gave to Israel at Sinai as one might give a book to a friend. But neither is it a book that the ancient Israelites simply dreamed up on their own. Rather it was only out of the encounter between God and Israel, out of the dialogue between God and the Jewish people in which each played an active role, that Torah emerged. Torah is neither purely divine nor purely human. It results from the encounters of ancient Israel with God. It is these encounters—or this relationship—that have produced Torah and continue to produce it in the present and the future.

In order to fully understand the nature of this relationship we must introduce one more important concept: in Hebrew *berit*, in English covenant. In Judaism covenant refers to the nature of the ongoing relationship of mutual obligation between God and Israel. A religious Jew feels himself or herself to be in covenant with God. The covenantal relationship with God requires Jews to perform commandments (in Hebrew: *mitzvot*), some of a ritual nature, others moral in character. The Torah indicates the nature of those obligations that God has placed upon Israel in order to fulfill its side of the covenant and likewise states God's promises to Israel. The records of our earliest encounters with God, embodied in all three parts of the Hebrew Bible, are uniquely important to us as Jews and therefore regular study of the Bible is a religious imperative.

For Judaism, whether Reform, Conservative, or Orthodox, the study of scripture is not something done merely out of intellectual or aesthetic interest, as one reads a book of history or a play by Shakespeare. The Jew reads the Bible because he or she is religiously obligated to do so. The 1976 platform calls it a practice that is our "chief means to holiness." Unlike truth, which is a cognitive category, and goodness, which refers to morality, holiness is a religious category. If a Jew wants to be a religious person, to be counted as part of the holy people of Israel, then understanding scripture is essential.

"Rabbis and teachers, philosophers and mystics" in the text of the platform refers to the Oral Torah, to the various streams within the later tradition, and to all the Jewish teachings that have gained veneration down through the centuries. In each age religiously gifted Jews amplified the Torah tradition. The creation of Torah has not ceased; Jewish creativity in our time, as well, is adding to the "chain of tradition."

That metaphor of a chain deserves a moment's thought as well. It suggests that from Moses, through the prophets and the rabbis of the Talmud, and down to our own time, we understand our tradition to be like a chain to which we, through our own religious actions, attach the most recent links. In scriptural terms, we are the Bible's contemporary expositors, attached to all those commentators that came before us and, in turn, a link to which the next generation can attach itself.

Moshe Greenberg, Abraham Cronbach, and Martin Buber on Scripture

Representing very different approaches to the text, three important modern Jewish thinkers are among those who have forged significant new links in the chain of tradition as it applies to Jewish scriptural interpretation. Moshe Greenberg (born 1928) grew up in New York, earned his doctorate from the University of Pennsylvania, where he became a professor of Bible, and then moved to Israel where he taught Bible at the

Hebrew University in Jerusalem. Although associated with the Conservative movement in Judaism, some of his ideas are applicable to the modern Jewish approach to scripture in general.

In his article "On Teaching the Bible in Religious Schools" (*Jewish Education* 29 [1959]: 45–53) Greenberg asks: How can one who is teaching scripture within a religious setting present it in a way that will be intellectually honest and yet at the same time fully convey its religious meaning? How can the teacher of religion avoid being dogmatic but still inspire religious faith? Greenberg suggests that in order to convey the meaning of a scriptural text the teacher must not only transmit the information and facts contained in it, but engage in a personal and public struggle to evoke its contemporary religious significance. The student must become aware that the teacher really cares about scripture religiously, that he or she regards it as personally of the highest importance and hence feels the need to reconcile the text with science, history, and conscience. Only if the Bible is alive in the teacher will the Bible come alive for the students. Here, I believe, is a lesson for Jews and Christians alike. Greenberg suggests that the historical approach to the Bible is indispensable even though it may not always be possible to harmonize historical data in the Bible with facts that originate from outside of it. But what is really of primary import is not the precise date when the Israelites left Egypt or how many of them participated in the exodus (whether it was really 600,000 or some smaller number), the importance of the exodus is its religious message: the liberation from slavery. Likewise, what matters about the creation story is not whether creation occurred in six days. What matters with regard to the biblical creation story is what it conveys about the centrality of humanity in God's creation, about the purpose of the world in God's eyes, and about human beings as created in God's image. According to Greenberg, it tells us

> that the world has a creator and is not a product of chance or merely mechanical forces; that the ultimate principle of the cosmos is one and moral; that evil is not rooted in the nature of things; that men are free in the sense that they are capable of making moral decisions which are decisive for their well-being. (p. 48)

Similarly, the importance of the parting of the Reed Sea lies not in its being a miracle contravening the laws of physics. Its message is about God's saving power, and that message is what should be imparted when teaching this passage from scripture. In sum, Greenberg suggests that it is possible to derive spiritual meaning even from scriptural passages that are difficult to accept literally if we concentrate on the ideas that they presuppose and the consequences for humanity that follow from them.

The second religious thinker, Abraham Cronbach (1882–1965), presents a very different approach. Cronbach wrote an essay entitled "What May We Expect from the Study?" as the introduction to a volume entitled *The Bible and Our Social Outlook* (1941). Rabbi Cronbach, who taught at the Hebrew Union College in Cincinnati during the 1920s and 1930s, represents the most radical extreme of Reform Judaism, somewhat analogous to Unitarianism within Protestantism. In his view, the Bible itself possesses no independent authority. Instead, ultimate authority rests in the human conscience. Like Walter Rauschenbusch and the Social Gospel movement in Protestantism at the beginning of the twentieth century, Abraham Cronbach believed that the task of religion was to make the world a better place in which to live. Like the ancient prophets, Cronbach was willing to take very unpopular positions if his conscience required it of him. During the Great Depression he was an uncompromising advocate of the poor and a champion of the downtrodden.

Cronbach's approach to the institutions of the Bible could be highly critical. He would ask rhetorically: What about those biblical institutions that conflict with what I believe society requires today? What about slavery? What about polygamy—which the Bible tolerates freely? Even the great biblical heroes Abraham and David, he noted, had more than one wife, to say nothing of Solomon. The Bible also provides for the extensive application of capital punishment, applying it even to the Sabbath violator and to the idolater, to persons whom we might today call heretics. Cronbach believed capital punishment to be especially repugnant from a moral point of view and could not accept it as an institution that should outlive the biblical period. When biblical laws conflict with moral convictions that we hold deeply, then, according to Cronbach, our own God-given conscience must be the ultimate authority, not the biblical text. In fact, in his writings, Cronbach does not begin with the Bible, but with his own moral values and then enlists the Bible in support of them wherever he can. In other words, he seeks confirmation in the Bible for his own convictions.

Of scripture in general Cronbach wrote: "The Bible helps us appreciate the heights that Judaism has attained by showing us also the depth out of which it has struggled." Thus, a great deal in the Bible is not "Jewish," because while it is part of Jewish history it is no longer part of the ongoing Jewish chain of tradition. That chain is composed only of those elements that do no violence to contemporary conscience. For Cronbach, in contrast to Greenberg (and, as we shall see, also to Buber), the Bible gives historical sanction and Jewish legitimization to our own visions of social progress. It provides us with scriptural proof texts for our most deeply held religious and moral convictions.

The last and most challenging of the three thinkers, Martin Buber (1878–1965) is arguably the most significant Jewish theologian of the twentieth century. He has been widely read not only by Jews, but also by Christians. His little book, *I and Thou*, has sold millions of copies in many languages and greatly influenced religious people of different religious faiths. Buber was neither Orthodox, Conservative, nor Reform in that he did not believe in the value of organized religion. But he was deeply religious and deeply Jewish. As a writer and scholar, he wrote about Hasidism and contemporary Jewish life; his most lasting fame is as a philosopher and theologian. But he also wrote about the Bible and participated in a novel translation of the Hebrew Scriptures into German. He spent the last years of his life in Israel as a professor of social philosophy at the Hebrew University.

For Martin Buber all of religious life consists of encounter and dialogue. It is composed of what he called I-Thou relationships, by which he meant relationships in which the one side does not exploit the other for its own purposes, where genuine mutuality reigns. Such relationships Buber considers religious in character, for God is involved in them. Along these lines, he understands the Bible as a religious encounter or dialogue between God and the Jewish people. Buber's position here was influential for the third of the Reform platforms according to which, as we have noted, God and Israel together create Torah out of their covenantal relationship.

Buber notes, however, that the relationship between the modern Jew and scripture has become strained. Why? Because contemporary individuals are so scientifically oriented that they fail to encounter the Bible as whole human beings. We approach the text with our intellect alone, the same way we approach a book of science, a textbook in physics. We do not hear the scriptural message because we do not open ourselves up to it. What Buber is suggesting is that somehow we need to get across the abyss between scripture and ourselves. How does one get across that abyss? Buber suggests that the first step is to realize that the Bible does not separate intellect and emotion. The Bible addresses the entire person, and we cannot understand it by our intellect alone. What is required, according to Buber, is a way *in* to scripture, not just a way *back* to it, a way to the interior of the Bible.

And what is our way in? How can we reestablish a religious relationship to the Bible and through the Bible to God? Buber's answer does not rest upon the idea of creation, nor on that of redemption, but upon the idea of revelation. It is because God is not absent from our own lives that we can hope to understand what revelation meant for our biblical ancestors. But that requires us to encounter the Bible, not just with our minds, but also with our hearts. Once we have entered the biblical domain through our own awareness of God's presence, specifically of God's revelation in our relationships of trust and mutuality with other people and with the world around us, we can then, from our own experience of revelation, come to an understanding of creation and of redemption as well.

Thus, Buber's approach to the Bible brings us back to the beginning of this essay, the fact that the term for scripture in Hebrew has nothing to do with script, has nothing to do with writing, but rather with calling out, with a voice. Buber is saying that the way to open ourselves up to the Bible is to avoid treating it as a text, as something that is written down and fixed, but rather to relate to it as something that is alive and addresses each one of us. Or, put theologically, the Bible is one of the ways that God speaks to human beings who are willing to listen. Buber's own words on this subject provide a fitting conclusion for this essay. He wrote ("People Today and the Jewish Bible" [1926], in *Scripture and Translation* [1994], 21):

> Do we mean a book? We mean the voice. Do we mean that people should learn to read it? We mean that people should learn to hear it. There is no other going back but the turning around that turns us about our own axis until we reach, not an earlier stretch of our path, but the path on which we can hear the voice! We want to go straight through the spoken-ness, to the being-spoken, of the word.

What, then, is scripture for modern Jews? It is the words that continue to address Jews even as they speak to modern Christians according to their modes of understanding. Scripture is composed of those words that remain alive for us today as they were for Israel in ancient times.

Suggestions for Further Reading

Buber, Martin, and Franz Rosenzweig. *Scripture and Translation.* Trans. L Rosenwald with E. Fox. Bloomington: Indiana University Press, 1994.

Greenberg, Moshe. *Studies in the Bible and Jewish Thought.* New York: Jewish Publication Society, 1995.

Kugel, James L. *The Bible as It Was.* Cambridge, Mass.: Belknap Press, 1997.

Meyer, Michael A. *Response to Modernity: A History of the Reform Movement.* New York: Oxford University Press, 1988. This volume contains the platforms of Reform Judaism cited on pages 387–94.

Sandmel, Samuel. *The Hebrew Scriptures.* New York: Oxford University Press, 1978.

---

[1]Max Wiener, ed. *Abraham Geiger and Liberal Judaism* (Philadelphia: Jewish Publication Society, 1962), 6.